AN OUTLINE HISTORY
of the
JAPANESE DRAMA

THE ANGEL IN "HAGOROMO"

AN OUTLINE HISTORY OF THE
JAPANESE DRAMA

BY

Frank Alanson Lombard

Formerly Professor of English Literature, Doshisha University;
lecturer in English Literature, Imperial University,
Kyoto, Japan; sometime Lecturer in English
Literature, Peking University, Peking, China

WITH AN INTRODUCTION BY

George Pierce Baker

Director of the University Theatre; Professor
of the History and the Technique of the
Drama, Yale University

HASKELL HOUSE
Publishers of Scholarly Books
NEW YORK
1966
n. d.

published by

HASKELL HOUSE
Publishers of Scholarly Books
30 East 10th Street • New York, N. Y. 10003

FOREWORD

THE drama in its varied forms constitutes one of the richest Arts in the possession of the Japanese people. The history of its development in Japan is strikingly parallel to that of the Western drama, while at the same time it reveals much that is significant of the peculiar character and spirit of the Japanese.

The richness of her dramatic repertoire compensates in large measure for Japan's relative poverty in other forms of literature, and will reward greater study than has yet been given it by Western students.

The following History is merely an Outline, ambitious only to lift the curtain and, by the presentation of material in illustration, to incite interest in those who may study further and enjoy more deeply.

The writer's debt is great : to Professor George P. Baker, of Yale University, for inspiration and encouragement ; to many whose books, especially in Japanese, have been used for reference ; to Mr. Tetsuo Fukawa and Mrs. Haruyo Fukuhara, for able secretarial assistance, without which much material would have remained beyond his reach.

FRANK ALANSON LOMBARD

NEWTONVILLE, MASSACHUSETTS
    January 1928

CONTENTS

LIST OF ILLUSTRATIONS

(The line drawings are by S. Tomita; the *Niwabi* from *Nen-jū Gyoji Taisei* (Book of Annual Observances); the *Kawara Shibai* from a seventeenth-century screen by an unknown artist; the others from photographs or composite sketches.)

INTRODUCTION

STUDENTS of international drama are turning more and more to study of Japanese drama, desirous to know to what extent its development duplicates or differs from the evolution of drama in other countries. Stimulated by the colour, originality, power, or poetry of the few specimens they know, they are steadily more anxious to know it well in all its branches.

Professor Lombard comes with special fitness to his task as translator and historian. His long association with university work in Japan has given him unusual opportunities to know the Japanese drama at first hand. Deeply interested by it and keenly sensitive to its beauties, he has had, too, the background for a comparative study of it, for he has been a student of the English and Continental drama for many years—not satisfied merely to know the printed play, but judging the play as, above all, something to be acted. He has had, too, exceptional chances to learn just what the older and basal forms of the Japanese drama mean now, and have meant historically, to the priests or other special groups who still maintain the older forms. Carefully he traces for the Japanese the passage from song or symbolistic mimicry to popular plays of crude types, and from these to something of as definite rules as the *Noh* dramas on the one hand or the *Kabuki* plays on the other. Reading his pages one sees that, whatever the differentiations between the Japanese and other great national dramas, the evolution is really the same—from song and mimicry through drama perfected according to artistic standards of the nation out of which the drama in question grows, to the desire for a drama which, though it must remain thoroughly Japanese in essence, may yet take its place in the world drama of to-day as explaining that people, not only to themselves, but to the world at large.

We have had books before dealing with particular periods of the Japanese drama, or particular types such as the *Noh*. We have had very rapid sketches of Japanese drama as a whole. Here is a book, written by a person particularly fitted for the work, which not only traces the general development of the drama of the Japanese, but in the course of that tracing contributes some very sympathetic translations for a knowledge of the various forms which at different periods have been dominant. It should be very welcome, not only to special students of the world drama to-day.

GEORGE P. BAKER

NEW HAVEN, CONNECTICUT
April 2, 1928

[NOTE.—In the pronunciation of Japanese words it should be remembered that the language is free from accent, except such as is given by the length of its vowels, which are sounded uniformly, as upon the Continent of Europe. Each syllable contains but one vowel or diphthong. This concludes the syllable, except when followed by *n* or a double consonant, the first of which should be pronounced with the preceding vowel.

In the names of individuals the given name follows that of the family and is united thereto by the post-position *no*, signifying *of*, or by *a-*, when *no* is omitted.]

AN OUTLINE HISTORY OF THE JAPANESE DRAMA

CHAPTER I

ORIGINS AND EARLY FORMS

THE origins of speech are probably to be found in emotional exclamations and the imitative sounds which accompany imitative action. The inner urge to self-expression, joined with capacity for mimicry, not only led to language, but also, we may be confident, made natural the union of song and dance in which we have the primal elements of the drama.

The expressive moments of primitive life were essentially dramatic ; and the primal elements of the drama may be found wherever ethnic societies have had their beginnings, for, whatever may have been the influence of later contacts, each primitive society held within itself the germ of dramatic culture. Thus we may find not one but many distinct origins of the drama as a form of human expression ; and need feel no surprise at the discovery of marked similarities in the development of the drama among widely scattered peoples, for parallel development is natural, within the limits of experience, and does not demand the explanation of inter-operating influences. Such similarities are but evidence of the essential oneness of human nature in its reaction to similar conditions, whether in India, Greece, or Japan.

It is usual to trace dramatic art to an origin in forms of

religious worship. Religion itself, however, is an expression of the social mind; and the social mind, in its self-expression, provided the material which, under religious patronage, took form in art. Life in expression is dramatic ; and that dramatic expression, under the inspiration of high social contacts in the exercise of religion, invariably takes on forms of beauty which constitûte art. It is difficult for Japanese writers to break away from the conventional loyalty which tends to emphasize the uniqueness of their cultural beginnings ; but it is increasingly evident that the primitive Japanese were far more democratic than their later records admit, and that their social instincts were merely human, and hence of universal character. Thus we may say, with little fear of contradiction, that the origin of the Japanese drama was socially religious. Religious and social customs are so united in the culture of the Japanese race that it may be impossible to state with assurance that either exercised determining influence upon the other ; but it seems reasonably certain that the social life of a simple, agricultural people provided the material which religious ceremonies of worship wrought into the forms of art which we find still preserved in *Kagura* and *Noh*.

The earliest written testimony of the Japanese people concerning their ancient history is the *Ko-ji-ki*, or *Record of Ancient Matters* (A.D. 712). This is in three volumes, and may be called the Bible of Shinto.[1] The first volume contains, in the form of confused and often contradictory myths, truths which are fundamental in the faith of every Japanese. It identifies racial origins with natural forces, and finds kinship, with subordination as in a family, between the human and divine. The second and third volumes contain a record of increasing historicity from the time of

---

[1] Shinto, now held by many as a patriotic cult and not a religion, seems to consist of ancestor-worship grafted upon an original stock of nature-worship in which the sun was the chief object of reverence.

Jimmu Tenno (660 B.C. ?) to that of Empress Suiko, who reigned from A.D. 593 to A.D. 628.

The following passage, as translated by Basil Hall Chamberlain, from Vol. I, sec. xvi, is worth quoting in this connection, not so much because it is taken as authoritative by Japanese writers upon dramatic history as because it is a revelation of early conceptions which throw light upon still more primitive customs. Ama-terasu-oho-mi-kami, the Heaven-Shining-Great-August-Deity, the shining one from whom descended Japan's line of illustrious rulers, had been offended and frightened by the rude pranks of her impetuous brother, and had taken refuge in the retirement of a Heavenly-Rock-Dwelling.

Then the whole Plain of High Heaven was obscured and all the Central Land of Reed-Plains [1] darkened. Owing to this, eternal night prevailed. Hereupon the voices of the myriad deities were like unto the flies in the fifth moon as they swarmed, and a myriad portents of woe all arose. Therefore did the eight hundred myriad deities assemble in a divine assembly in the bed of the Tranquil River of Heaven,[2] and bid the deity Thought-Includer, child of the High-August-Producing-Wondrous-Deity, think of a plan,[3] assembling the long-singing birds [4] of eternal night and making them sing, taking the hard rocks of Heaven from the river-bed of the Tranquil River of Heaven, and taking iron from the Heavenly Metal-Mountains, calling in the smith Ama-tsu-ma-ra, charging Her Augustness I-shi-ko-ri-do-me to make a mirror, and charging His Augustness Jewel-Ancestor to make an augustly complete (string) of curved jewels eight feet (long), of five hundred jewels, and summoning His Augustness Heavenly-Beckoning-Ancestor-Lord and His Augustness Great-Jewel, and causing them to pull out with a complete pulling the shoulder (blade) of a true

[1] An ancient poetic name for Japan.
[2] Stony river-beds, largely dry during summer and autumn, provided a wide expanse for the erection of temporary play-houses. They are so used even in modern times.
[3] What follows appears to be the plan.
[4] Cocks, whose crowing might assist in calling forth the sun.

stag from the Heavenly Mount Kagu,[1] and take cherrybark
from the Heavenly Mount Kagu, and perform divination, and
pulling up by the roots a true *cleyera japonica* [2] with five hundred
(branches) from the Heavenly Mount Kagu, and taking and
putting upon its upper branches the augustly complete (string)
of curved jewels eight feet (long), of five hundred jewels, and
taking and tying to the middle branches the mirror eight feet
(long), and taking and hanging upon its lower branches the white
pacificatory offerings [3] and the blue pacificatory offerings, His
Augustness Grand-Jewel taking these divers things and holding
them together with the grand august offerings, and His Augustness Heavenly-Beckoning-Ancestor-Lord prayerfully reciting
grand liturgies, and the Heavenly-Hand-Strength-Male-Deity
standing hidden beside the door, and Her Augustness Heavenly-
Alarming-Female [4] hanging (round her) the heavenly clubmoss
from the Heavenly Mount Kagu as a sash, and making the
heavenly spindle-tree her headdress, and binding the leaves
of the bamboo-grass of the Heavenly Mount Kagu in a posy for
her hands, and laying a sounding-board before the door of the
Heavenly Rock-Dwelling, and stamping till she made it resound,
and doing as if possessed by a deity, and pulling out the nipples
of her breasts, pushing down her skirt-string *usque ad privates
partes*. Then the Plain of High Heaven shook, and the eight
hundred myriad deities laughed together. Hereupon the
Heaven-Shining-Great-August-Deity was amazed, and, slightly
opening the door of the Heavenly Rock-Dwelling, spoke thus from
the inside : " Methought that owing to my retirement the Plain
of Heaven would be dark, and likewise the Central Land of
Reed-Plains would all be dark ; how, then, is it that the Heavenly-
Alarming-Female makes merry, and that likewise the eight

[1] This, according to a book of ancient legends (*Yamato Fudoki*), fell
from heaven and became two mountains : Kaiyama in Yamato and
Fuzan in Iyo.

[2] The *Sakaki*, a tree with glossy evergreen leaves, much used in
ceremonial, and often planted near Shinto shrines.

[3] Originally actual products of land and sea were offered in sacrifice ;
but later, in place of these, symbolic gifts were presented, white and blue
cloth. *Gohei*—racemes of white or coloured papers cut into inch-wide
strips—are still used symbolically.

[4] Ame-no-usume-no-mikoto, who thus danced for the delight of the
deities, was the first *geisha* (dancing-girl), the possessor of polite accom-
plishments. After her supposed dress and conduct those of modern
entertainers are often modelled.

hundred myriad deities all laugh?" Then the Heavenly-
Alarming-Female spoke saying : " We rejoice and are glad
because there is a deity more illustrious than Thine Augustness."
While she was thus speaking His Augustness Heavenly-Beckoning-Ancestor-Lord and His Augustness Grand-Jewel pushed
forward the mirror and respectfully showed it to the Heaven-
Shining-Great-August-Deity, whereupon the Heaven-Shining-
Great-August-Deity, more and more astonished, gradually came
forth from the door and gazed upon it, whereupon the Heavenly-
Hand-Strength-Male-Deity, who was standing hidden, took her
august hand and drew her out, and then His Augustness Grand-
Jewel drew the bottom-tied rope [1] along at her august back, and
spoke, saying : " Thou must not go back farther in than this ! "
So when the Heaven-Shining-Great-August-Deity had come
forth, both the Plain of High Heaven and the Central-Land-of-
Reed-Plains, of course, again became light.

In this myth, explanatory of a solar eclipse, we have an
account of what is called by the Japanese the first *Kagura* or
Kami asobi, a play of the gods to beguile rather than to
propitiate the angry Sun-Goddess. The explanation itself
is almost buried beneath a mass of detail which is of great
value as showing a naïve effort to account for social and
religious customs, the true origin of which had, even at that
early time, been long forgotten. Customs already ancient
at the date of this composition, stereotyped in ceremony,
prove the antiquity of certain elements apparent in later
dramatic art, as well as of worship in which music and
dancing formed a conspicuous part.

The word *kagura* (神 樂) may be read *kamigaku*, and
signifies god-music. It is used to designate an entertainment of music and dance offered in the presence of deity ;
but the equivalent expression, *kami asobi* (神 遊), as well
as this account taken from the *Ko-ji-ki*, seems to imply

---

[1] The *shiri-kume-naha* is a rope made 'of untrimmed, twisted straw
rolled from right to left in strands of three, five, and seven. Still suspended before Shinto shrines, they are, at the time of the New Year,
hung before public buildings and private dwellings.

music and dance in which the gods themselves engage. The gods of the ancient Japanese, being ancestral as well as cosmic, may naturally be supposed to have entered freely into exercises held in their honour ; and thus the earliest reference to dramatic performance may be considered social as well as religious in its connotation.[1] However that may be, the more formal meaning appropriate to worship (*matsuru*) apparently gave significance to both words, as an early conception of social communion was lost in that of separation between men and gods.

Kagura, though considered by some to be played in its purity only at Court before the gods on earth, is still conspicuous in the ceremonial of all great Shinto shrines ; and, in addition to the body of Court *kagura*, each shrine has its own inherited forms, among which may be found approximately primitive vestiges. The earliest *kagura* was probably merely rude music and dancing before the shrine. It was held at night between twilight and cock-crow. This early *kagura*, if it did not arise directly from popular forms of entertainment, soon took to itself many elements of everyday origin, and, thus enriching itself, perpetuated these in forms of art through priestly patronage.

The popular forms of entertainment thus received into *kagura* arose from the experiences of daily life and labour. In the social emotions associated with labour may be found early incentives to song and dance. Primitive genius gave these emotions spontaneous expression ; and eager imitators established more or less stereotyped forms. The simplest of these forms is, doubtless, the rhythmic chant to which the movements of labour naturally set themselves, and by which those movements are harmonized and made less toilsome. Such chants are found among all peoples—mere

[1] This and many succeeding points of interesting comparison with the development of the Greek and Western drama, would, if amplified, extend this Outline beyond due limits, and must be left for the reader's own recognition and comment.

rhythmic exclamations that in some instances have developed into forms of art.

The ordinary building in rural Japan is of light-frame construction, placed upon stones which are driven into the surface of the ground. For all but the simplest structures, a log, to which ropes running over a pulley are attached, serves as a pile-driver. The ends of the rope are held by women ; and, while a leader chants, the women, joining in chorus, hoist the log, and let it drop upon the stones. The leadership passes from one to another in a rude democracy of labour ; and the chant, while not the same in all localities, seems reminiscent of primitive times, when labour was co-operative and not a matter of wage. As these lines are being written, in the midst of a city of seven hundred thousand, the chant of women driving in the foundation of a neighbour's house comes to the ear.

This is an *Ishi-tsuki-uta*, a song for driving in the stones, a series of rhythmic exclamations having only emotional meaning.

Owada-Tateki, a good stylist and interpreter of Japanese classical literature, has, in his *Japanese Songs (Nihon Kayo Ruiju*, 1898), collected from observation and research in country districts a large number of folk-songs, among which are the following *Ishi-tsuki-uta*, which, while evidently modern, illustrate the general type in which some meaning more or less fragmentary may be found. The form is invariably a combination of five- and seven-syllabled phrases.

In translation, appropriately rude, they read :

I

Now let us congratulate
This house of all houses—
The house which is fortunate !
Long life and prosperity,
Like plants here upspringing,
How full is the favour !
Oho, there, the wine, the wine !
Yea truly, yea truly !

II

May the house-wife here,
When we come to call,
Be robed in sashes red,
With chink aplenty !
Interesting, so !
Oho, there, the wine, the wine !

III

Out in the garden yonder,
When we admire it,
Peacocks in shining splendour
Dances are doing.

IV

To-night in here I slumber,
To-morrow night, I know not—
To-morrow night my pillow
A clod along the furrow.

At the raising of the heavy timbers which form the skeleton of the roof, the union of many sturdy arms is needed ; and the roof-raising is an occasion of mutual helpfulness and of festivity in which similar songs have had their part traditionally from most ancient times.

From the days portrayed in earliest mythology the Japanese have been an agricultural people, making rice their staple production. The irrigation of their diminutive fields has, therefore, been a matter of serious concern ; and the simple ideograph (田) by which a rice-field is designated shows, as in a picture, the low, encircling banks of earth which divide the fields, and yet allow the flow of water from one to another. Social ceremonies in connection with rice-culture have had in Japan all the significance which attended those associated with the culture of the vine in Ancient Greece. The time of planting the rice and certain periods in its growth, especially the 210th and 220th days after the turn of the season (Setsubun), which, according to the old reckoning, comes on December 30th, or, according to the new reckoning, on February 4th, are considered most important ; and then, as at the end of the harvest, the farming communities feel a peculiar oneness that expresses itself in song and dance.

Extant songs of the rice-planting (*Ta-ue-uta*), though usually of modern composition, point to primitive origin, especially as methods of planting are still primitive. The seed is sown thickly in beds to ensure a good start before the fields are cleared of their crop of winter grain and duly irrigated ; and the young plants, when about six inches high, are transplanted to the prepared and half-submerged fields. In the process all members of the community, women as well as men, work from dawn to dark, wading in the muddy water half-way to the knees. This is during the rainy season of the late spring ; and certain of the songs which break the tedium of toil are vivid pictures.

I

Oh dear, how my legs do ache !
The weary ridges, how long !
The days of May and April,
Are long, unending !

II

Whether falls the drenching rain,
Whether shines the burning sun,
Mid fields of growing greenness,
Monotonously,
The farmer folk live out their
Lives of weariness.
Do not forget, O masters,
Masters, their toil and pain !

III

Up in the early morning,
See through the open doorways
Over the landscape gleaming,
Richer than shining gold, the
Sun in the morning !

IV

Planting the young, growing rice,
Setting the seedling grain—
Maidens and mothers,
From hand to hand tossing—
Catch and catch quickly again.

V

Along toward the end of May,
I wish for a 'fretful babe
To nurse at my breast, while I
Sit by the field-side.

The naïve, spontaneous dance of labour, and the simple
celebration of occasions significant in agricultural life,
readily and naturally passed from being mere expressions
of personal or social joy into entertainment or the occasion
of joy in others. First there were the children and neigh-
bours, those of the immediate environment not actually
engaged in the labour or the celebration ; then those

more remote, as joy is always contagious ; until the spectators became in turn the object and inspiration of the performance.

Of this development, in such a society as that of Old Japan, we may not expect to find written record, except as the attention of the nobility was drawn to this source of entertainment. Much, therefore, may be inferred from the fact that there is record of Imperial interest in field dances (*Tamae*) as early as A.D. 671, when, according to the *Chronicles of Japan* (*Nihon Shoki*), A.D. 720, Emperor Tenshi saw them performed for his pleasure. These *Tamae*, called also *Denbu*, became a recognized form of Court music during the Nara Period, A.D. 708-794, and therefore were dropped, under that name at least, from popular use.

Field or Farm Dancing, however, continued in less-stereotyped forms among the common people. In the thirty-first volume of *Ruiju Kokoshi*[1] it is recorded that Emperor Seiwa, in A.D. 864, went to see the cherry blossoms at the residence of a high official, and was entertained by the farmers at work in the fields. The nature of this entertainment is unknown ; but it is reasonable to suppose it may have been a folk-dance elaborated for the occasion.

Dengaku (Field Music), a spectacular mime of the simplest nature, developed from beginnings probably identical with those of *Tamae*. Nothing survives of primitive *Dengaku* which can be declared free from later modification ; but, in the thought of the common people, the term still signifies a display of acrobatic skill ; and, in the language of the street, handed down from generation to generation of children, a slice of bean-curd with a skewer through it

[1] *Ruiju Kokoshi*, a collection, made in the Tokugawa Period, and published in 1816, of the scattered fragments of an earlier collection of writings on history made by Michizane by order of Emperor Uda, A.D. 889-897.

is *Dengaku*, from its likeness to a man balancing on a pole.

Takano-Tatsuyuki, in his *Considerations of Music and Dancing* (*Kabu Ongyoku Kosetsu*), 1915, says that the first known description of *Dengaku* is to be found in the nineteenth volume of the *Ega Monogatari*, a story by an unknown author in the reign of Horikawa (1086–1106), portraying the life of the Fujiwara family, especially of Fujiwara-no-Michinaga (965–1027). According to the story, *Dengaku* was performed in May 1023 for the entertainment of the Court in the rice-fields of Fu-no-mi. Koyata-Iwahashi, in his *History of the Japanese Dance* (*Nihon Buto Shi*), 1922, claims that the term *Dengaku* there used has reference to a drum and not to the dancers ; but his is merely one interpretation of an ambiguous passage ; and there is no good reason to suppose that dances of a similar nature had not been used in entertainment even previous to this date under the name *Dengaku*.

Freely translated, the story runs as follows. The Kamo Festival had passed, and the month of May had come. Michinaga was puzzled as to what could be done to entertain Omiya, the mother of Emperor Go Ichijo, who still remained at the Tsuchi Mikado Palace. Remembering that the rice-fields at North Segai, where supplies for his menage were raised, were about to be planted, he called his overseer and said to him : " On the day when you plant those fields, mind you, do not have the farmers behave in any unusual manner, but let them act and dress as usual, however awkward and rude they may appear. Have them enter by the gate on the south side of the riding-field, cross the boundary, and scatter over the field on the north. I shall have the earthen wall pulled down at the north-east corner so that Her Imperial Highness may come down and see, possibly from the eastern pavilion." The overseer, being thus instructed, planned well ; and when the day came the earthen wall was pulled down at that corner ; and Her Imperial Highness, with Her Imperial Son, descended to the eastern pavilion attended by the ladies of her retinue.

Then on to the field came young women, fifty or sixty in number, clothed in white, with blackened teeth and rouged lips. Behind them walked an old man, whom they called the field-master, in strange clothes, left unfastened here and there, holding a broken umbrella in his hand and wearing high clogs upon his feet. He was followed by women in black, with faces painted white, wearing false hair and carrying umbrellas. They in turn were followed by a party of about ten men whom they called *Dengaku*, with strange hand-drums (*tsuzumi*) fastened by cords to their waists, playing flutes, carrying sticks, and moving their arms and legs incessantly in a manner of dancing. They had a rough appearance and seemed slightly drunken, their drums beating *gobo*, *gobo*, quite unlike ordinary drums.

The farmers, busily engaged in planting the rice, grew warm, and began to shout aloud. The musicians and dancers of *Dengaku* also, though they had been very orderly in coming in, let themselves go, and shouted and yelled as they pleased, to the great amusement of the spectators. At last rain began to fall, and the planters' sleeves seemed wet and heavy ; but they kept at work while some sang of their labour :

> Wet with falling rain,
> In water we plant the rice,
> Hoping here to make
> Support for our lord's estate
> Into the far future years.
>
> Setting the plantlets here,
> Whose number we cannot count,
> Lo, we behold a store
> To fill heaven's barn of blue,
> In autumn, for him, our lord !

Then it chanced that the sweet, elusive notes of an *hototogisu* (cuckoo) were heard ; and one of the Court ladies sang :

> Hototogisu !
> Heard when the farmers are out
> Setting their rice-plants,
> Well by our fathers wert call'd
> Master of Shide's [1] far field.

The *Saibara* and the *Azuma mae* were evidently social in their early forms, and performed by the common people for their own pleasure upon the streets and in open fields. Concerning the origin of the name *Saibara*, there are various opinions. The oldest theory is that which regards it a literal name (Get-ready-horse-music) for the popular music rendered by the people in the olden time when they were about to carry tribute to their lords and rulers. . A second theory finds its origin in the name of a certain class of *Kagura*, called *Saibari*, which employs similar music. Motoori, a great authority upon the Japanese classics, though recognizing the fact that *Saibara* became closely associated with *Kagura*, inclines to the older theory, broadly interpreted.

The earliest collection of *Saibara* songs to which reference can be found is that by Mifume of Awaji (A.D. 723–785) ; and even this seems to have contained pure *Kagura*, as well as certain songs of a more unpolished, popular nature, fittingly called *Saibara*. Tachibana's collection includes some of gross vulgarity, and many which voice illicit love. A few have a lyric rather than a dramatic quality ; and all are evidently from the bold lips of unrefined folk. No certain date for the adoption of *Saibara* into association with *Kagura* can be set ; but, as the flageolet (*hichiriki*)

---

[1] *Shide* is the mountain barrier which divides the spirit-land from earth, the barrier over which in springtime the cuckoo comes to call the farmers to their rice-planting.

is invariably used in the accompaniment of *Saibara Kagura*, and as that instrument was added to the original *Kagura* orchestra of harp (*wagoto*) and flute (*wabue*) by Chinese influence at least as early as the middle of the ninth century, it seems safe to say that *Saibara* became more or less identified with *Kagura* at about that time.

The *Azuma mae* (Dances of the Eastern Provinces) were, as the name implies, the rude revels of country-folk from provinces at that time untouched by the culture which, originating in China, was transforming the western part of Japan.

The exact origin of such songs as these, likely long to have been transmitted in oral tradition, cannot be determined. In the Bunka era (1804–1817) there was a great revival of ancient ritual ; and at that time some songs may have been rescued from oblivion without reference to their history. According to an old book of the Tenji era (1124–1125) an Imperial collection of songs was made in the Enge era (901–922) ; and it is not unreasonable to suppose that some may have survived from that collection, especially when the primitive character of extant examples is noted. Owada includes the following in his collection of *Kagura*, under the subtitle *Azuma Asobi* ; but they clearly indicate a social origin which antedates their ceremonial use.

> O ! O ! O ! O !
> Ha re na !
> Arms in unison moving,
> Now let us sing together—
> Voices loud and high.
> O ! O ! O ! O !

The first and last lines are probably the notes of the chant. The second line has no known meaning ; and the rest appears to imply a confusion of voice and action being brought into harmony.

Eh !
Oh ! sweetheart of mine,
Thy koto-playing this morn,
Is it a seven,
Is it an eight-string'd *koto*,[1]
That koto-playing of thine ?

*   *   *

Ya !
Along the sandy
Shore of Uda's beach at Suruga
The waves come rolling, rolling in.
All-perfect darling of mine,
Ah ! sweet are thy words.
Thy words, they are sweet.
When we shall meet,
Shall we not couch together ?
All-perfect darling of mine,
Oh, sweet are thy words !

Along with this song from a forgotten past there grew
up a tradition that once in ancient days an old man saw an
angel dance upon the shore at Suruga. The legend is
probably the same as that which is immortalized in
Hagoromo, one of the most beautiful of the *Noh*.   As
elaborated by Seami (1363–1444), this *Noh* has been
pleasingly translated by Arthur Waley in *The No Plays
of Japan*, 1922; but no rendering, not even the libretto in
Japanese, can awaken in those who have not seen and
learned to love it any conception of its beauty, which is
primarily the beauty of a dance so delicate, so refined, so
almost imperceptible in motion, as to be lifted above all
human passion into the cool realm of the spirit. The outline
in story is simple : A rude fisherman finds an angel's feather-
robe hanging upon a pine by the sea, and refuses to restore
it until she dances the Heavenly Dance. It is the Dance
which makes this *Noh* (see Frontispiece).

[1] The *koto* is a recumbent harp.

Later references to these dances are intimately associated with occasions of Buddhist or Shinto ceremonial; and it is evident that a study of their development must include a recognition of the part played by religion as a patron of art in early Japan. Japanese culture in general cannot have reached a very high level before it received the quickening influence of China. The written characters of the Japanese language are a product of contact with Chinese culture; and, although the *Ko-ji-ki*, the earliest written record in the Japanese language, was not produced until A.D. 712, the beginning of Chinese influence reached Japan through Chosen at least as early as A.D. 284. The most vital element in all this influence was Buddhism; and as early as the regency of Shotoku Taishi (593–621) that religion had gained a position of Imperial sanction and favour.

Buddhism is characterized by its ability and its willingness to recognize and utilize elements of value outside itself; and one secret of its early strength in Japan was its recognition of the essentials of Shinto and its utilization of social customs in the spread and support of its religious teachings. Although formal recognition of Shinto by Buddhism did not take place until early in the ninth century, when Kukai (Kobo Daishi), a Buddhist priest of great learning and culture, opened the way by the recognition of Shinto deities as avatars (incarnations) of the numerous Buddhas, the adoption by Buddhism of social dances, already having a place in Shinto ceremonial, or popular with the common people, seems to have been much earlier.

Shinto, incited by Buddhism to greater self-consciousness as a religion, continued to enrich its services from various popular sources; and the social dance in turn, wherever played, took on a more distinctively religious character, as it came under the patronage of the Buddhist temples and the Shinto shrines. Some of these dances, with their songs

c

still social in character, assumed, under the patronage of Shinto, the name *Kagura*, and, becoming stereotyped in form, gradually usurped the ceremonial place of the more primitive *Kagura*. Others, under the influence of ethically inclined Buddhism, developed as instruments of popular instruction.

Though no clear line of demarcation can be drawn, because of the blending of the two religions, we will take into consideration first those dance-songs most intimately associated with Shinto ceremonial and grouped under the general name of *Kagura*, and thereafter those which, with the addition of more evidently dramatic elements, developed under Buddhist patronage. Though at present interested not so much in the ritual of the dance as in the songs themselves with their evidences of social origin, we must remember, in connection with both groups, that the verbal meaning of the songs was distinctly subordinated by their religious patrons to the movements of the dance, and utilized largely as a musical scaffolding for the support of liturgic action. The fact that the word for dancing (*mai*) rather than that for singing (*utai*) is in common use to designate even spoken plays, strengthens the belief that the early ceremonies were dances accompanied by music but lacking in all except exclamatory utterance.

CHAPTER II

KAGURA

Kagura, as we have noted, was originally an entertainment of music and dancing in the presence of some Shinto deity. It was given from the ground or from a temporary platform. As now presented at Shinto shrines it is given

KAGURA PROPERTIES.
Showing, in addition to the harp, flute, and hand-drums of the musicians, the fans and bells (upon the stand) used by the Maiko.

from a platform or stage, which forms a permanent part of the establishment. The *Kagura* stage faces the shrine, as the performance is designed primarily for the pleasure of deity ; but the curtains, which enclose the rear and sides, are usually arranged so as to allow spectators freely to observe the plays. *Kagura* are evening entertainments, beginning usually at twilight and closing at morning cock-crow. They are given most frequently, though not exclusively, in the late autumn or early winter.

Slightly previous to a performance a garden fire (*niwabi*) is lighted on the ground in front of the shrine. This is tended by special attendants. At the appointed time the singers, musicians, and director enter the platform and take their seats upon either side at right-angles to the shrine. Players of the flute (*wabve*) and harp (*wagoto*) sit upon the left, players of the flageolet (*hichiriki*) upon the right. The singers are divided for antiphonal purposes, those upon the left being called leaders (*motokata*), those upon the right, followers (*suikata*). When all have been seated the players ceremonially test their instruments ; the director rises and, going to the fire, orders the attendants to tend the fire. At his command an introductory ceremony is given. This is usually the *Niwabi* or the *Achime* ; and it is followed by the evening's series of *Kagura*, each being rather brief.

In the performance of true *Kagura*, dancing has a large part ; and with the growth of *Kagura* as a regular ceremonial a special group of trained dancers, as well as players and singers, was developed. These were called *Maiko* and *Kagura Oh*. The former were young women of good social standing, who upon examination were given diplomas admitting them to the privilege of dancing in Kagura as regular attendants at the shrine. The latter were men and less permanently attached to the shrine.

According to Tachibana, the ancient *Kagura* songs, which are now extant, may be arranged in groups, each having a distinct and appropriate name. The first group, called simply *Kagura*, contains only two songs, *Niwabi* and *Achime*. These are of great interest because of their primitive character ; but they might better be called *Introductory Kagura*, since they serve usually to introduce a *Kagura* service, and are in themselves of the utmost simplicity.

NIWABI (GARDEN FIRE).

Amid the mountains
Wintry hail may be falling,
Along their slopes . . .
Bright the leaves of the dogwood
Flame in festoons of glory.

This stanza is a *Tanka*, or composition of thirty-one
syllables, and is found also in the *Kokinshiu*, which was

THE NIWABI.

compiled in A.D. 922. The name—Garden Fire—suggests
to the Western mind the bonfire in which the garden refuse
is burned in autumn amid the shouts and laughter of children,
while the chill of winter is felt among the hills, and the
flame of the foliage along the uplands tells that the year is
growing old. From such a commonplace origin may well
have developed the use of fire in the garden for illumination
upon festive occasions, even though there is nothing in the
customs of present-day Japan to give ground for such a
theory. As we have noted, *Kagura* were played at night.

This necessitated artificial lighting ; and naturally fires were kindled before the shrine. These fires for illumination, essential to the success of the performance, might easily have become associated with the opening ceremony, and have been made the subject of a *Kagura*. Even in the modern rendering of this *Kagura* a tradition of simplicity is followed. There is no beating of time by the director. The flute, flageolet, and harp are first played in successive solos ; then the flute and the flageolet are played in duet. The words are then sung as a solo, first by a member of the *Motokata*, and again by a member of the *Suikata*, to the accompaniment of the harp. There is no dancing, beyond the ceremonial handling of the sacred *Sakaki* branches by the director.

The music, rewritten in modern notation from ancient *Kagura* notes by Tanabe-Hisao, gives some idea of the fragment which alone is played in the presentation of this *Kagura* (see page 39).

The *Achime* is the most tenuous of all extant *Kagura* forms. Its origin is lost in antiquity ; but it is based traditionally upon the dance of *Ame-no-uzume* before the rock-cave in which the Sun-Goddess was hiding. It is no real song, but merely a cry or shout :

> Achime ! Oh, Oh !
> Oke, Oke !

Some have considered this merely a ceremonial in which two groups of singers antiphonally cry. *Achime* is supposed to be a corruption of *Uzume*. *Oh, Oh !* is the laughter of the eight hundred myriad deities ; and *Oke, Oke !* for which no good explanation has been proposed, may, as suggested by Tachibana, be a corruption of *Oh, Oh ! Okashi, Oh, Oh !*—*Okashi* meaning " How funny." In any case, the entire *Kagura* is hardly more than a shout of introduction or transition, after which the director says : " We will now have *Kagura*."

THE NIWABI.

TORIMONO UTA.

The second group of *Kagura*, called *Songs of Offerings* (*Torimono Uta*), contains eight or ten songs. The *Torimono* are offerings presented to deity ; and each song is named after, and celebrates, some special gift. The songs are of two stanzas each, the first being sung by the *Motokata*, the second by the *Suikata*, while *Maiko* dance appropriately in the centre front of the *Kagura* stage.

SAKAKI (God's Tree).

Led by the odour
Sweet of the evergreen leaves,
Longing I come . . . ;
Lo, in a circle to find
Family folk at their prayers.

In the holy grove
Upon the lofty mountain,
Sacred evergreens
'Fore the face of deity
Grow thick, luxuriantly.

The *Sakaki* (*Cleyera Japonica*), or God's Tree, is a glossy-leaved evergreen associated from prehistoric times with Shinto shrines and ceremonies. One cannot read these lines without having his imagination stirred to interpret them. Yet whose interpretation shall be judged correct ? *Family folk* may mean the members of some country hamlet, all united by ties of blood, or the official representatives of some larger community ; but with them in either case a lonely wanderer finds satisfaction in worship before the shrine to which the smell of the sacred *Sakaki* has led him.

NUSA (THE WAND).

This wand, full laden,
Dedicate, is not for me ;
To one in heaven,
Goddess Toyooka, dear,
Belongs this token.

This wand, full laden,
Dedicate, I'd like to be ;
So might I, lowly,
Still be held in hand divine,
Dear familiarity.

The *nusa* is a *gohei*, or wand, laden at one end with strips
of white or coloured paper, symbolic of primitive offerings ;
and it is used upon all occasions of Shinto worship.

TSUE (THE STAFF).

This staff, behold it !
Whose, I wonder, can it be ?
To one in heaven,
Goddess Toyooka, dear,
Belongs it wholly.

This morning, as I
Wandered o'er Mount Osaka,
A mountain hermit
Gave this staff to me, and said—
" A thousand years."

The *tsue* is a stick or staff such as a pilgrim might use,
and it is a not infrequent offering at shrines by pilgrims
frequented.

SASA (THE BAMBOO).

Behold the bamboo !
Whose, I wonder, can it be ?
It is a bamboo ·
Hanging from an archer's waist,
From Mount Tome, distant, brought.

> If through the bamboo
> Grass I push, my sleeves are torn ;
> So by the Tone
> River bed I'll make my way,
> Though I stumble over stones.

The *sasa* is a bamboo grass which may be used for the making of arrows. All bamboos, even such as attain in their single season's growth a height of sixty or more feet, are grasses ; but this seems more appropriately so called. There is more than a touch of artificiality in these last two selections; but in the second stanza of *Sasa* there is something quite other than ritualistic. It is a love poem, and may be an example of the adoption into Shinto ritual of folk-songs such as later came to be used with no apparent sense of incongruity.

YUMI (The Bow).

> Speaking of a bow,
> There seemeth to be but one ;
> Yet from varied wood
> Come names that are manifold ;
> The bows, too, are different,
> The bows, too, are different.

> Strongly drawing out
> Michinobu's mighty bow,
> Wrought in ebony,
> It gradually responds,
> Stealthily . . .
> Stealthily.

TSURUGI (The Sword).

> Bearing upon him
> A sword with gorgeous hilt
> Of silver, richly chased,
> Through Nara's royal highway
> Whose son goes proudly walking ?
> What youth goes proudly walking ?

Antiquity . . . !
Had I an ancient sword
So tempered, truly
I'd wear it on its hanger,
And walk the Capital streets,
And walk the Capital streets.

HOKO (The Halberd).

Behold this halberd !
Whose, I wonder, can it be ?
To one in heaven,
Goddess Toyooka, dear,
Belongs this holy halberd,
Belongs this holy halberd.

A halberd, turning
Every way, protecting all
The people—
I have lifted up to God ;
Lo, on high I've lifted up,
Lo, on high I've lifted up !

The bow, the sword, and the halberd, dear to the warriors
of old, were acceptable gifts ; and many weapons made
famous in battle were dedicated to those by whose divine
aid success had been attained.

HISAGO (The Gourd).

From Ohara's well,
Where the clear water floweth,
Bearing our beakers,
Though the birds be awakened,
Let us play drawing water,
Let us play drawing water.

The clear water well,
Wooden curb'd at my gate-side,
Far from the village,
No one draws water from it ;
And the weeds grow within it,
And the weeds grow within it.

The *hisago* is a gourd, in ancient use for the carrying of water and an object of beauty because of its graceful shape.

These eight *Torimono Uta*, with the two *Introductory Kagura*, appear to make up the formal or ceremonial *Kagura* songs. Some collections give two additional fragments, much resembling *Hisago*; and the following song shows clear evidence of Buddhist influence, in that *Karakami*, the foreign gods, are Buddhist deities introduced from the Continent of Asia.

KARAKAMI (Foreign Gods).

Mishima Ivy
Over our shoulders throwing,
Gods from beyond the sea-waves,
Rattling the reeds we worship,
Rattling the reed wands,
Rattling the reeds we worship.

Bearing on hands uplifted
Trays with their votive gifts,
Gods from beyond the sea-waves,
Rattling the reeds we worship,
Rattling the reeds we worship.

These ceremonial *Kagura* betray something of popular influence; but it is much more apparent that popular desire and priestly favour met in the inclusion of the *O* and *Ko* (large and small) *Saibari* within the body of *Kagura* songs, for each of their songs bears clear internal evidence of its original character. The name *Saibari* may have come possibly from the fourth song in the *O Saibari* group, or from the fact that both collections are made up of songs of popular origin such as are commonly called *Saibara*.

O SAIBARI.

1. *Miyabito*—(The Courtier).

Of a courtier
The ceremonial dress
Is long and flowing ;
Flowing and comfortable,
His ceremonial dress.

Ah, long and flowing,
Flowing and comfortable,
His ceremonial dress.

2. *Naniwa Gata*—(Naniwa Bay).

In Naniwa Bay,
When the tide flows full and free—
The rain-coats of straw,
The rain-coats of straw,

The rain-coats of straw !
O'er the Isle of Tamino
Wild geese fly screaming,
Wild geese fly screaming.

3. *Yushide*—(Guardian Gifts).

Made sacred by gifts,
In the field blessed by Heaven,
All the heads of rice,

All the heads of rice,
All the heads of rice,
To maturity come—
Not a one being mildewed,
Not a one being mildewed.

4. *Saibari*—(Early Elm Leaves).

With early elm leaves
Let us dye our garments ;
Even if it rains,
Even if it rains,

Even if it rains,
Hardly will their colour fail
So deeply do we dye them,
So deeply do we dye them.

5. *Shinage Tori*—(Flying Waterfowl).[1]

Flying waterfowl !
Aha there ! into harbour ;
Oho ! as the boat enters ;
Steady, keep the tiller straight ;
Don't let the boat be upset !
Don't let the boat be upset.

Green are the spring-time grasses !
A sweetheart of mine would ride.
Oho ! so would I, so would I.
Don't let the boat be upset !
Don't let the boat be upset !

6. *Inano.*

Swift-flying waterfowl !
Aha, the reedy marshes !
Oho, there they come flying !
Snipe with their wings aflapping ;
Delightful to me the sound—
Snipe with their wings aflapping !

Swift-flying waterfowl !
Aha, the reedy marshes !
Oho, spread the nets abroad !
Lover, O lover of mine !
How many has he taken ?
How many has he taken ?

[1] The title of this song, used as the introductory expression from which the title is taken, is what the Japanese call a *pillow*, an expression used as a euphonious filling with no reference to meaning. In most cases it is absolutely impossible to produce the same effect by any substitute rendering in another language. A transliteration or a literal translation must be accepted with recognition of the fact that the word or phrase is not supposed to add to the intelligent significance of the passage.

7. *Wagimoko*—(My Sweetheart).

Oh, sweetheart of mine,
One night's passionate meeting !
Alas, since I made that mistake,
Not a bird I've been able to catch !
Not a bird I've been able to catch !

Whatever you may say,
Lover, O lover of mine,
Most surely five birdies,
Six birdies,
Perhaps seven or eight,
Nine or even ten, you've taken ;
Yes, ten you have taken.

KO SAIBARI.

1. *Komo Makura*—(A Pillow of Straw).

A pillow of straw !
Along the marshy Yodo,
Whose servants are they ?
Throwing the nets, large and small,
And spearing the snipe,
As they walk, as they walk on,
Whose servants, indeed, are they ?
Throwing the nets, large and small,
And spearing the snipe,
As they walk, as they walk on ?

To one in Heaven,
The Goddess Toyooka,
These serving men belong,—
Throwing the nets, large and small,
And spearing the snipe,
As they walk, as they walk on ;
Her serving men, indeed, are they,
Throwing the nets, large and small
And spearing the snipe,
As they walk, as they walk on.

2.   *Shizuya*—(Low-lying Land).

> Sedge of the low-lying land,
> When cut by the reaping scythe,
> Quickly upspringeth ;
> Quickly upspringeth the sedge.
>
> Skylark in heaven high,
> To earth return, O Skylark,
> The blessed rice,
> The blessed rice down bringing.

3.   *Isora*.

> Off the Cape of Isora,
> Fishermen angling sea-bream,
> Angling sea-bream,
> Angling sea-bream.
>
> For the sake of my sweetheart,
> Fishermen angling sea-bream,
> Fishermen angling sea-bream.

4.   *Sasanami*—(Ripples).

> Ye Ripples !
> At Karasaki,
> In the Province of Shiga,
> There are some pretty girls
> Grinding the rice, grinding rice.
> This one I desire,
> That one I desire,
> Object of my heart—
> My very own dear one to make.
>
> In the marshy fields,
> Even the rice-grinding crabs,
> Having no wives to embrace,
> Erect themselves and let themselves fall,
> Let themselves fall and erect themselves,
> As if 'twere arms they lifted.

5. *Uetsuki.*

In Uetsuki,
By groves of Tanaka—
By forest groves—
There grow in Kasa's field the grasses wild.

Abandoning me,
Are you taking another ?
Take not, I say.
There grow in Kasa's field the grasses wild.

6. *Agemaki*—(The Lover Laddie).

My lover laddie
They have sent to the rice-fields !
When I think of him,
When I think of him,
When I think of him,
When I think of him,

When I think of him,
I feel like doing nothing
Through the long spring day,
Through the long spring day,
Through the long spring day,
Through the long spring day,
Through the long spring day.

7. *O Miya*—(The Royal Court).

Little attendant
Archer of the Royal Court,
In my hand I would . . .
In my hand I would . . .
As if a jewel,
In my hand I would . . .

D

As if a jewel,
By day I'd hold in hand,
By night with thee entwine.
In my hand I would . . .
By night with thee entwine,
In my hand I would . . .

8. *Minatoda.*

Off Minatoda
Are loons, loons eight in number ;
I wish I could catch them,
I wish I could catch them,
Eight altogether,
I wish I could catch them.

Eight altogether
Calmly floating so care-free,
Eight altogether,
I wish I could catch them,
I wish I could catch them.

9. *Kirigirisu*—(The Grasshopper).

A grasshopper,
Provoked and very angry,
Into the garden
There has come hopping.
Grass-roots he has dug up to eat
Funny, oh, funny !
Antennæ broken,
Funny, how funny !
Antennæ broken !

Provoked and very angry,
Into the garden
He has come hopping.
Grass-roots he has dug up to eat
Funny, how funny !
Antennæ broken !

In addition to these ancient *Kagura*, used in Court ceremonies and generally available for all shrines, each important shrine has such *Kagura* as may be called locally canonical.

In the city of Nara, capital of the Empire from A.D. 708 to A.D. 784, and now a provincial capital or county seat, stands the *Kasuga*, founded in A.D. 768 by the Fujiwara family as a titulary shrine. It is in reality a group of four shrines, the third of which is dedicated to *Koyane*, the supposed ancestor of the Fujiwara chieftains, who, according to the Ko-ji-ki, prayerfully recited grand liturgies before the rock-cave in which Ama-terasu-oho-mi-kami had hidden herself.

In A.D. 1122 a *Kagura* Hall was built in front of the *Koyane* Shrine. In A.D. 1135 the *Wakamiya* (Young Shrine) was dedicated to the son of *Koyane*; and there, in A.D. 1137, national prayers were offered for deliverance from bad crops and strange illnesses. Conditions improved; and in thankfulness the people sought to express their gratitude in an entertainment of thanksgiving in which each took part according to his ability. This service evidently included a procession and various forms of popular dancing associated with *Kagura*.

In ancient times the shrine had a *Kagura* Department, sustained by popular subscription; but in the time of Hideyoshi it was given grants of land, from the income of which the *Kagura* came to be supported, and thus, through endowment, to lose much of their natural spontaneity as expressions of popular feeling. The practice of *Kagura*, inclusive of popular forms, appears to have been generally continuous at this shrine; but the confusion attendant upon the Restoration of 1868 destroyed most of the documentary data; and the present system at Nara dates from the revival in 1874, at which time a priest of the shrine compiled a collection of songs and costumes from various sources of traditional authority into a closed canon of official *Wakamiya Kagura*.

In the text, courteously loaned by Chishima-Sukemune, priest-in-charge, the arrangement of the stage is as follows— the hand-drum (*tsuzumi*) being substituted for the flageolet.

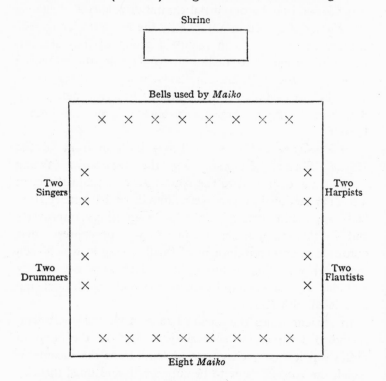

The songs are all of local colour, and are relatively modern in their self-conscious loyalty to the Imperial House. Thus they have interest in this study chiefly as an illustration of *Canonical Kagura*, in distinction from those of unknown, popular origin. They show the degree to which patronage had stereotyped the spontaneous dance-songs of the people, and mark the limit beyond which *Kagura* never developed in dramatic power.

CANONICAL KAGURA OF KASUGA.

OPENING WORDS.—These eight maidens standing before the Shrine, whose eight maidens are they ?   They are eight maidens in bloom.

FOUR SONGS, EACH WITH ITS SPECIAL DANCE.

I

Wakamiya.

The flawless mirror,
Which reflects the image clear
Of Wakamiya,
May not be clouded ever.
Look upon us, we beseech thee !

II

Wonderful.

Oh, so wonderful
Are the eight precious maidens
Of this *Kagura*,
That Deity beholdeth them
With the greatest of pleasure !

III

Where Deity Dwells.

These eight fair maidens,
Standing in Kasuga's fields
Where Deity dwells,
These eight beautiful maidens
Are Deity maidens fair.

IV

Whom we Adore.

Maidens and flowers
All beautiful are blooming
Before the presence
Of him whom we adore,
Of him whom we adore.

THREE SERIES OF SONGS.

First Series.

I

A. Just for a token
    Of the long eternity
    Of this great Empire,
    Deity may have planted
    The Pine of Sumiyoshi.

B. Although the pine-tree,
    Rock-rooted in the stony
    Slope of Kasuga,
    Speaketh no word,
    We know its age
    From its shade of green.

C. The sound of the mountain wind
    Is not what I hear—
    'Tis the surge of the shouting
    Falling full on my ear.

II

As each separate
Branch upon Mount Mikasa's
Growing trees of green,
Shalt thou prosper ceaselessly—
In all thy ways, ceaselessly,
Shalt thou prosper ceaselessly.

III

The still unchanging
Evergreen pine and bamboo,
Evergreen pine and bamboo,
Evergreen pine and bamboo,
Which in the future
For long years may survive,
For long years may survive,
You alone will live to see,
You alone will live to see ;

For long years may survive,
For long years may survive,
You alone will live to see,
You alone will live to see,
You alone will live to see.

Second Series.

I

A. Through eternal years
   When we pray that thou may'st live,
   From the echoing
   Crest of great Mikasa's height
   There breaks forth the one grand cry,
   The one cry, the one grand cry.

B. Happy the pine-tree,
   The symbol of great blessing,
   Happy the little pine-tree
   On Kasuga's peak ;
   Happy the stork, through ages
   Long on earth dwelling,
   And the sea-turtle
   Off Nagai !

II

The child of the stork,
Yea, the grandchild of the stork,
And its great-grandchild—
Through all their generations
May our Royal Lord live on,
May our Royal Lord live on,
May our Royal Lord live on !

III

A. The young Court noble,
   With his printed garments gay,
   With his printed garments gay,
   With his printed garments gay !

B. A humble sleeve-cord,
Whose garment shall I fasten ?
An empty bosom,
Whom, O whom shall I embrace ?
To whom shall I give my heart ?
To whom shall I give my heart ?
To whom shall I give my heart ?
An empty bosom,
Whom, O whom shall I embrace ?
Whom, O whom shall I embrace ?

Third Series.

I

A. Through countless years, and,
As the thick-growing pine groves,
Very prosperous,
We pray thy rule may extend ;
Yea, even through eternity,
Yea, even through eternity.

B. Since God with loving power
Stands in his place,
No prayer is needed ;
Neither need any fear.
The warning drum
Need not be sounded.

II

Within the garden
Of my home, an old bamboo,
Long-jointed, groweth ;
And its leaves far up extend,
A future long foretelling,
A future long foretelling,
A future long foretelling !

PRESENTATION OF ANNIVERSARY OFFERINGS AT NARA

III

Each joint of bamboo,
Each joint of bamboo,
In the hedge I am planting,
In the hedge I am planting,
In the hedge I am planting,
In the hedge I am planting,
In the hedge I am planting,
Contains a thousand
Years which only thou shalt see ;
Which only our Lord shall see,
Which only our Lord shall see ;
Contains a thousand
Years which only thou shalt see ;
Which only our Lord shall see,
Which only our Lord shall see.

Benediction.

For ever—
For ever and ever,
And still for evermore,
Time without end !

Words of Conclusion, to be spoken at the close of the Dancing :—

Favourably receive
These our *Kagura !*
Grant us long life ;
And the prayers we have offered,
Graciously fulfil !

The same canonical book contains, as in an appendix, four *Denbu* (Field Dances) and a group of ten songs of no particular character—some seem meaningless, some are counting songs, and three are from old literary sources. Concerning the *Denbu*, it is stated that they were played at the Kasuga Shrine for the first time in A.D. 1163, and

that the manner of presentation has been preserved.   The
dancers carry farm-tools and baskets of young rice-plants.
Both the men and the women wear white clothes and farm-
hats, the sleeves of their garments being fastened back with
cord—white for the men, red for the women.   An ox,
masked and wearing a black cloth, forms a part of the
procession.

DENBU SONGS.

I

O come, let us plant the rice,
Let us plant the young rice shoots ;
The girls, coming hand in hand,
Will gather up the bundles.

II

Behold the hands
That gather up the seedlets,
That gather up the dew-drops,
The bright and quiv'ring dew-drops,
The flowers of the thriving grain.

III

Planting the rice,
For a mighty yield,
Over all the Land,
Let us gather the seedlings.

IV

If it were not
For the ancient shrine,
We would be planting millet
In Kasuga's fields.

From the group of ten, one song is from the *Ko-ji-ki*,
where it is recorded as the composition of Susanowo, brother
of the Sun-Goddess.   He had descended to the province

of Idzumo and built a palace. Enfolding clouds arose, and he sang :

> Where rise the eight-fold
> Clouds at Idzumo, I build
> Secure an eight-fold
> Fence wherein to hide my love—
> Yea, this eight-fold fence of cloud.

The pathetic longing of a woman for her native land is voiced in the song attributed to Obake, who, with her husband, had been captured in an attack upon Chosen about A.D. 540.

> Within the shadow
> Of a foreign fortress strong,
> Obake prostrate
> Falls, facing her native Land—
> Yamato's Land of Longing.

From *Hyaku-nin-isshiu* (a collection made in A.D. 1235) is taken a stanza supposed to have been composed by Munesada Yoshimune, upon seeing a dance, some time before A.D. 850.

> O wind of heaven,
> Together bring the cloudy
> Barriers of the sky,
> For we would keep these maidens
> Fair from flight away.

In addition to *Court Kagura*, and *Kagura* which are locally canonical, there are non-canonical *Kagura*, which have their immediate origin in the desire of local communities to celebrate, in approved fashion, incidents in the history or mythology of local heroes. Such *Kagura* are played in private and in public upon occasions of rejoicing, as well as before shrines in personal petition or in personal thanksgiving. They appear also as popular offerings in connection with ceremonial celebrations at shrines, both large and small, and afford interesting evidence of those elements which went to make up ritualistic *Kagura*—examples of remnants which, escaping the deadening touch of patronage, might be expected to appear elsewhere in forms of freer evolution.

On the 17th of each December an anniversary *Kagura*, at which non-canonical as well as canonical *Kagura* are greatly in evidence, is held at Kasuga. In 1920 the occasion was of special interest, as great effort was made to reproduce ancient forms and to allow spontaneous participation.

At a distance from the permanent shrine had been erected a temporary shrine of primitive construction, with unhewn posts and uncoloured mud walls. Its overhanging roof of thatch was supported in front by two tree-trunk pillars, from between which straw-covered steps led to the altar. The structure, resting directly upon the ground, which had been built up about six feet, was about eight feet by ten, exclusive of the steps and overhanging roof. In front of the steps, to the west, an inclined, grass-turfed descent led to a turfed square about thirty feet on a side, which in turn had been built up some three feet from the ground-level. From this square a second incline led to the ground-level on the west. Surrounding the elevated square on three sides was what might be called the pit, some thirty feet wide ; and outside of this, on the north and south, were crude roofed shelters for participants and guests of honour. On a line with the back of these shelters, and extending a little to the west, the entire ground was enclosed by a bamboo fence, which permitted free observation without entrance.

All-day processions and dancing upon the avenue entertained the thousands who thronged the park. At about three-thirty ten priests passed through the pit and ascended to the square. All were richly dressed in old-style ceremonial robes. Upon the elevated square they formed two rows facing each other at right angles to the shrine. Then up the incline attendants brought standards laden with offerings of varied kinds—a large fish, a gorgeous pheasant, vegetables, and confections. These were handed by the priests from one to another, and by the head-priest presented at the altar. When the offerings had all been presented, *norito* (prayers) by the head-priest and various high officials concluded the formal opening of the evening's entertainment.

At once the populace began to take a more vital interest in the proceedings. Various actor groups, *samurai* in old costumes, wrestlers (naked except for loin-cloths) and horsemen, presented themselves before the shrine, and at once withdrew to engage in sports for the people in the adjoining park. In the meantime dancers robed themselves in the shelters which skirted the pit. These were private citizens of good family who provided their own heirloom robes of great beauty and richness. By five o'clock it began to grow dark; and on all sides were suspended large white paper lanterns, bearing the Imperial crest in black outline. Six iron net-braziers were hung about the elevated square, and in them fires of pinewood were lighted. These were kept brightly burning, and added greatly to the primitive effect.

The elevated square was now covered with straw mats, and a series of *Kagura* were danced by young *Maiko* to the accompaniment of flute and harp. These were followed by a second series performed by older women. Both were apparently canonical in character, but soon gave place to more popular forms. The *Dengaku* was presented by eight farmers, grotesque of dress and walking intentionally out of step, but with every motion harmoniously inharmonious. Six musicians and two dancers performed *Sarugaku*. Some of the movements were exceedingly difficult in their simplicity, demanding both physical strength and the most perfect nerve-control ; but only by name, for the most part, could the different forms—*Azuma Mae, Dengaku, Sarugaku,* and *Saibara*—be distinguished.

CHAPTER III

MATSURI AND STREET PLAYS

Matsuri, or processions in honour of deity, have from ancient times in Japan been occasions of great popular rejoicing. Priests might act as official participants ; but the entire local population was expected to bear a part, and the processions themselves to be an expression of the popular will in its desire to please and honour the gods. This popular participation was originally spontaneous, and quite as naïve as the merry dancing of children ; and, although studied contributions and imitations of ceremonial forms were gradually added to increase the dignity of the occasion, and participation in some form by all came to be officially required, the *Matsuri* still afford excellent opportunity for the study of spontaneous dramatic action on the part of the common people.

The city of Kyoto is divided into three sections, each forming the special territory of an important Shinto shrine. The northern third of the city is under the protection of those deities enshrined at Goryo ; the central third, under those at Gion ; and the southern third, under those at Inari. The *matsuri* of these three great shrines, held annually on May 18, July 17, and May 7 respectively, are events of popular interest even in the modern city with its universities of world learning and culture. Each has its contribution to make towards an understanding of how primitive instinct and priestly patronage united in the development of the dramatic art in Japan ; but the contribution made by Gion is the most significant, since that alone of the three is celebrated with floats accompanying the sacred palanquin (*mikoshi*).

The deities enshrined at Gion are *Susanowo-no-mikoto*, brother of the Sun-Goddess, and his wife, *Inada-hime*, with their five children. The shrine was established probably in A.D. 656; and the *matsuri* is said to have originated in A.D. 869, when *Urebe-no-hinomaru*, in his effort to obey an Imperial order that he should check the plague which was then raging in the city, presented to the shrine sixty-six halberds, one for each province of the Empire.[1] The youth of the city, with farmers from the outlying districts, then carried the sacred palanquin in honour through the streets. No record in detail remains of that early *matsuri*; but the plague is said to have been averted and a memorial ceremony established. In A.D. 999 a float on wheels was presented to the shrine for use in the procession as a stage for a *Dengaku*. This was at first prohibited by the Government, as it seemed a discourteous imitation of floats already being used in Imperial ceremonies; but as a disaster came upon the city the prohibition was removed, and the *Dengaku* player with his acrobatic feats contributed greatly to the popularity of the festival.

The enrichment of this *matsuri* continued until there were floats for musicians, for the dancing of *Kuse mae*, and primitive *Sarugaku*, as well as for *Dengaku*. The nobility and members of the Royal family watched the procession from a special reviewing-stand; and even the Emperor sent his ceremonial greetings. In addition to floats, upon which dancers performed to the delight of the people and the consequent prestige of the festival, there were halberd-crowned cars (*hoko*) in which various scenes and events were depicted by the use of dolls, or enacted by human actors. Chief of these was the *Naginata hoko*, which is still given the privilege of leading the procession. According to

[1] The long halberd (*naginata*), being a modified phallus recognized in Shinto as prophylactic, is efficacious in averting disease. This probably accounts for its presence in all *matsuri*.

tradition, a famous sword-smith of the eleventh century presented to the shrine a *naginata* of finest workmanship in gratitude for the recovery of his daughter in answer to his prayer. This *naginata*, in the Kamakura Period (1186–1334), was loaned to a famous warrior that he might quell an insurrection. By its aid he was successful ; and the *naginata* was returned to the shrine with even greater sanctity attached thereto. So precious did it become that its place upon the *hoko* was taken by a *naginata* of lacquered bamboo, while the original reposed within the shrine. The mighty warrior still is depicted in the float, holding a halberd in one hand and the model of a boat in the other.

After some years of apparent neglect this *matsuri* was revived in the sixteenth century by Oda Nobunaga (1533– 1582) ; and from that time floats for dancers seem gradually to have been replaced by *yama*, platforms carried upon the shoulders of many bearers for the display of various scenes in tableau.

The deities in residence at Gion have a very central part in this *matsuri* ; but for many years there have been two processions—one in the morning, of *hoko* and *yama*, to herald the coming and to welcome the deities who in the afternoon are brought in three ornate sacred palanquins from the shrine to their *Otabisho* (Place of Sojourn) in the central part of the city, where they remain for a week, and thence are then returned to their shrine with similar ceremony. The afternoon processions may have a deeper interest for the strictly religious ; but for the common people the morning processions of *hoko* and *yama* are the chief attractions.

The *hoko* and *yama* of the morning processions are provided by different wards of the city, some being decorated with almost priceless treasures of old brocade—each ward, naturally, taking pride in its own contribution. The *hoko* are heavy, four-wheeled carts having enclosed bodies, draped with rich hangings of brocade and embroidery,

NAGINATA HOKO

and flat roofs with canopies, which in turn are surmounted each with a lofty halberd. The enclosed bodies may be entered from the rear ; and the flat roofs are filled with boys and young men trained for the occasion in the rude music of flute, drum, and beaten bell. In front of these musicians, upon the roof, under the canopy, stand dolls or human figures in portrayal of that which the special *hoko* represents ; and these dolls or children in costume, judging from old pictures and models of old-time *hoko*, appear to be survivals from a time when a larger part of the space was occupied by actors rather than by musicians. The *hoko* are drawn through the streets by hand—two long ropes being manned by an enthusiastic populace, while three men attend with heavy wooden blocks to brake the wheels and a pointed wedge wherewith to steer the car.

The *yama*, or portable stages, though usually less ornate than the *hoko*, are of interest for their tableaux, which depict scenes in the lives of old heroes, or legends of general didactic value. The Empress Jingo (A.D. 201–270), for example, before starting upon her military expedition against Chosen, wished to forecast her success, and went fishing in a river in Matsura, using a common needle for a hook and a thread from her garments for a line. Such was her catch that none could doubt of her future success. One *yama* represents the famous warrior-empress holding a bent rod in one hand and a large fish in the other.

Kakkyo was very poor, but very good to his aged mother. The support of his only son, a little boy, made it impossible, he thought, to care for his mother as he ought ; and he resolved to sacrifice his child. While digging a grave wherein to bury the boy he found a pot of gold with an inscription stating that it was for a dutiful son. Rejoicing in this favour of Heaven, he found it unnecessary to kill his child, but was able to care for his mother more faithfully than before. The boy, and the father digging the grave,

E

appear upon a *yama* ; but Heaven's intervention in the affairs of this Chinese Abraham seems less emphasized than the filial piety which forms the heart of the lesson.

In the city of Otsu, ten miles from Kyoto, is an old shrine in which four deities are honoured. It is, therefore, known as *Shinomiya* (the Shrine of Four). The first of the four is *Hikohohodemi-no-mikoto*, a son of *Ninigi-no-mikoto* and the grandfather of the first Japanese emperor, Jimmu Tenno ; and it is probably in his honour that the shrine is also called the *Shrine of the Imperial Grandson*.

In the archives of a family of unbroken history through many centuries is an interesting manuscript, dated September 13, 1635, concerning the development of the *matsuri* observed in connection with *Shinomiya*. It reads in translation as follows :

TO BE REMEMBERED

Several years ago, on the 10th of September, at the *Shinomiya matsuri*, *Jihei-dono*, a pedlar of salt from this street, danced in the horse-field of the shrine, wearing the mask of a racoon. His dancing proved so attractive, and the people enjoyed it so much, that he danced again the following year, again attracting a large crowd. The next year the people of this street, wishing to make a stage of bamboo bound with ropes and to bear it through the town, asked the local authorities for permission. This was granted, as the intent was to increase the attractiveness of the *matsuri*. Therefore the people made a stage of bamboo bound with ropes, with curtains of cotton-cloth, and bore it through the streets with the ringing of bells and the beating of drums, while *Jihei-dono* in a racoon mask danced upon it, shaking branches of the holy tree in his hand.

This they carried from street to street in the parish during the *matsuri* for about ten succeeding years, until *Jihei-dono* asked to be excused because of his increasing age. There being no one upon the street to take his place, for the *matsuri* of 1622 they made a racoon of wood and by means of strings caused it to beat its abdomen with its hands. This they carried upon the platform each year until the present, when we put wheels to it and allowed the children to draw it through the parish for the more enthusiastic celebration of the *matsuri*.

THE SENIOR OF KAJIYA STREET.

September 13, 1635.

From this old record it is evident that the custom of *matsuri* had become well established in Otsu by the beginning of the seventeenth century, that the populace were responsible for its success, and that the simplest of mimic dances were thought worthy of a place therein. The example of this street, or section of the parish, was evidently followed by others, for at the present time thirteen floats from as many different sections of the city are drawn in procession at the *Shinomiya matsuri*. That from Kajiya Street is still given the place of honour at the head of the procession ; but the racoon now perches upon the very top of the canopy, while his place in the open part of the car is taken by a life-sized doll, representing Priest Saigyo (A.D. 1118–1190), whose fame rests for the most part upon his skill as an itinerant poet.

This *matsuri*, unlike those in Kyoto, contains no *hoko*, or halberd-crowned cars. In fact, the halberd does not appear in the procession. The original *yama*, or portable stage, has given place to floats on which musicians are drawn about the city, and in which a prominent place is given to dolls in dramatic representation. The decorations are in character not unlike those of Gion, but the dolls are the centre of attraction ; and, as the cars are halted every few rods, the dolls by the pulling of strings are made to go through simple motions suggestive of the characters which they represent. The position of the cars in the procession is determined, with the exception of the first, by lot. The priest of the shrine has only very indirect charge of the celebration ; and the crowd of people attending the procession is a rejoicing, well-mannered mob.

In this *matsuri*, also, Kakkyo, the filial son, appears ; but here he is much more dramatically represented accompanied by his wife, who carries the child in her arms.

Murasaki Shikibu, the famous Court novelist, who at Ishiyama at the close of the tenth century wrote *Genji Monogatari*, is shown standing thoughtfully before her desk in another float ; and with every car is associated some event of legend or history in which the people take natural pride. The float called *Seseho Seki* shows the dramatic moment of an old story, at which, at the prayer of a holy priest, the spirit of a woman, imprisoned in a mighty stone because of her sin, is released.

In Nagahama, a small town not far from Otsu, a similar *matsuri* is held ; but this differs in that children, instead of dolls, present the dramatic action. It is not known which of these *matsuri* is the older ; but natural supposition leads one to think that the first actors were children, or adults, and that the introduction of the dolls may have been in imitation of the doll theatres, of which we shall have occasion to speak later.

Although these *matsuri* may be taken as typical of thousands, and as affording evidence of popular interest in dramatic presentation, many of the more important *matsuri* now devote themselves almost exclusively to the exhibition of old costumes and customs—affording no mean opportunity for the study of period history of the last four hundred years, but relatively little for an understanding of dramatic development. From ancient times the Japanese Court has been as it were a Shinto Holy of Holies, the Emperor being a national high priest as well as the human link in the unending chain of deity which all should worship. As an inevitable result the best of the performances before the shrines were taken over as parts of the Court ceremonial entertainment—true *Kami Asobi*. Others remained as *Kagura* attached to local shrines, and still others dropped

RACOON FLOAT, SHINOMIYA MATSURI

back to the popular level from which they sprang, carrying with them Shinto accretions. Those held under Imperial or priestly patronage became fixed in form and underwent no further development; but those which dropped back into popular use, though retaining the name *Kagura*, remained more or less plastic. This may be illustrated by the *Iwato* and *Sato Kagura*.

The former, as played at the opening of the New Year, was a kind of serenade, of a purely social and mercenary character, for the purpose of paying respect and soliciting gifts. It was performed by non-professional folk with no set form of action, though a lion-mask was often worn, and juggling tricks displayed to the rude accompaniment of drum and flute. The latter were rural presentations of mythological stories, danced with masks and often without dialogue.

Other New Year congratulatory dances akin to *Kagura* were danced to rhythmic chanting, with most expressive movements in imitation of labour, by artisan groups from door to door during the first few days of the new year. For twenty years, to the writer's personal knowledge, the same dance was given upon a certain Kyoto street on the 3rd of January by a group of from six to eight men in work-clothes, each emphasizing his movements with a light wand of wood.

CHAPTER IV

DENGAKU AND OTHER ANTECEDENTS OF NOH

RETURNING to a further consideration of *Dengaku*, we find that by the middle of the Heian Period (794–1129) six different names were employed to designate these dances, according to their character and special circumstances.

The *Shiba* (Lawn) *Dengaku* is mentioned as early as 1095 as an entertainment, together with racing,[1] in thanksgiving for a royal recovery from illness. The name, taken together with reference to the absence of mats in the performance, makes clear that the dance was performed upon the lawn or turf.

The *Dai* (Great) *Dengaku* was probably nothing more than a very elaborate presentation of *Dengaku*. In connection with this, reference is found to athletic sports, to rich costumes of gold and silver, to the participation therein of *samurai* and the higher nobility, and to rude revels which filled the streets and broke both social order and moral restraint. They seem to have possessed all the rude freedom of masques, in which all classes of society mingled without restraint.

The *Sho* (Small) *Dengaku* and the *Maiko* (Dancing-Girl) *Dengaku* appear to have been such as were ordinarily given in close association with Shinto shrines and with less of popular participation, though any *Dengaku* played by women may have been called *Maiko*, as when, according to the record

[1] The horse is the first and only domestic animal mentioned in the *Ko-ji-ki* ; and its mention there, in connection with the heavenly deities before the creation of the earthly islands, may be taken as evidence of its great antiquity among the Japanese. The horse, as a semi-sacred creature, is often found in Shinto establishments ; and the running or racing of horses seems from the most ancient times to have been a popular sport for the entertainment of gods as well as men.

of an Imperial outing (1180), the Court ladies are said to have blackened their teeth, dressed in flowers, and performed *Dengaku*.

The *Kachi* (Walking) *Dengaku* by its name implies the existence of a *Dengaku* played upon horseback. There is mention of such a *Dengaku* in connection with a Gion festival in 1246. Original *Dengaku*, however, was certainly played on foot ; and the special name probably designates merely ordinary *Dengaku* in distinction from *Dengaku* played upon horseback by *samurai*, or members of the warrior class.

Mura (Village) *Dengaku* is a relatively late designation of *Dengaku* as played purely for personal entertainment in small rural communities ; and its use serves merely to point out the fact, already noted, that these dances, once taken into patronage, tended to fall back into purely popular sports.

The *Kasuga* shrine at Nara and the *Gion* shrine at Kyoto were the chief patrons of *Dengaku* ; and to such an extent was patronage carried that *Dengaku* dancing became practically a profession. Before A.D. 1150 two rival schools, the *Honza* and the *Shimza* (the Root and the Branch) arose among the players, each striving for favour with the shrines and with the nobility. *Dengaku* reached the height of its development in the Kamakura Period (A.D. 1185–1332), and towards the end of that period it was particularly popular among the *samurai*. Provincial lords maintained their own players, who were known by their patrons' names and played at their banquets. Guests and patrons often gave the players in reward the rich apparel they themselves were wearing. The crest of patronage was reached in the time of Takatoki, the last of the Hojo Shoguns (A.D. 1316–1325) ; and thereafter *Dengaku* gradually lost favour, as *Sarugaku* took its place in the patronage of the nobility.

Throughout its history *Dengaku* remained characterized chiefly by its dancing ; but, as was inevitable under the patronage of the warrior class, its songs tended more and more to epic recital, seldom to dramatic portrayal by means of dialogue. The epic element in *Dengaku*, however, could not compete for popular favour with the greater freedom of recital in the *Monogatari*, which by the fourteenth century had gained a considerable standing, and was to prove a much more influential factor in dramatic development.

While primitive *Dengaku*, which originated as a spontaneous rural sport, was being formalized by Shinto shrines in close association with *Kagura*, or was enjoying a very limited freedom along epic lines under the patronage of the nobility, the common people were finding expression for their emotions in various dances, such as *Kuse Mae*, *Ennen Mae*, and *Sarugaku*. These, in contrast to *Dengaku*, were exceedingly plastic. Their music was simple, not to say rude ; and their chanted songs tended to the dramatic. The dramatic element was most apparent in *Kuse Mae*, which became an important influence in the development of *Ennen* and *Sarugaku* during the Muromachi Period (A.D. 1336–1440). The popularity of *Kuse Mae* in the later Ashikaga Period (A.D. 1440–1574) is evidence of the appeal made to the nobility, as well as to the common people, by its detailed stories of faithful children and its emphasis upon sustained emotion, such as we have preserved for us to modern times in the *Kuse* sections of *Noh* written in that period.

Furthermore, while *Dengaku*, under the patronage of priests and nobles, was reaching a level of development upon which it became stereotyped, that remnant of *Dengaku* which fell back into the hands of the common people developed more freely and incorporated with itself elements of simple dialogue. Thus, popular *Dengaku*, *Ennen Mae*, and *Sarugaku*, with its inclusion of *Kuse Mae*, came to exist side by side with little to distinguish them one from another. These under favourable circumstances might have reached a high degree of dramatic excellence ; but they, like their predecessors, were doomed to formalism under the influence of Buddhist priests and men of letters, through whom alone any literary perpetuation could be expected.

Buddhism gained its first firm foothold in Japan under the favour of Shotoku Taishi, regent from A.D. 593 to A.D. 621. He not only gave it his personal faith, but also encouraged its spread by sending priests to study its doctrines in China, and by inviting Chinese teachers to propagate them in Japan. The success of the new religion was great ; and its contribution was the greater because its propagandists were wise enough to utilize whatever could be found of local worth.

In connection with Buddhism there developed in Japan the practice of *Zushi*. This originally was the practice of *In-yo-do*, the No-yes-way ; and its practitioners, by the recital of incantations and the use of hypnotic arts, gained a standing as faith-healers and fortune-tellers. These came to be attached to the staff of various temples, and proved of service in extending the influence of the temples over their adherents. As might be expected, degeneration took place ; and these temple *Zushi* became mere entertainers engaged in attracting adherents by their plays and dancing. Through these, in part at least, popular sports found admission to temple ceremonies ; and, a beginning once made, progress was rapid, until all forms of popular entertainment were gathered under the patronage of Buddhist temples and of Shinto shrines as well, since the shrines had already received Buddhist recognition under the influence of Priest Gyogi (667–749).

Buddhism, however eclectic, was yet a religion, and in many particulars highly ethical, so that a process of selection and exclusion began ; and, while the ruder sports were relegated to the position of side-shows, *Dengaku*, *Ennen*, and *Sarugaku* were taken into favour and carried forward, with a large mixture of Chinese material, for the purpose of enriching the services and of teaching Buddhist principles to the common people.

The word *Noh* signifies accomplishment, and early came to be used of various dramatic dances which had attained a degree of acknowledged grace ; but in the adoption of *Dengaku*, *Ennen*, and *Sarugaku*, the elements of humour, often rude and vulgar, which had characterized their popular forms, were gradually cast off by Buddhist reformers until the title *Noh* came to be reserved entirely for those plays which, of a serious nature, tended to inculcate ethical, if not religious, principles. Thus, as the freedom of primitive dance became set in the art forms of Shinto, so by a gradual process, as didactic words in prose or verse were set to music by Buddhist priests, *Ennen*, *Dengaku*, and *Sarugaku* came to have a highly conventionalized form of presentation called *Noh*. *Ennen-no-Noh*, *Dengaku-no-Noh*, and *Saru-gaku-no-Noh* are thus merely highly developed, dignified, and artistic forms of *Ennen*, *Dengaku*, and *Sarugaku*.

The very elasticity of the term *Noh* makes historic dating impossible. Records of *Ennen* and *Dengaku* antedate those of *Sarugaku* ; and such is the generally accepted order of their development, under Buddhist patronage, into *Noh* ; but by the middle of the fifteenth century their *Noh* was scarcely distinguishable in art or substance, being kept distinct merely by the hereditary groups to which the players belonged, until the *Noh* of *Ennen* and *Dengaku* suffered almost total eclipse before the *Noh* of *Sarugaku*, as developed by Kiyotsugu, a Shinto priest of Kasuga (A.D. 1333-1384), and his son, Seami (A.D. 1363-1444), into the *Noh* of later years, in which the word came to mean, not the perfection of an art, but a particular art of dramatic presentation.

By the early years of the Kamakura Period (A.D. 1185-1329) *Zushi* entertainments of song and dance had come to include stories taken from Indian Buddhism, such as stories of Monju Bosatsu, Shakamune's great disciple, and to bear the name *Zushi Sarugaku*.   *Zushi* players, according to Motoori, were known as *Dai* and *Sho* (large and small), being priests or boys.   *Ennen*, which in early forms was a disordered entertainment of dance and miscellaneous sports, developed similar characteristics—possibly from the influence of *Zushi* ; and, when used as entertainment wherewith to conclude Buddhist services, had old men and boys who took appropriate parts in dialogue.   These also presented Indian stories and quoted bits of Chinese verse, becoming *Ennen-no-Noh* through such enrichment.   The use of young boys in the presentation of *Ennen* may account in part for the fact that these plays were particularly popular in Kyoto and Nara, where the priests are reputed to have been over-partial to the presence of youth in the temples ; and in this also we may find a beginning of those immoral customs which later shamed the records of the Japanese stage.

There were at least three distinct forms of *Ennen* at the time when, or just before, it assumed the name *Noh* : *Tsurane*, *Kaiko*, and *Furyu*.   The *Tsurane* were dialogues or series of conversations setting forth supposedly historic stories, interspersed with verses set to music. *Kaiko* were congratulatory addresses, humorous in nature, in introduction to more general entertainments ; and the *Furyu* also were dialogues in introduction to musical selections.

In A.D. 1544 there was published a collection of *Tsurane*, *Kaiko*, and *Furyu*, many of which were taken from older sources.   This collection contains thirteen titles of *Tsurane*, all of which are clearly vehicles for the conveyance of Buddhist teaching ; but they must have been quite incomprehensible to the common people of an age in which literary culture was confined almost entirely to the priesthood. Doubtless the dances in rich costume were attractive to the uneducated ; but, as in Europe of the Middle Ages, religious scriptures and services were beyond the intelligent comprehension of the mass of the people. Thus did Buddhism, as well as Shinto in its patronage of a popular art, withdraw that art from the intelligent interest of the common people, and doom it to a limited and specialized future.

Of the *Ennen* in the 1544 collection many were from *Kofukuji*, the chief temple of the Hosso sect, founded at Nara by the Fujiwara family in the early eighth century ; and, though neither author nor exact date is known, *Konron zan ni Shugyoku wo Tazunuru* (Seeking Jewels in Mount Konron) may be taken as an early example of *Pre-Noh-Ennen*, of the *Tsurane* type.

SEEKING JEWELS IN MOUNT KONRON [1]

PROLOGUE (*in chant or recitative*).

Although there are many forms of religious service there is nothing superior to the Lotus Service.[2] Although there are various entertainments, there is nothing finer than an entertainment of *Ennen* song and dance. This evening our hearts are to be moved by a service of mystery and revelation, and by a musical entertainment.

*   *   *   *   *

ONE PERSON.

As you say, the ceremonies which are held in this temple are not inferior to those of the olden time. This is because of the prosperity of this temple.

---

[1] At least two characters and a chorus are required for the presentation of this *Tsurane* ; but the characters are unnamed and entirely without individuality. Each is called merely *One Person*.

[2] *Renge Tai E.* The *Renge* (lotus) is the symbolic flower of Buddhism. *Tai E* signifies a great meeting ; and the entire phrase here refers to the service which is about to be held at the temple.

ONE PERSON.

The restoration of the temple buildings is almost finished ; but I fear the decorations are not in keeping. If only we could secure an abundance of the seven jewels ! [1]

ONE PERSON.

I have heard that there are many jewels in Mount Konron, in China. You would better go to that sacred mountain and get material wherewith to decorate the temple.

ONE PERSON.

Your words have the sound of wisdom ; but I have heard that in ancient times Emperor Boku, of Shu, reached that mountain only after having travelled over all the earth in a chariot drawn by eight divine horses. I doubt that any ordinary mortal may hope to reach it.

ONE PERSON.

No, no ; our purpose is unselfish ! Trusting in divine aid, you well may cross to China and seek the jewels there.

ONE PERSON.

Indeed, it seemeth reasonable.

(Song, with Dancing.) [2]

Solo.

We seek a foreign land, three thousand *ri* away ;
Through smoky waves on struggling we come.

Chorus.

Our native land is distant far, oh, far away ;
The mountains crossing, thence we come, we come.
How shall we find again our homeward way ?

---

[1] Gold, silver, emerald, mother of pearl, agate, amber, and coral.

[2] The song is a *Shirabyoshi*, or Chinese poem in lines of seven, five, seven. five, five words respectively. By it, and by the succeeding song it is made clear that the characters, after great difficulty, have reached their destination.

(Song, with Dancing.)

Solo.

Still on and on we go, through valleys dim,
Moon-shadow'd, where never comes the dawn.

Chorus.

Yet now at last, along the wind-swept shore,
The deeper evening shadows silent fall.

.   .   .   .   .

Where is the mountain ?
  Still from early dawn through many days,
We strive on toilsome
  Boat, or weary steed, or painful feet.
How much we long for
  Jewels fair from Konron's holy mount !

ONE PERSON.

At last we have come to the Jewel Lake upon Mount Konron.
Let us at once seek for the jewels.

ONE PERSON.

According to my understanding of an ancient song, the Jewel
Lake is but a common pond. The brightness of this night is
better far than any jewel. It seems to me, indeed, that no gem
is fairer than the moon's clear light.

ONE PERSON.

That is interestingly true ! All night long, by the shore of
the lake, let us sing songs to the moon.

ONE PERSON.

So let us do !

(Song.) [1]

Chorus.

Along the shore of the lake
It is delightful
To watch the little ripples,
As they come and go,
Gathering jewels in the light
Of the evening moon.

[1] The song is *hayauta* in rapid 7, 5, 7, 5 syllabic verse.

An Old Man.

> Dewdrops are pearls,
> The moon a shining mirror !

Chorus.

> Only to enlightened eyes,
> Glorious appear
> Jewels white from garments rare—
> Gifts of the dragon maid.

Postlogue.

> Indeed, it is true ; indeed, it is true.

*   *   *   *   *

The same collection from which *Seeking Jewels from Mount Konron* was taken contains seven *Kaiko* and thirty-nine *Furyu*. The *Kaiko* are merely introductions ; but the *Furyu*, though employed in introduction to musical entertainments, possess elements of dramatic interest. Vague hints of *Waki* and *Shite* and even of the *Ghost*, familiar in *Noh*, appear in *Renshobu Biwa Kyoku no Koto* (Music for the Biwa by Renshobu).

MUSIC FOR THE BIWA BY RENSHOBU [1]

Prologue.

This is Emperor Tenryaku.[2] The waves of his benevolence flow forth beyond the main island, and the breath of his virtues

---

[1] The date and authorship of this *Furyu* are unknown. At least two characters, though unnamed, appear, together with a speaking ghost and a silent emperor.

[2] The Emperor is thought of as passing at a distance. The name is that of an era (947–956). To have used the name of Emperor Murakami, who reigned during that era, would have seemed discourteous ; but this reference to an emperor and era noted for peace and the patronage of the arts may assist in giving a probable date to this composition, as within the next hundred years peace gave place to petty strife, and the conditions at *Kofukuji* became such as to make this *Furyu* inappropriate. The reign of Murakami, though noted for peace and literary patronage, is one upon which no Japanese looks with pride, for it records the lowest ebb of Imperial slavery to the will of the Fujiwara family, which reached the height of its prosperity in Michinaga's time about forty years after the Tenryaku era.

bloweth throughout the whole empire. Because of this, high officials are in harmony, and the wild barbarians are peaceably inclined. Truly, it seems to me that there has been before no age so holy.

*   *   *   *   *

ONE PERSON.

As you say, the just administration of the present time makes the effortless influence of *Gyo* and *Shun* [1] seem insignificant. Furthermore, in time of leisure from duties of State the Emperor rejoices in the beauties of Nature and the pleasures of the banquet. He has announced that he goes to-night to the Seiryo Palace to play the *biwa* and to enjoy the cloudless moon. Noblemen all, I beg you to accompany him.

ONE PERSON.

Truly, in the beauty of this evening it is hard to refrain from rejoicing ! Please, at once request his presence with us.

> (*Stage directions : Build Seiryo Palace upon the stage.*
> *Enter* EMPEROR, *playing upon the* biwa. *In the court-*
> *yard, before the palace, enter* RENSHOBU, THE SPIRIT.)

ONE PERSON.

The Emperor has already come to the Seiryo Palace, and is now playing upon the *biwa*. The sound of his plectrum is clear and full of feeling. The autumn moon shines cloudless. Night deepens and all is still. A bank of cloud draws near and hovers in the courtyard. What can it be ? Some evil one with plot to seize the Royal throne ! Away ! at once, away !

RENSHOBU, THE SPIRIT MASTER OF MUSIC.

Be not affrighted ! 'Tis Renshobu, the hermit, the player of *biwa* from China. Drawn by His Majesty's playing, this night I have come. In the era of Showa [2] I taught three *biwa* selections—*Ryusen, Kaiboku,* and *Yoshin*—to Teibin, your envoy to China, that he might in turn introduce them unto this land. There remains yet one other—*Seigen Sekijo*—which now I would teach to His Majesty.

---

[1] The first and second emperors of China, rulers of mythically divine power.
[2] Era of Showa, A.D. 834–847.

ONE PERSON.

How strange ! It must be because the Emperor is devoted to music as well as most faithful in administration.

＊　　　＊　　　＊　　　＊　　　＊

ONE PERSON.

We have reported your courteous desire. His Majesty is graciously pleased. You will kindly at once teach that remaining selection.

THE SPIRIT.

Then to the Palace I'll go, and on his own instrument teach him.

> (Hashirimono—*birds and beasts, familiars of the hermit— gather about, while the* SPIRIT *enters the Palace and plays upon the* biwa *If the young players of* Ennen *cannot perform upon the* biwa, *it may be played by others behind the scenes*.)

ONE PERSON.

That a saintly hermit thus should come to teach His Majesty must be an omen good of his and of the country's long prosperity. Let us entertain the Spirit with music and with dance.

ONE PERSON.

Play, and perform the dance !

＊　　　＊　　　＊　　　＊　　　＊

Of popular *Dengaku* which under Buddhist patronage developed into *Dengaku-no-Noh*, there are very few literary remains, fragments of only three plays remaining out of some three hundred titles. On a picture of *Dengaku-no-Noh*, as supposed to have been given at Wakamiya in Nara, where *Dengaku* survived longest, appears a list of titles with the statement that six selections were given annually, there being a change from year to year.

One year : *Kikusui, Matsudomo ei, Tsunemasu, Furugori, Shinobu*, and *Kappo*.

One year : *Hakozaki, Ukioni, Tsunemasu, Furugori, Hashiwa*, and *Kappo*.

F

It is to be noted that even in these lists the titles are somewhat duplicated. Other titles are given in other lists ; but, of them all, *Kikusui, Nisei,* and a fragment of *Kappo* alone are extant. Even when titles are given on festival programmes, the plays may not be given, for in this connection a pleasing little fiction is maintained. After a beginning has been made, one of the players goes to the priest in charge and begs that they may be excused from further acting as the players are ill.

In 1756, the Tokugawa Government ordered an investigation of the history and condition of *Dengaku,* with a view to including it in the ceremonial of the Nikko Shrines. An evasive answer was sent from Nara, where alone *Dengaku* players could be found, to the effect that there were several selections and that the plays could be given upon request. Further investigation revealed the fact that only *Kikusui* could be found. In 1915 there were said to be in the region of Nara seven men who had old costumes and instruments and possessed some knowledge of the *Dengaku* art ; and in 1920, upon an occasion of special celebration, the writer saw eight actors who in *Dengaku,* so called, presented a brief dance which, however, was entirely lacking in dramatic character and intelligible significance. Thus it seems clearly evident that *Dengaku,* as a primitive dramatic form, is no longer extant.

The *Kikusui,* the sole surviving example of *Dengaku,* has nothing which even suggests the popular origin of the *Dengaku* dance. It shows the art in its utter subordination to Buddhist purpose. The story is Chinese, scarcely modified in transition ; and its chief interest lies in the introduction of character parts which took definite place in later *Noh.* Here the *Waki,* or first actor, whose business is to explain the circumstances, is a hermit, who performs his part largely by asking questions. The *Tayu,* who seems to occupy the place later taken by the *Shite* in *Noh,* is an attendant priest of the Royal Court ; and the Sashi Goe are holy hermits.

KIKUSUI

CHRYSANTHEMUM WATER.

PART I.

WAKI.

Happy the reign whose sovereign liveth long ! I am a subject of Emperor Bun [1] of China. Although our Lord is young to rule, he is far more merciful to his people than were those three emperors and five kings of old, famed for their mercy. Our age is fortunate, indeed !

Having been summoned to the Court by His Majesty, we hermits from many mountains are hastening to the Steel-sword Mountain.

How many years may he reign ?
'Tis said our Lord shall reign
A thousand years,
Rather—eight thousand,
Till pebbles on the shore become rocks,
Moss-grown.

Passing shore after shore,
Rock-strewn through many years,
To the Steel-sword Mountain we have come,
We have come.

Having made haste, I have arrived at the Steel-sword Mountain. After resting here a little, I want to call upon certain people of the place.

TAYU.

O chrysanthemum, blooming ever, even for a thousand years ! Tribute to our Lord's gracious reign !

SASHI GOE.

Although our Lord is young to rule, he is far more merciful to his people than were those three emperors and five kings of old, famed for their mercy.

[1] Emperor Bun, 178–158 B.C.

To him we owe thanks, indeed ! To him we offer up this water of chrysanthemum, that he long may live. He who drinks this water of chrysanthemum shall escape all disease and, though lightly clad, shall not feel the cold.

Therefore is it a cordial of eternal youth, water of chrysanthemum known to all.

Having gathered this water, we have come to the Court ; we have come.

WAKI.

Whence came these hermits, who have just arrived ?

TAYU.

They have come to offer our Lord life's elixir.

WAKI.

That's good ; very good, indeed !

It's a sign of a peaceful age when hermits come from the mountains and saints find position in the State.

Who are these people, anyhow ?

TAYU.

That one is Jido, a subject of Emperor Boku Shu, who, having lived seven hundred years, is now called Hoso.

WAKI.

What ! If he were a subject of Emperor Boku Shu, [1] how can he have lived till now ?

TAYU.

There is no peculiar reason ; it is merely because he drank chrysanthemum water such as he has just brought.

WAKI.

Indeed ! If anyone drinks that water of chrysanthemum, will he live many years ?

TAYU.

Of course, there is no doubt about it. You'd better try it. Without doubt, if one drinks chrysanthemum water, the

[1] Emperor Boku Shu reigned about 950 B.C., some four hundred years before Gautama's birth ! Need the drama be free from anachronism ?

chrysanthemum water of Nanyoken, it will, as medicine, preserve his life. Though this man has lived seven hundred years, he is as young as ever.

May our Lord deign to drink !

We, his faithful subjects, sing the praises of chrysanthemum water. If one drinks, surely it will remove all shadows which darken life, remove and cause them to be forgotten.

> Plucking chrysanthemum—
> Plucking their flowers—
> Delay we the passing years,
> Turn back their numbers.

PART II.

WAKI.

Please tell us more fully how it is that this man has lived so long.

TAYU.

When Great Gautama was expounding the Law upon Mount Ryoju, Emperor Boku, drawn by his preaching, came quickly on horseback to listen. The Buddha told him that the teaching was for him alone, but that, for future rulers, he would give two phrases—they are found in the *Fumon-bon*.[1]

Thereafter the fame of the Emperor increased. Jido at the time was in great favour at the Court ; but one day he carelessly stepped over his royal master's pillow, and for that was banished to Steel-sword Mountain. That mountain was several hundred miles from the palace ; and there were tigers and wolves with sharp teeth, but not a human being upon it. In pity the Emperor taught Jido the two sacred phrases—they are found in the *Fumon-bon*. These, lest he should forget, Jido wrote upon the leaves of a chrysanthemum growing by a brook on Steel-sword Mountain ; and, gazing all day long upon them, spent many days repeating them.

Thereafter the dewdrops on the chrysanthemum turned to water of chrysanthemum and became an elixir of life. Drinking this, Jido prolonged his days.

---

[1] *Fumon-bon* : the scriptures in which it is declared that the repetition of Kwanon's name will bring salvation.

So, as I've told you, it became an elixir of life for all who drink of it. They say that the power of the Doctrine clings to the chrysanthemums of the Steel-sword Mountain and makes them life-giving.

> May our Lord accept
> The chrysanthemum water !

WAKI.

Thanks, many thanks ! Surely, our Lord will himself visit the Steel-sword Mountain. Be thou his guide.

TAYU.

Surely ! Going to the Steel-sword Mountain, and calling Hoso's friends together, we will make pleasant our Lord's journey.

Already I am upon my way.

Our Lord's reign is like a chrysanthemum seen upon the clouds, a white chrysanthemum in the light of the evening stars.

       *   *   *   *   *

We have come to the Steel-sword Mountain, we have come to the Steel-sword Mountain.

Praise be ! The water falling from the leaves will keep our Lord's reign ever pure. The promise of a long reign fills the sky.

> Upon Arashiyama
> The maple gleameth,
> The folded clouds are redden'd
> In evening's glow—
> The water freshly falleth,
> Aglint the sunlight ;
> And that which laves the blossoms,
> We'll take and bear it
> To him, our Lord, in prayer
> For life unending.

CHAPTER V

SARUGAKU AND NOH

IN contrast to the *Noh* of *Dengaku*, the *Noh* of *Sarugaku* left an abundant literary legacy, now carefully cherished by devotees of *Noh* as a dramatic art. Originally, the characters which are read *Sarugaku* (猿 樂) and which signify *monkey music*, were used to designate spontaneous actions of a humorous or comic nature. To this popular *Sarugaku*, dialogue had been added before the beginning of the fourteenth century ; but gradually, under the influence of literary priests, the dialogue lost its comic nature and gave way to a more poetically austere recital, in the interpretation of which the action also became refined, while still retaining the original name.

The various great shrines had in their service families whose hereditary duty it was to present contributions of *Noh* upon festive occasions. Such were found at Ise, Kamo, Sumiyoshi, as well as at Nara ; but in connection with the *Kasuga* shrine in Nara, there were four families of special note, whose descendants alone have preserved the art. The Emani, Yusaki, Toyama, and Sakado families, now known as *Konperu*, *Kwanze*, *Hosho*, and *Kongo*, together with *Kita*—an outgrowth of *Kongo*—form in reality two schools, the *Shimogakari* and the *Kamigakari*, according to their method of acting. Of these families, the *Kwanze* and the *Kongo* are the most prominent, and representative of the *Kamigakari* and the *Shimogakari* schools respectively.

Kwanami Kiyotsugu and his son, Seami, were members of the *Kwanze* family, and by them *Sarugaku* was brought to its perfection. Seami (A.D. 1363–1444) considered it a

Noh or art, under the name *Sarugaku no Noh* (申 樂 の 能). In this connection it is of interest to note that Seami rejected the character signifying *monkey*, and substituted 申 which, while read *saru*, is derived from the character for deity (神) which is used in the term *Kagura* (神 樂), from which more elementary form of entertainment he thought, or assumed to think, that *Sarugaku* had been developed. The increased dignity, in greater harmony with the acquired character of his *Sarugaku*, is at once perceived.

Seami's Sixteen Booklets (*Seami Jurokubu Shu*) throw much light upon his contribution to *Sarugaku no Noh* ; and by inference, though not from direct statement in this, we may judge that he definitely rejected all lighter elements in early *Sarugaku* which his father had in a degree favoured through the influence of Itchu, his teacher, himself a noted player of *Dengaku*. In spite of Seami's serious-mindedness, however, he did much, through the inclusion of more human elements, to free *Sarugaku no Noh* from the crushing domination of the Buddhist priesthood, which sought to use it almost exclusively for purposes of religious propaganda ; and, since it still retained greater plasticity than did *Kagura* or *Dengaku*, he was able to make of it an entertainment which, however saturated with the more austere elements of Buddhism, appealed to men as no temple ceremony had ever done or as no simpler *Kuse* had ever aspired to do. As this style of entertainment developed in his hands, Seami began to drop the extended title and to call it simply *Noh*, the entertainment *par excellence*.

Before the end of the fifteenth century, four types of *Noh* were clearly discernible : *Shinji Noh*, dealing with mythological subjects, including the supposed origins of certain shrines and temples ; *Shugen Noh*, celebrating customs or occasions and brought to its perfection for the entertainment of the Shogun and his military associates ; *Yurei* and

THE NOH STAGE

(1) Stage proper.   (3) Shite Pillar.   (5) Rear wall, with painted pine.   (7) Chorus
(2) Approach from dressing-room. (4) Waki Pillar.   (6) Musicians.   (8) Audience boxes.

Seirei Noh, in which ghosts and spirits have part, and by which the stern hearts of the warrior class were supposed to be softened and turned to spiritual things ; and *Genzai Mono Noh*, dealing with human passion, things of the present life, and filled with moral purpose.

Although Seami's name is associated more closely with the *Shugen Noh*, neither school confined itself to the production of any one type, practically all types coming to be used in the presentation of a complete *Noh* performance ; and the types themselves cannot be regarded as of chronological order of development, but rather as expressive of varying taste, in part according to the temper of different localities. However, whether emphasis were placed upon the sense of mystery and art or upon the skill in mimic action, Seami was insistent that the emphasis must be given from inner conviction and with depth of feeling. In him *Noh* found a creator who was a master ; but even he could not confer a vitality capable of continued development. The art became fixed and changeless.

A full *Noh* programme consists of a series of individual plays, some of which may be understood and appreciated separately, some only in connection with their setting in the series. The order of performance (*Ban-gumi*) usually includes five or six *Noh*, with lighter *Kyogen* as interludes to break the strain of serious attention. Of these *Noh*, the first must be a *Shinji Noh*. The second is a *Shura*, or selection wherein the chief character is a warrior. The third features a female character ; the fourth an evil spirit ; and these three may be taken from any one of various *types* of *Noh*. The fifth is a *Genzai Mono Noh*, and will be followed by some formula of congratulation or by a *Shugen Noh*, if that element has not been sufficiently emphasized in the earlier selections.

Others have given for English readers excellent translations of *Noh* ; [1] but the following representative selections may serve to make the plays stand out more vividly as the final form of still another line of development which, like that in the *Kagura*, was doomed to become stereotyped through lack of contact with life.

For better understanding of *Noh* in translation, it should be noted that a practically changeless form governs all libretto (*Utai*). The opening verse (*Jidai*) is abrupt and often difficult of understanding. This is followed by the self-introduction of the first speaker, in matter-of-fact prose. A travel song is then intoned, and gives a series of dissolving views which serve to awaken the imagination in preparation for the spirit of the *Noh*, which is presented subtly and indirectly, never directly, to the appreciation of the audience.

The actors in *Noh* may be two or more. The first to enter is *Waki*, or *Side*, an assistant. He introduces the situation and acts throughout as a foil to the second or chief character, the *Shite*, the Doer. Both of these may have attendants, *Tsure*. The Chorus (*Ji*), consisting of eight or more men, sit at one side and chant when the nature of the dance makes it difficult for the actor to deliver his own part. Occasionally, also, like the Chorus of the Greek Drama, they serve as direct interpreters of the action.

The terms *actor* and **action**, furthermore, must not mislead the Western reader. The *Noh* is not like anything of which the West has first-hand experience. It is not a lyric drama, though its lines are chanted rather than spoken. The characters are often masked, always when representing women ; and their movements are formalized to the last degree in stately posturing, which is designed to reveal the spirit rather than the body of the story. The effect produced

---

[1] None surpass, in literary scholarship, those by Arthur Waley in *The Nō Plays of Japan* (1922).

must be experienced to be appreciated. It grows upon one with strange hypnotic power.

Shinji Noh, though holding high honour at Shinto shrines because of the character of its themes, is too lacking in spontaneity to be counted as among the most primitive forms. It seems to have been built up with clear purpose from more popular models. Of the *Shinji Noh* the *Okina* is thought to be the most ancient. Of its origin and significance there are many theories, none of which are convincing. Some would trace it to the same origin as *Kagura*, and find in it representation of characters present at the dance by *Uzume* before the Rock Cave ; but, in objection to that, it may be stated that the chief character in *Okina* has no counterpart in the myth, and that the words spoken in the *Noh* can have no possible reference to that story. Others would find in it an inheritance from Persian influence which reached Japan through India ; but of that the evidence is too slight. At least it can be said that the *Okina* is traditionally ancient ; that it is given, when played in a service of *Noh*, the position of honour corresponding to that given *Niwabi* in *Kagura*, and that its character betokens a ritualistic rather than a social development.

Okina, *Senzai*, and *Sanbanso* appear to be three possible names for the same *Noh*, each being the designation of a character : an old man, an echo-like follower, and a comic clown. It is to be noted, however, that, in all extant *Okina*, *Sanbanso*, the one character whom the common people would enjoy, has disappeared, leaving only a name and a memory of comedy. His certain presence as an element of rude jesting in early forms, and his later reappearance in many *Kyogen*, is evidence bearing upon the rejection of the comic by *Noh* and its separate development as *Kyogen*, which we shall consider later.

OKINA

Characters :

SHITE.
TSURE.
CHORUS.

SHITE.

> To to tarari tararira
> Tarari agari rararido ! [1]

CHORUS.

> Chiriya tarari tararira
> Tarari agari rararido !

SHITE.

> Even for a thousand years,
> May life be granted,

CHORUS.

> Through a thousand autumns long,
> May we continue,

SHITE.

> With the endless years of the
> Tortoise and the crane. [2]

CHORUS.

> Hearts o'erflowing happily,
> We joy, rejoicing.

SHITE.

> Do do tarari tararira

CHORUS.

> Chiriya tarari tararira
> Tarari agari rararido !

[1] Exclamatory expressions of unknown meaning, possibly corrupted from a foreign liturgy.
[2] Both noted for long life.

TSURE.

> 'Tis the water of the fall that sounds,[1]
> 'Tis the water of the fall that sounds.
> Although the sun shines,

CHORUS.

> Ceaselessly it rusheth on—
> Aryuto, aryuto, aryuto !

TSURE.

> Ceaselessly it rusheth on,
> Ceaselessly it rusheth on.
>
> Long may he, our Lord, live on,
> A thousand years,
> Guardian maids from heaven high,
> With wings empowered !
>
> 'Tis the water of the fall that sounds.
> Although the sun shines,

CHORUS.

> Ceaselessly it rusheth on,
> Aryuto, aryuto, aryuto !

TSURE.

> My hair-bound lover— [2]
> Ha ha !

CHORUS.

> So closely lying—
> Ha ha !

SHITE.

> Although I am old,

CHORUS.

> Yet will I go.
> Ha ha !

[1] This is a song from *Ennen Mae*, interrupted by exclamation and a prayer which may be from some old liturgy.   The song appears in other *Noh*, all, probably, quoting from a single older source.

[2] These phrases are from a Saibara song, and possibly suggest that which the dignified *Noh* may not express.

SHITE.

> From unrecorded
> Ages, men have sought in prayer
> For added yéars—
> For added years—
> Through the ages men have sought.

CHORUS.

> Soyo ya riichi ya !
> 'Tis so.

SHITE.

> The aged crane doth sing his song
> Of years, ten thousand ;
> And the tortoise in the ancient pond
> Doth bear upon his back
> All heaven, and earth, and man.
> The clear sands of the shore
> Reflect the light of the morning sun ;
> And the cool waters of the fall
> Reflect the evening moon.
> Peace on the earth, and safety o'er the Land !
> This is our prayer to-day.
> Old men,
> Old men from everywhere.

CHORUS.

> Ah, old men from everywhere—
> Old men from everywhere.

SHITE.

> In celebration of a thousand years,
> Let me dance the dance
> Of years ten thousand.

CHORUS.

> The dance of years ten thousand !

SHITE.

> The dance of years ten thousand !

CHORUS.

> The dance of years ten thousand !

CHIKUBU SHIMA [1]

Characters :

WAKI, *an Official.*
WAKI TSURE, *a Servant to the Official.*
SHITE OF FIRST PART, *an Aged Fisherman.*
TSURE OF FIRST PART, *a Fisher Wife.*
SHITE OF SECOND PART, *the Dragon God.*
TSURE OF SECOND PART, *Benzaiten, Goddess.*

PART I.

WAKI AND WAKI TSURE.

Let us make haste to visit
Chikubu Shima,
Where Uguisu— [2]
Where Uguisu are born
In bamboo groves.

We are subjects in the service of Engi's virtuous lord. By our master we have been given release from duty, and are on our way to Chikubu Shima in Omi, whose deity is a wonder-working God.

By its river-bed
We found the Shrine of Four,[3]
Then quickly came where
In the water clear
Of a swift-flowing well-spring
Could be seen the moon
Below, as in the heaven.
At Seki's lofty
Shrine, on Mount Osaka, next
We humbly worshipped.
Beyond the mountain ridges
Then, descending low,
A town we reached in Shiga,
By the shore, the shore
Ye know as Nio.

[1] This is a *Shinji Noh* by Ujinobu (1404–1469), in which deity appears and tells of the divine character of the shrine on the Island of Chikubu in Lake Biwa.

[2] The *Uguisu* is the Japanese nightingale, falsely so called.

[3] *Shinomiya*, a Shrine in Otsu. See page 66.

Since we have made haste, we have arrived at the shore of Nio.   Behold !   There comes a fishing-boat.   Here let us wait awhile, and ask for passage.

> SHITE (*in the boat*).
>> A day of marvel !
>> Midway nature's month of birth,[1]
>> The lake lies sleeping,
>> Its quiet surface scarcely
>> By ripples broken.
>
> TSURE.
>> The dawn's clear brightness veiled
>> In misty beauty !
>
> SHITE.
>> The pathway of the boats—
>> So calm in motion !
>
> SHITE AND TSURE.
>> Indeed, it seemeth truly
>> There are no troubles !
>
> SHITE.
>> Ah, we are they who long have lived
>> Along this shore,
>> And all day long
>> The burden of the scaly fish have borne.
>
> SHITE AND TSURE.
>> Weary, indeed, the wretched poor,
>> Who spend their nights and days upon the lake,
>> Merely to live.
>>> (*To be sung softly.*)
>> E'en though monotonously,
>> We toil unceasing,
>> On this clear lake 'tis better
>> Far, than elsewhere,

[1] The month of March.

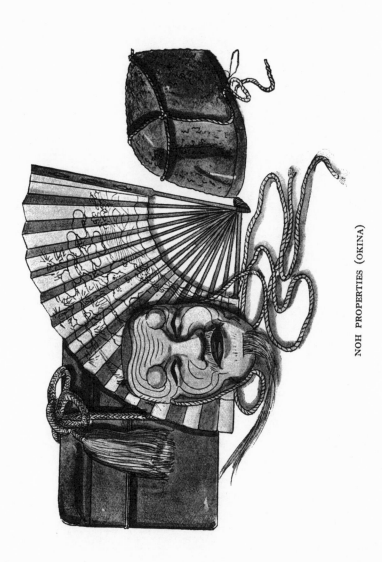

NOH PROPERTIES (OKINA)

(More loudly.)

Because, along the coast line,
And among the hills,
Are famous places
Many for us to look at.
There are flow'ring fields
In Shiga's central city ;
The mountain cherries
Are beautiful as ever ;
The white-sailed ships and
Little boats dot Mano's bay.
Some one upon the shore is calling ;
Let us draw near and question, question him.

WAKI.

I pray you, let us take passage in your boat.

SHITE.

This is no ferry.   Look ye well.   This is a fishing-boat.

WAKI.

Indeed, it is because we know that yours is a fishing-boat that
we ask for passage.   We are ones who for the first time visit
Chikubu Shima ; and we must take the heaven-sent boat which
first appeareth.[1]

SHITE.

Of a truth this place is holy ; and if we show contempt toward
those who turn their footsteps hither, it may offend the gods.

TSURE.

Yes, we will take you on our boat.

WAKI.

How fortunate !   This boat must have been sent to welcome
us.   I think it comes driven by the power of Buddha's teaching.

---

[1] *Chikai no fune* may mean the *nearest boat* or *Buddha's boat of
promise,* according to reading.   Shaka is reputed to have sent a boat
from the other world with promise of salvation for all.

SHITE.

To-day is unusually calm ; there is no wind to cause anxiety.

CHORUS.

Though its name means *little waves*, there's scarce a ripple on the lake to-day. May those folk upon the shore, I wonder, be from the city ? I hope they go on board and enjoy the views.

> They are on the lake, the lake ;
> The country yonder
> Lies near the bay of Omi.
> Spring amid the hills !
> Like snow appear the blossoms.
> Can it be snowing,
> Or is it winter's remnant ?
> The mountain that knows not the seasons
> Must surely be Fuji near Kyoto.[1]
> Though cold the wind that bloweth
> From Hira's summit
> Down, the day is bright with spring.
> Out upon the lake
> We cannot count the vessels.
> Like country tourists,
> Those fisher-folk are meeting
> Great ones whom they scarce
> Dreamed of seeing.
> Now the boat has floated far,
> Chikubu Shima sighting.

SHITE.

> As green trees sink their shadows [2]
> Deep beneath the waves,

[1] *Miyako no Fuji* is Mount Hiei ; and the quotation is from the *Ise Monogatari*, a story of Narihira, of disputed date and authorship.
[2] This appears to be a free quotation from an old poem by a priest upon visiting Chikubu Shima.

> Green trees sink their shadows down,
> And fishes climb ; the rabbits
> Of the floating moon do race
> The waves ; sacred lights, holy
> Places, unsurpassed !
> Ceaselessly the wind of God
> The Boat of Mercy wafteth.

CHORUS.

> The moving fish do seem
> To climb their branches ;
> But when upon the water
> The moon rides floating,
> Can it be her rabbits play
> With sporting wavelets ?
> Island of wonders !

SHITE.

> Our boat has now arrived.   Please disembark.

WAKI.

> Oh joy, that soon we'll see great Deity !

SHITE.

> My own, old, humble self will show the way.
> 'Tis very Benzaiten !   Ye both should pray.

WAKI.

> 'Tis finer far than we'd been told.
> But this is strange !
> We'd heard the Island to be closed
> To women, all.
> How came that woman there ?

SHITE.

> The rumour of a fool, in sooth !
> I'm glad to say that women, most,
> May come, since this is dedicate
> To Kyosho Nyorai's second birth.

WAKI.

> 'Tis hard, indeed, to understand !

CHORUS.

> Great Benzaiten,
> A woman, truly,
> A woman, truly,
> Of wonder-working power,
> From heaven comes, an angel, here ;
> So here there's no distinction drawn
> Forbidding women.

Those only who know nothing
Such tales repeat.
Her merciful desire has long been granted.
From the time of Shakamune she hath wrought
For the saving of women.

SHITE.

Truly, truly, there is no doubt of that.

CHORUS.

Into the pine shadows
Of the rocky coast
The fishing-boat has faded ;
And the woman old
Has opened wide the door
Of the holy shrine,
And entered, saying—
" I am no woman born."
The aged fisherman,
Into the water plunging,
Has disappeared.
In a wave's white crest
His face, turned back, revealed
The Dragon of the Lake.

PART II.

CHORUS.

A rumbling is heard
From the Shrine's inner chamber ;
And, like to the sun
Or the moon on the mountain,
The Goddess appears,
In her radiance gracious.

TSURE.

Benzaiten am I,
And I dwell in this Island,
Protecting the Land
Through my reverence, tended
The Gods who are great.

CHORUS.

> Now music is heard
> From above, and the music
> Resoundeth.
> From the flowers the petals
> Are falling like rain
> In the spring-time ; and over
> Her bright waving sleeves
> The evening moon shineth.
> Wondrous the vision !

Dancing.

CHORUS.

> The time for the dance,
> And the music at evening,
> Is over and gone.
> In the gleam of the moonlight,
> The waters, wind-blown,
> Are a-rustle and quiver ;
> The earth's Dragon God,
> On the face of the water,
> The earth's Dragon God
> In his glory appeareth,
> To all lifting high,
> As a gift, precious jewels
> Of silver and gold.
> The vision a marvel !
> Adore ye, and praise !

SHITE.

> Salvation for all !
> Is the promise of old—

CHORUS.

> Salvation for all !
> And in manifold ways from
> Of old hath the pledge
> Been redeemed. An Angel
> Now granteth the prayers
> Of the people ; a Dragon
> Protecteth the Land,
> And the promise fulfilleth.

The Angel returns
To the Holy of Holies ;
The Dragon God flies
To the lake ; and, with smiting
Of water and waves,
To his home the Great Guardian
Hasteth.

CHAPTER VI

SHUGEN, YUREI AND SEIREI NOH

HIMURO [1]

Characters:

WAKI, *an Official.*
SHITE OF FIRST PART, *an Aged Keeper of an Ice-Shelter.*
TSURE OF FIRST PART, *his Servant.*
SHITE OF SECOND PART, *the Deity of Ice-Shelters.*
TSURE OF SECOND PART, *an Angel.*

PART I.

WAKI.

One lord of all the Islands,
Of them all, one lord,
By whose fair favour
All nature tranquil smileth,
In spring-time smileth.

A subject am I of Kameyama, the retired Emperor.
To-day I have come to Kusenoto, to Tango ; and, as I have
already travelled far, I am planning to take the Wakase
road and have a look over the mountains, Irie of Tsuda,
Aoba and Nochise. After that I will return to the city.

Spring-flowers, surely
The jewel-white camellia !
Eight thousand years— [2]
Eight thousand years—
Are over : the sky is blue !

[1] This is a *Shugen Noh* of unknown authorship dating from about
A.D. 1300.
[2] The long, long winter is over.

Range after range of
Mountains in the glad spring-time !
Through the green shadows
Of Aoba I'm passing ;
The end of the cloud-road,
The road to the Palace, nears !
Now, on Tamba's [1] road,
Not far from the Capital,
I am journeying ;
To the hill of ice-shelters
I have come at last,
I have come at last.

As I have hurried, I have arrived at the hill of ice-shelters in Tamba. I will wait for one of the townsmen of the place and ask the history of these ice-shelters.

SHITE.

Amid the mountain shadows,
Late in the spring-time,
From flowers which are blooming
Snow we can gather.

TSURE.

In the midst of the mountains,
The shade of the pines

SHITE AND TSURE.

The resemblance of winter
Retains through the spring.

SHITE.

If there blooms one single blossom,
All the world has spring ;
But the pine-trees add the colour
Of eternal things.

[1] Tamba and Tango are regions lying to the north of the Capital.

SHITE AND TSURE.

> Down the green slopes of the hill of ice-shelters
> Loudly the valley wind blows ; and, like rain-drops,
> Hail with the gentle snow falleth, falleth.
> Surely the era of plentiful harvests
> Smiles 'neath the blessing of Majesty's favour.
>
> May the Land through endless years
> In bounty prosper,
> Like the deep green of the mountain
> Which still unchanging
> Its greenness keepeth.
> Spring in beauty gleameth there,
> But in the valley
> 'Tis as in winter.
> Year by year an aged man,
> With head frost-laden,
> Gathers snow in winter deep
> To keep as treasure ;
> And he guards it as a gift
> In ice-store shelters—
> With care he guardeth.

WAKI.

> Oh ! There is something I want to ask this old man.

SHITE.

> Do you want me ?   What would you ask ?

WAKI.

> Are you the keeper of this ice-shelter ?

SHITE.

> Yes, I am the keeper of this ice-shelter.

WAKI.

I have often had the honour of seeing the annual offering of ice ; but this is the first time I have seen its place of shelter. I pray you, tell me by what means you keep the ice into spring and summer.

SHITE.

In olden times there was a hut under a grove, in the vast moorland set aside as an Imperial Hunting Ground ; and once, though in mid June, the wind blew cold across the Emperor's sleeves, as though he hunted over a wintry field. To his surprise, he found an old man storing snow and ice within the hut. The old man said that holy hermits in their homes were wont to keep both red and purple snow as medicine ; and that he stored the snow for the same purpose. To His Majesty he offered ice ; and thus began the custom of Imperial Ice-offering.

WAKI.

The story which I have heard is very interesting. But the location of the ice-shelters has been changed quite frequently since ancient times, I suppose.

SHITE.

During the reign of Emperor Nintoku, ice was sent from shelters in Tsuge, Yamato ;

TSURE.

Matsugasaki,
Listening for royal news,
Then, 'mid its snow-drifts,

SHITE.

Shadowed by mountains northward,
Was made an ice-shelter ;

TSURE.

> Lastly to this province,
> Brought were the ice-shelters,
> Here to this valley,
> Wind-swept and cold, for winter

SHITE.

> E'en till now famous.

SHITE AND TSURE.

> And for the future,
> Here in Kuwata of Tamba
> Shelters are standing,
> Offering yearly gifts.

WAKI.

> Indeed, I believe
> The old man speaketh truly !
> Since mountains and all
> Hereabout, as with garments,
> In forests are clothed,
> And the sun in the valley
> Shines not, 'tis not strange
> That the ice and the snowflakes
> Melt not till spring,
> Till the hot summer cometh.

SHITE.

You err. Saying that in some places ice does not melt would imply that the will of His Majesty is needless, powerless there.

WAKI.

> Ordinary snow and ice,

SHITE.

> When the year changeth,
> Though it be in one night time,

WAKI.

> Would melt in the wind,
> The wind that bringeth the spring.

SHITE.

> As in a poem

WAKI.

> Tsurayuki sang—

CHORUS.

> Though, from sleeves dipped in water,
> The drops froze to ice,
> The drops froze to ice,
> To-day's wind, bringing spring-time,
> Would melt them—he sang.
> In the breath of the spring-time,
> That comes in one night,
> 'Tis the usual thing for
> The ice all to melt.
> Till the spring-time has vanished,
> And the summer has grown
> Into June, why the ice does
> Not melt—can it be
> That the offering is sacred ?
> What else can it be ?
>
> Take heed, note it well :
> How they make His Majesty
> Lord of the whole earth,
> Of heaven and the people.
> The life of all things,
> In the seas and the shorelands,
> Is the fruitage of his reign.

SHITE.

The Imperial Line is long and well-established ; the Imperial Design is far-reaching and beneficent.

CHORUS.

> The light of Buddha's sun increases ;
> His wheel of truth turns ceaselessly.

SHITE.

> The favour of the sun fails not its seasons.

CHORUS.

Rain and dew, frost and snow, have their appointed seasons.

> E'en in mid-summer
> Winter ice still unmelted !
> Spring winds in blowing
> Must have shunned it completely,
> Must have shunned it completely.
> Is it not wondrous?

> Though a season to all things
> By heaven is given,
> A marvel is granted
> In His Majesty's favour.

> Under the forest
> Shadows, deep and green,
> On this side and on that
> Of neighbour mountains
> That skirt the royal city
> On the north, we gather in
> The fallen snowflakes.

Surely the trees,
The very ground itself,
Upon this mountain,
Have not been o'erlooked in the mercy
Of our Lord !

In truth, my work is humble ;
Yet His Majesty
Appreciates our offering :
Ice, sacred, holy,
Like to no other gift ;
And we, in bearing,
Have the joy of worship
Before his face.

SHITE.

So in the first month of the New Year, .

CHORUS.

On the very first day of the Rat,[1]
We take a broom of seedling
Pine—a jewel broom—
And make its jewels quiver.
Snow that's fallen now,
As in the last year's winter
'Neath mountain shadows,
The old man gathers up,
Putting it under water
And piling upon it frozen snow and ice.
While he is waiting,
Spring has passed, and summer comes
Upon the mountains ;
So he builds a shelter cool
In summer shadows—
The never-changing shade.

[1] Rat, one of the twelve figures of the zodiac in accord with which the years, months, and days are grouped in cycles of twelve.

> The keeper of the shelter,
> Though living near the water,
> Wears summer clothing ;
> But his garments, waving free,
> Seem to feel the cold.

'Tis well ! I will at once return to the Imperial City by the straight path over which the offerings are taken.

SHITE.

Please wait a little. Deign to witness this evening's festival of ice-offering.

CHORUS.

> Indeed ! What is this festival of ice-offering?

SHITE.

> Others may not know ;
> But, here upon the mountain,
> Tree and mountain gods,
> Who guard the shelter, nightly
> Hold high festival.

CHORUS.

> While still he speaketh,
> Dark it grows upon the height ;
> The cold wind whistles
> Through the pines, making the snow
> In unexpected
> Flakes to fall. Ice covers all
> The trees, the mountain,
> Making them a jewelled shrine.
> On ice-glaze stepping,
> Now, the keeper enters in
> The low ice-shelter,
> Enters in the shelter.

PART II.

CHORUS.

> Swaying to the music, free
> Swing the dancer's sleeves ;

TSURE.

> Changeless lies the deep, dark green
> Of the mountain-side.

CHORUS.

> Dancer's sleeves that swing the snow !

TSURE AND CHORUS.

> Shines the light of a cloudless age
> Over all the sky—
> While they offer sacred ice,
> Offer sacred ice.

CHORUS.

> Offer ! Offer ! The sand lies
> Clear beneath the wave,

TSURE.

> Sand that grows to rock whence

CHORUS.

> Bright appeareth the God of Ice-
> Shelters, wearing for
> Headdress ice from hell-caverns ;
> Mountains, rivers shake,
> Earth and heaven tremble while,
> Cold with winds that blow,
> All the people stand in awe.

SHITE.

> Over the valley, the wind
> Freezeth the water.

SCENE FROM NOH DRAMA (" NAKAMITSU ")
Showing Nakamitsu about to behead Koju

CHORUS.

> Over the valley, the wind
> Freezeth the water.

SHITE.

> Even the moon has a sheen
> Bright as an ice-field,

CHORUS.

> Like to a mirror reflecting
> All that man doeth.

SHITE.

> Cool breezes blow through the trees ;

CHORUS.

> On the door of the deep
> Shadowed valley,

SHITE.

> Splasheth the snowflake,

CHORUS.

> Cutteth the hailstone.
> Drops which now fall from the rocks
> Freeze on the pebbles
> Lying down deep in the well.
> Breaking the ice-bonds,
> Up to the surface the wind-
> God of the mountain
> Riseth, exclaiming—'Tis cold,
> Oh, it is freezing !

SHITE.

> Gifts for our Master and Lord !

H

CHORUS.

Gifts for our Master and Lord !
'Tis snow that quiets the waves,
'Tis snow that stilleth the waters.
Day to day added, the months
Pass ; and still, as if
Years, do they wait for the time
When the ice may be offered.
" Offer it, offer it now ! "
Sings the servant whose
Long dancing sleeves swing the snow.
" Break not at all, do not break,
Neither melt the thin
Ice on the sleeves," saith the God,
God of ice-shelters—
Guarding the ice from the sun,
Pouring cold water,
Blowing the breezes that cool,
Parting the snow, on their way
Up to the city—
Capital City of flowers.
Lifting the clouds on the north,
Lo, the city revealed !
Hasten, make haste, I command;
Offer the ice to our
Lord at Otagi, to the
Lord of the Sunrise Land—
Offering most holy !

EGUCHI [1]

Characters :

    WAKI, *a Travelling Priest.*
    SHITE OF FIRST PART, *a Woman.*
    SHITE OF SECOND PART, *the Ghost of Eguchi.*
    TSURE, *Ghosts of Dancing-Girls.*

WAKI.

> How, since the moon was my chum
> In the good old days,
> In the good old days,
> Can I escape from the world
> And its luring snares ?

I am a priest on a pilgrimage over all the Land. As I
have never visited Tennoji, in the Province of Tsu, I have
made up my mind to go there upon this occasion.

> From the Capital,
> While still it was deepest night,
> Having set forth,
> Having set forth,
> My boat on Yodo's stream
> Floated onward
> To where might dimly be seen
> Udono's reeds—
> The smoking torches and the waves
> Where they lap the shore.
> To Eguchi's hamlet now
> I have come at last,
> I have come at last.

[1] A *Yurei Noh* by Ujinobu (1404–1469).

So this is the place where Lady Eguchi dwelt ! Her name is remembered even until now, though she has been dead for many years. It is sad, indeed, to behold the scene of the story.

Once when Priest Saigyo asked for a night's lodging here, the mistress of the house was hard-hearted ; so he composed a stanza :

> To forsake the world
> May be difficult, indeed ;
> But that you deny
> To me shelter from the rain
> For a night is passing strange !

This might be the very spot. Alas for them !

SHITE.

My honoured priest, why did you but now repeat that stanza old ?

WAKI.

'Tis strange ! There came a woman from where no house is seen, and asked me why I repeated that stanza old. Why do you question me ?

SHITE.

> Years have passed away
> Since it has been forgotten ;
> But your saying that
> The world to all forsake—
> Dew from shady fields—
> May be full difficult—
> While a shelter from
> The rain denying—
> —Recalled it all.

His words were false, declaring
I denied him—
So I come again
To say that not exactly
Him did I deny.

WAKI.

I cannot understand. While, recalling Saigyo, I repeat
his stanza on the woman who refused him shelter from the
rain, who on earth are you declaring that you did not exactly
deny him ?

SHITE.

But, why did you not recite the answering lines declaring
that I did not deny ?

WAKI.

Indeed, the answering lines :
One who had renounced

SHITE.

The world, as I had been told,
Surely should not more
Upon the pleasures of life
Set his heart's desire—
Was my only thought.

As I wished the priest to preserve his blameless purity,
how could I give him lodging in a woman's home ?

WAKI.

Indeed, you were right.

Saigyo declared himself to have renounced the world.

SHITE.

And my home was a place well known, where many a
sensual deed remained unknown.

WAKI.

    Not more to set his heart,

SHITE.

    I said, because I wished his good.

WAKI.

    But you refused, he said.

SHITE.

    His words !

CHORUS.

    Deny him I did,
    Because it was a worldly place ;
    I could not receive—
    A worldly place—
    Why did he say that I denied him ?

Remember not, I pray, the priest's account of days beyond recall.

A tale, indeed, of old romance !

While he was listening to her, her form grew dim.
Who can the woman like a shadow be ?

SHITE.

    This shadow that is standing,
    Dimly in the twilight
    Appearing, disappearing,
    At the river bend,
    He may perchance now think it
    A woman of the highway—
    Oh, the shame, the shame !

CHORUS.

    Oh, 'tis doubtless she !
    Of old she vanished 'neath the waves.

SHITE.

> In my house I lived a worldly life.

CHORUS.

The branches of her garden plum may still be seen.

WAKI.

> How strangely

CHORUS.

> Did she come !
> If you but rest beneath the shade
> Of yonder plum, or try
> From that same spring refreshment,
> The Spirit of Eguchi
> You then will recognize.
>
> She vanished, speaking,
> In silence vanished.

PART II.

WAKI.

Surely the Ghost of Lady Eguchi appeared and talked with me. I will pray for her soul that she may rest in peace.

> No sooner had I ceased
> From speaking—
> How marvellous !
> How marvellous ! than yonder,
> Where flows the river,
> All bright in gleaming moonlight,
> A boat of singing
> Women is seen in moonlight.
> A marvel, surely,
> To see it in the moonlight !

CHORUS.

> They are stopping their boat for the night;
> They would sleep with the waves for a pillow,
> With the waves for a pillow.
> How like the waves are they
> Who wake not from the dream
> Of worldly life!
> The Lady Sayo, too,
> Who wet her sleeve with tears,
> When sailed her lover's boat
> For China's shore,
> And Lady Hashi, sad,
> At Uji waiting long
> For one who ne'er returned,
> Were both like these, like these.
> Laments are useless. Ah!
> We only long for happy hours:
> Each season in its prime,
> With blooming flowers and falling snows,
> With wave and wind.

WAKI.

> How strange! Upon the water,
> In the bright moonlight,
> The dancing-girls are singing;
> And their waving forms—
> Whose boat is that, I wonder!

SHITE.

> Indeed, and do you question
> Whose this boat may be?
> I tell you promptly 'tis a pleasure-boat
> Belonging to Eguchi.
> In the moonlight, yonder,
> Look ye well upon it.

WAKI.

> Eguchi, truly ?
> The one of olden story ?

SHITE.

> Say not—of olden story !
> Hath the moon, to-night,
> Lost aught her old-time glory ?

TSURE.

> We look like this—
> And yet ye speak of us
> As women of an olden time !
> We cannot, will not bear it.

SHITE.

> Whatever you may say—

TSURE.

> We'll neither hear nor answer.

SHITE.

> 'Tis hard !

SHITE AND TSURE.

> Rivers in Autumn
> Brim to o'erflowing;
> Yet but the swifter
> Speed our boats onward.

SHITE.

> Thus do we sing in the moonlight.

CHORUS.

> Sing, O sing of the longing
> Of days that are gone,
> The boating of women for pleasure
> In days that are o'er.

> Let us sing of life's mysterious ways.

Now the change of the twelve courses is like a wheel that turns in the garden ;

SHITE.

> Or like birds that flit in the forest.

CHORUS.

> A former life, a life still more remote—

SHITE.

> We never knew the dawning of our lives.

CHORUS.

> A future life, a life still more remote—
> We'll never know the ending of our lives.

SHITE.

> Among men, some have gained good hope of heaven ;

CHORUS.

> Yet have they failed, through error and deceit,
> To plant the seed of long salvation,

SHITE.

> To ruin falling and to depths of hell,

CHORUS.

> Blinded by fate, all saving guidance lost ;

SHITE.

And we, though hardly into human form,

CHORUS.

Are women born, and famed in all fame, ill.

> Sad, indeed, to think
> Of life's stern retributions
> Though in morning light,
> Spring blossoms red emblazon
> Bright high mountain slopes,
> The evening breezes tempt them
> To their final fall ;
> Though in the evening splendour
> Leaves of autumn tint
> And dye the forests wholly,
> Frosts of morning blight
> Their beauty all.
> The guests that talked of gentle
> Things, the whispering pines,
> The moonlight on the twining
> Vines, are gone for aye.
> To lovers, linked in slumber,
> Curtained richly
> The parting comes untimely
> E'er they sense its dawn.
> No heartless grass, or man of
> Feeling deep and strong,
> Escapes the touch of sorrow ;
> This we know, but yet

SHITE.

> Sometimes we are enamoured—
> Beauty is so fair,
> And love is deep, unsounded ;

CHORUS.

> Sometimes the voices of women
> Take us captive, and
> By subtle spell confine us ;
> We think in our hearts and we speak with
> Our lips of the things
> Which lead to delusion.
> In truth there are none but who suffer
> Misleading, amid
> The objects of sense, and
> Commit the sins of the senses.
> All this must be caused by the mind which
> Is driven in doubt
> Concerning the things which it seeth,
> The things which it heareth.
> How great is our task !

SHITE.

> Over the ocean of truth,
> Bloweth no storm wind,
> Passionate, full of deceit ;

CHORUS.

> Yet from the depths of life,
> Daily there riseth
> Waves that are terribly real.

SHITE.

> Why do our hearts beat like waves ?
> 'Tis that we backward
> Turn to illusion.

CHORUS.

> If for that world we care not,
> Surely it is not.

SHITE.

> We'll neither worship nor pine,

CHORUS.

> Waiting at evening,

SHITE.

> Feeling the storm of farewell.

CHORUS.

> Flowers and leaves of autumn,
> Snow and the moonlight,
> These are frivolities, all,
> Subjects of chatter ;

SHITE.

> If we believe it,
> All is but vanity.

CHORUS.

> Of a truth it was I that
> Advised him to think
> Not at all of illusion.
> It is finished and over !
> Return will I now—
> And, so saying, the angel
> Fugen Bosatsu—
> She it was, and her vessel,
> An elephant white—
> With the rays of the morning
> On clouds that were white,
> Fled away to the westward.
> O wonder divine !
> O wonder divine !

FUJI

THE SPIRIT OF THE WISTARIA.[1]

Characters :

 WAKI, *a Travelling Priest.*
 SHITE OF FIRST PART, *a Woman.*
 SHITE OF SECOND PART, *the Spirit of the Wistaria.*

PART I.

WAKI.

> Over mountains and mountains,
> Endless, unending,
> On my pilgrimage far and
> Far do I journey.

I am a priest from the capital city. Recently I have visited the various famous places in the Province of Kaga, and now I am on my way to Zenkoji.

> The breezes blowing
> Cool from mountains white,
> Where melt the snows, are
> Very pleasant as I go.
> Beyond the village,
> Where the sun shines long, Nagae,
> I've journeyed onward ;
> Through the barrier gate, whose doors
> At Tonami are
> Shut not day or night, I've passed ;

[1] A *Seirei Noh* by Yasukiyo (1382–1458).

> And, catching glimpses
> Fair of crimson-maple-brook
> 'Neath leaves that still are
> Green, I come at last to see,
> By Himi's shore, the
> Far-famed Tago-no-ura.

I have already come to what I take to be Tago-no-ura in
the Province of Etchu.   I have heard that the place is famous
for its wistaria ; and, indeed, the wistaria yonder is in its
prime.   I will go near and take a look.   Truly, it blossoms
wonderfully.

> The leaves at the ends
> Of the waving wistaria,
> By waves like their own,
> Are all withered and worn, so
> That I'm angry at Tago.

I am reminded of the old poem.

SHITE.

Sir, there's something I would say to you.

WAKI.

To me ?   What is it ?

SHITE.

This is a place well known for its wistaria.
According to an old poem—

> While bloom by the shore
> Of Tago-no-ura the
> Wistaria vines,
> All the bloom of the sea waves
> With their purple is dyed.

Forgetting that stanza, you recalled the lines :

> The leaves at the end
> By the waves are all withered.

What a thoughtless stranger !

WAKI.

I repeated without expecting anyone to hear—

SHITE.

How about the flowers themselves—

WAKI.

That the leaves are all withered.

SHITE.

> Was it not a grief to them ?

It was very unfortunate !   The poem by Tsunomaro—

CHORUS.

> Wistaria sprays
> That make fragrant the sea-depths,
> Tago-no-ura,
> Will I carry to many
> Who're unable to see them.

It is too bad that you spoke of the flowers thoughtlessly. Is it not true, as one said, that

> Only the sympathetic
> The beauty and the perfume
> Of flowers can fully know ?

WAKI.

It is strange !   Who can be repeating so many verses old ?

SHITE.

> Do you ask who I am ?
> A girl with flowers
> That shine in her hair, purple
> Like dusk of the evening, and
> Do not forget it.

CHORUS.

> Do not forget it !
> The wistaria branches,
> Wavelike in motion,

SHITE.

> By the famous coast-line of
> Tago-no-ura.

CHORUS.

> The spirit of the flowers,
> Thus speaking, quickly,
> As a cloud of the evening,
> Blown by the sea-breeze,
> Nearer drew and then vanished.

PART II.

WAKI.

> Though dim be the night,
> Dim though the moon hath arisen,
> There singeth a bird.
> Like to the doctrine doth ring
> The voice of his song.
> Spring breezes blow and they bring
> Comfort where flowers,
> Ruined, have vanished away.
> From transient dreams, .
> Awful the roar of the sea
> Awakens the dreamer.

I

SHITE.

> Why, oh why, in days of old,
> Was I entranced
> With the charm hypnotic of
> Flowers against an empty sky ?

WAKI.

> Strange ! A figure in the light
> Of midnight moonbeams
> Standing. Her face I find to be
> So like the former !
> > Can it be thou art the spirit
> > Of earthly blossoms ?

SHITE.

> I shame to say it ;
> But I am their spirit.
> My eyes, like blossoms
> In the gentle rain of spring,
> Have opened widely,
> 'Neath the wondrous teaching, to
> New joys I knew not.
> So I here appear.

WAKI.

> His name be praised !
> But how is it that we here
> Can speak thus freely ?

SHITE.

> Because of the truth
> That all things have power to change,
> Remaining unchanged the while,
> I've come, all the night
> To dance by the changing sea.

WAKI.

> Of course !
> Wild and ordered words alike,

SHITE.

> Proclaim his praises ;

WAKI.

> There's no distinction.

SHITE.

> Purple,

CHORUS.

> That very colour,
> Dear to heaven, must have been
> A cause propitious.
> Her heart so flowerlike
> Opened to teachings broader
> Than those of Law and Doctrine ;
> And, thus, it seemeth,
> Trees and grasses without sense
> May come to sainthood !
> Truly deep, great Buddha's grace,
> As mighty sea-depths.

Yes, in farewell to the spring-time, we need no lordly ship or stately coach ; we merely say good-bye to the last nightingale, to the falling flowers,

SHITE.

To the colour of the blossoms that yet lingers in the dew upon the purple wistaria.

CHORUS.

Marvellous ! Spring, upon the surface of the sea,
revealed in the light of a veiled moon, a bright purple
headdress—such views are not of earth !

SHITE.

> The Bay of Nako
> Is not far from here.

CHORUS.

> Such sights as poets
> Sing, that men may read.
> How sweet to think it
> Has the hue of heaven !
> In vain the months and
> Years, day after day, like
> Wistaria waves,
> Come and go.
> The summer orange,
> When the flowers of spring-time all
> Have fallen, grows its
> Leaves of green which tell us once
> Again of days long
> Since forgotten.
> The very moonlight
> Brightens, as the falling leaves
> Foretell the coming
> Autumn.
> Sea-breezes usher
> In the night ; and, ere the dawn,
> A flock of plover,
> Calling o'er the waves at sea,
> Bring back their comrades,
> Frost and snow, and make us know
> That winter comes.

SHITE.

> The four seasons that thus change—

CHORUS.

> The morning mists, from
> Fair wistaria blossoms
> Lingering late till
> Summer comes, seem keepsakes of
> Departing spring.
> 'Tis well, indeed, the
> Purple blossoms, in such a world
> Of change, should climbing
> Cling to pines that, evergreen,
> Substantial stand.

SHITE.

> Behold ! By the breezes of spring

CHORUS.

> Though tempted to wander, the vine
> Embraces the century-old

SHITE.

> Pine-tree, and there hangs in full bloom.

CHORUS.

> The dancing-maiden with her sleeves
> Of cloud-like purple turning—

SHITE.

> Sing, oh sing of the
> Willow-picking, songs of the
> Falling plum blossoms,

CHORUS.

> Or of blossoming

SHITE.

> Fields of rank wistaria,

CHORUS.

> Deep in perfume and
> Hue as these before us here.
> Clearly sound the sea-
> Breezes from Ao's coast where the
> Lush weed flourisheth.
> Waving sleeves, that in
> Turning colour the waves
> Turn, in the moonlight.
> Into the low-hanging
> Mists of the morning, purple and
> Red, she entereth
> Now, her figure lost in their
> Glory.

CHAPTER VII

GENZAI MONO NOH

THIS class of *Noh* occupies a very significant position between *Noh* such as we have been considering and *Kyogen* or light comedy. It is conspicuous for its human interest and more evident dramatic quality. Its characters are often of a nature which permits comic as well as tragic treatment, as is shown conclusively by the fact that many of the stories utilized in *Genzai Mono Noh* appear, only slightly modified, in *Kyogen* and *Kabuki*. The proportion of conversational prose to poetry is far greater than in other forms of *Noh* ; characters of general utility and light nature are frequently called *Kyogen* ; and even leading characters are often designated by name, as is generally the case in *Kyogen*, instead of by conventional titles as in most other forms of *Noh*. Thus we have in *Genzai Mono Noh* what is apparently a surviving link which united earlier *Sarugaku* with later *Noh* and *Kyogen*, now recognized as distinct but practically inseparable art forms.

MANJU [1]

Characters :

MANJU, *a Nobleman.*
NAKAMITSU, *a Retainer to Manju.*
BIJO, *a Lad, Son to Manju.*
KOJU, *a Lad, Son to Nakamitsu.*
ESHIN, *Abbot of a Monastery on Mount Hiei.*

[1] A *Genzai Mono Noh* by Seami (1363–1444), based upon historic characters and events of the early tenth century. This *Noh* is also known by the name *Nakamitsu*, from the leading character.

PART I

NAKAMITSU.

Fujiwara-no-Nakamitsu is my name, a retainer of Tada-no-Manju, of the Province of Settsu. My master, on whom I rely, has a son whom he sent up to Nakayama Temple. The boy pays no attention to study, but day and night devotes himself to military sports. Often, with intent to punish, my master has sent for him to come down ; but he does not come. This time, I, Nakamitsu, myself am ordered to bring him.

I too have a son, Koju by name, who serves this youth at the temple. This is a good opportunity, and I am eager to see him.

   *   *   *   *   *

I have made haste, and so already have come to Nakayama Temple.

Excuse me ! Is no one at home ?

KOJU.

Who is there ?

NAKAMITSU.

Well, well ! I have not seen you for a long time. Is it Koju, indeed ? Tell your young master, Bijo, that I have come to escort him home.

KOJU.

I will, Sir.

Master, Nakamitsu has come to escort you home.

BIJO.

Show him in, please.

KOJU.

Please, come in this way.

NAKAMITSU.

Certainly, thank you !

It is a long time since I have seen you !

BIJO.

And now, why have you come ?

NAKAMITSU.

Why, it is merely that I am sent to tell you to return home with me at once.

BIJO.

Shall I not report anything of this to my superior ?

NAKAMITSU.

No, do not so. If you tell him, he will surely wish to accompany you as escort. You had better come home quietly at once.

BIJO.

Very well, I will come.

NAKAMITSU.

Koju, you will accompany him.

KOJU.

Certainly, Sir.

*   *   *   *   *

NAKAMITSU.

We have made haste, and so have already arrived at Tada's residence. Please wait a moment. I will announce your arrival.

Master, I have returned with Master Bijo.

MANJU.

Tell him to come here.

NAKAMITSU.

Certainly, Sir.

Please come this way.

MANJU, TO BIJO.

That you might study hard, I sent you up to the temple.
First of all, now, let me hear you chant the scriptures.

> (*Before* BIJO *is placed a red sandal-wood desk with the scrip-
> tures in gold characters upon it.*)

CHORUS.

> In reply to his father,
> Unable to read
> E'en a word of the scriptures,
> Not once having learned
> The rudiments,
> Bijo merely weeps.

MANJU.

I am not surprised. Being Manju's son, you have been
spoiled with petting by those priests, and so have not learned
to read the scriptures. How is it, then, about poetical composition ?

BIJO.

I cannot.

MANJU.

How about music ?
Though I question, no answer comes from that tongueless
child.

CHORUS.

> Why did he not accomplish
> The task assigned him ?
> I cannot introduce him,
> My son, to others !
> Thus saying, from its scabbard
> His sword he drew—
> But Nakamitsu, running,
> Held fast his garment.
> How pitiful, indeed,
> Is Bijo's fate !

MANJU.

> Why dost thou stay me, Nakamitsu?
> At once, with this my sword, behead him.

NAKAMITSU.

> I pray thee, think again!

MANJU.

> By a soldier's gods, I swear;
> If ye obey not,
> I myself will kill ye both.

NAKAMITSU.

> Each word of thy commandment
> I will perform.

*   *   *   *   *

Beyond expression great, his anger burns!
Truly, he said—kill him at once with this my sword, or I, myself, will kill ye both. Alas, what shall I do? Some way, surely, of escape I shall find for him.

Is Koju there?

KOJU.
I am here.

NAKAMITSU.
Where is Master Bijo?

KOJU.
In spite of my urging, still he lingers here.

NAKAMITSU.
Why have you not fled somewhither?

A messenger from my master!

BIJO.

When you restrained my father, I could have fled—I overheard him in anger tell you to kill me or that he would kill
us both with his own hand.

> For myself I care not at all ;
> But thinking of you
> Turned me back again from my flight ;
> Behead me at once,
> And to him my head you may show.

NAKAMITSU.

Fear not ; I will plan some means for your escape.

What, another messenger from your father !

> Indeed, all things must be
> In compensation ;

KOJU.

> And sins of former ages

BIJO.

> Were yet but earthly.

CHORUS.

> Not from another's sowing,
> The harvest groweth,
> But from one's own ill deeds——
> Think no perversion.
>
> O Nakamitsu !
> Let's not in idle talking
> The time consume ;
> Behead me quickly.

Thus ran their lamentation.

NAKAMITSU.

> If I were only
> Of age with thee, I'd gladly
> This life surrender ; 'tis sad
> That at this moment
> I cannot give my life.

KOJU.
My father ! There's something I would say to thee.

NAKAMITSU.
What is it ?

KOJU.
My ears overheard your words just now. You are, in very deed, Manju's vassal ; and I am Bijo's. This is a time of crisis. I am of age to serve. Behead me quickly, and to your master show my head, declaring that you have slain Bijo.

NAKAMITSU.
Ah, nobly spoken ! I will tell him what you have said.

I wish to tell thee my Koju bravely offers that I should take his head, wrapped in your flowing robe, and show it from a distance, in the dim light of night, when parental love will veil distinctions.

Well said, my son ! Now, then !

Drawing his sword, Nakamitsu steps behind his son.[1]

BIJO.

> Bijo in anguish
> Grasps his garment's sleeve, saying—
> " If Koju be slain,
> He himself will slay also."

With tears he restrains Nakamitsu.

[1] Here we have an illustration of how a *Noh* actor may, in spoken or chanted words, define his own action.

Koju.

No ; to die for one's master is the privilege of one who beareth the bow.

Bijo.

Those who serve have courage ; why should not I, who rule ? For me now to live is a disgrace.

Nakamitsu.

How sad to strive for precedence in death !

Koju.

Myself I offer.

Bijo.

I claim a greater right.

Nakamitsu.

He is my lord !

Koju.

I am thy well-beloved son.

Nakamitsu.

Between the two—torn with conflict, Nakamitsu——

Chorus.

> Values his own life less,
> Less than the children's.
> What's to be done ?
> What's to be left—undone ?
> Brave Nakamitsu
> Feels his heart sink within him.

Bijo.

> How his love tortures
> This being of mine ! O why
> Should he love me,
> Whose life hath no value
> In the eyes of my father ?

KOJU.

> 'Tis for my own sake,
> And not for thy sake
> Only, I offer.
> My death for thee, now,
> Saves from dishonour
> The name of a soldier.

CHORUS.

> Though they were children,
> Both with nobility spoke.
> Yet could he never
> Slay the dear son of his lord.
> Closing his eyelids,
> Calming his wavering mind,
> Quickly he struck where
> Judged he his son to be,
> Instantly making
> Life for that son a mere dream.

NAKAMITSU (*to* BIJO, *who would kill himself*).

Thou shalt not ! What wouldst thou do ?

For the sake of the one who has died in thy stead, make thy escape and finish thy schooling.

Attendant !

ATTENDANT.

Here, Sir !

NAKAMITSU.

Hide Master Bijo, and take my son's body away, lest the master should see it.

Now I will tell him.

My Lord, I have slain Master Bijo.

MANJU.

You have done well.   He was craven at the last, I doubt not.

NAKAMITSU.

No, quite the contrary. As, amazed at your order, I stood with your sword in my hand, he said, " Do not hesitate." Those were his last words.

MANJU.

Bijo is gone ; and, as you know, Nakamitsu, I have no other son. Bring Koju here ; I wish to make him my heir.

NAKAMITSU.

That is kind of you, indeed ; but Koju, in sorrow for the death of his young master, has shaved his head and left my home for ever.

MANJU.

What ? Did you say that Koju had shaved his head and left your home for ever ?

NAKAMITSU.

Give me also leave to go. I also would take the vows.

MANJU.

Though strong of will, to do as I commanded, he loved Bijo, whom he had brought up as his son ; and, now that he has gone, he loses both sons together.

CHORUS.

> Urged for permission
> Now to retire, Manju
> Firmly reminded
> Nakamitsu of sovereign
> Power with its claim,
> By much remonstrance even
> Hardly prevailing.
>
> Deathless the union
> Parent and child binding,
> Deathless the union
> Parent and child binding ;
> So for the fated
> Sadly a funeral,
> Fixed as by custom,
> Holy, was ordered prepared.

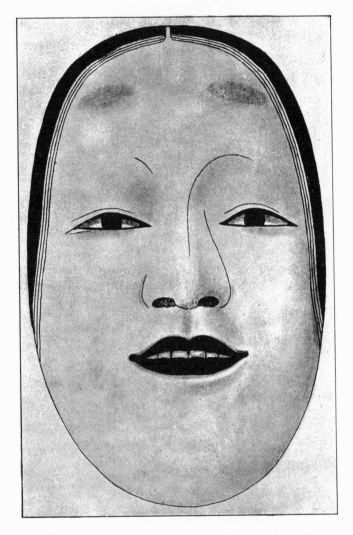

MASK WORN BY KENREIMONIN IN " OHARA GOKO "

PART II.

ESHIN.

I am Eshin-no-Sozu of Mount Hiei. I am hastening to the mansion of Tada-no-Manju.

Already I have arrived at his residence.

Excuse my call !

NAKAMITSU.

Who is it seeks admission ?

Oh, Eshin-no-Sozu !

Eshin-no-Sozu has come !

ESHIN.

I have heard of your Koju's sad end.

NAKAMITSU.

Ah ! be careful not to speak of it before the Master.

ESHIN.

Of course ; please announce my arrival.

NAKAMITSU.

Wait here a moment, please, and I will announce you.

My Lord, Eshin-no-Sozu has come down from Mount Hiei

MANJU.

Show him in.

NAKAMITSU.

I will, Sir.

Eshin-no-Sozu, this way, if you please.

ESHIN.

It is a long time since we have met.

K

MANJU.

What is your errand, Sire, to-day ?

ESHIN.

To say a few words concerning Bijo.

MANJU.

Oh, about him ! I told Nakamitsu to lose him.

ESHIN.

Though urged by your messengers to kill Bijo at once, Nakamitsu could by no means touch his master's son. Instead, he beheaded his own child, Koju, and showed you his head for Bijo's.

If it please my lord, pardon Bijo, for whom Nakamitsu felt such love as to kill his own son in his stead.

> ESHIN *presents* BIJO *to his father*.

MANJU.

Bijo's cowardice is once again proven !

Why did you not kill yourself, when Koju was slain ?

ESHIN.

Do not ask that ; but pardon Bijo, I beg you, for the sake of Koju, for whom we all mourn.

CHORUS.

> Eshin-no-Sozu
> Won from Lord Manju, by long
> Tearful entreaty,
> Pardon for Bijo.
>
> Glad that the death of
> Koju had not been in vain,
> Quickly a banquet,
> Rich with chrysanthemum wine,
> His father prepared.

That father and son,
Once estranged, again were united,
Filled all their hearts with great joy,
Like that of a hermit
Who seeth his son
Of the seventh generation.

There was feasting unending.

ESHIN.

Bijo, let me see you dance on this blessed occasion the dance of the mandarin duck ;—

Lonely the mandarin duck
Floats on the billow,
Floats and then dives 'neath the wave,

CHORUS.

Though in the shadow,
Fearful its feet are in motion.

NAKAMITSU.

Ah, were my son but alive,
Now would he dance with his lord ;
And for their dancing,
I would beat time with my hands.
Ah, were my tears but of joy,
Tears that I'm shedding,
Happy indeed would I be !

CHORUS.

Within are tears,

NAKAMITSU.

Without are waving sleeves.

CHORUS.

The long sleeves waving,
Now up, now down, they move
Like falling dew—
Like which our lives are spent
Early or late,
Departed sorrow, joy
Of this to-day.

Let the dance conclude !

Eshin-no-Sozu went back to the mountain with Bijo. Naka-mitsu walked by his young master's palanquin, urging him kindly never to think his father's anger for aught else but that he should give himself faithfully to study thereafter.

As with such words to the youth, Nakamitsu made his fare-well, there came the old longing :

> Were Koju alive,
> Alive to accompany !
> And he stood there alone,
> And disheartened,
> Looking after the figure.
> And he stood there alone,
> And disheartened,
> Looking after the figure.

OHARA GOKO [1]

AN IMPERIAL VISIT TO OHARA.

Characters :

> MARINOKOJI (*Waki*), *a Court Official.*
> WAKI-TSURE, *a Subordinate Official.*
> KENREIMONIN (*Shite*), *Retired Empress.*
> DAINAGON (*Tsure*), *a Lady-in-waiting.*
> AWANONASHI (*Tsure*), *a Lady-in-waiting.*
> HOO, *Retired Emperor Goshirakawa.*

PART I.

WAKI-TSURE.

I am a subject in the service of Retired Emperor Goshirakawa.

At the time when the whole Heiki Clan (from the Retired Emperor Antoku and Niinotsubone, wife of Kiyomori their

---

[1] A *Genzai Mono Noh*, by Seami (1363–1444). Kenreimonin, the heroine, was the adopted daughter of Goshirakawa and became empress in 1172, at the age of sixteen. Her son, Antoku, was born in 1178, and became emperor at the age of four. She became a nun in 1185, at the age of twenty-nine ; and the date of this visit to her was about 1186, when she was thirty years of age.

slaughtered chieftain, to the humblest follower) were driven
into the sea off the coast of Hayatomo in the Province of Nagato,
the Retired Empress Kenreimonin threw herself into the waves,
but was caught and rescued from pitiful death.   Noriyori, the
chief of Mikawa, together with Yoshitsune and his brother,
accompanied the Three Sacred Treasures in safety to the Capital ;
and it was expected that the Retired Empress would remain in
the palace.   She, having taken the veil, however, now lives at
Jakkoin, the Temple of the Lonely Light in Ohara, praying to
Amidha Buddha for the happiness of her son, the late Emperor,
and for her mother, Niinotsubone.

Hoo, the Retired Emperor, now an Imperial Priest, has issued
an order saying that he will visit Ohara to call upon her.   I am
on my way to give command that the mountain roads be all
examined.

" Proclamation to any and to all !

"Examine the roads and put them all in order, as His Majesty
is going out to Ohara."

          *   *   *   *   *

KENREIMONIN.

This mountain hamlet may be lonely, but it is far better than
the weary world outside.

KENREIMONIN AND DAINAGON.

> A woodman's hut of brushwood
> Makes pleasant shelter.
> Like scattered bamboo palings,
> Where fence is needless,
> The news from the great city
> Comes here but rarely.
> We have our sorrows, many
> As bamboo joints
> In posts that prop our dwelling ;
> Yet 'tis a comfort,
> In time of trouble, knowing
> No eyes are watching.

At times there cometh
Those who call upon us here,
All unintending.:
The sound of axes
Swung by humble cutters, poor,
The sound of axes ;
Storms that sing amid the trees,
And monkeys' screaming ;
And, besides these neighbour sounds,
The vines—Masaki
And the green Tsuzura.
The visitors are
Few who come of late to call ;
And thickly grows the
Grass, as on the road to Ganen's—
It well may be our
Anxious thoughts upspringing ;
It often rains, as
'Gainst the door of Genken's hut—
It well may be the
Spirit of our tears, our tears
Upon our sleeves—
Upon our sleeves.

KENREIMONIN.

Well, Dainagon, let us go up the mountain, yonder, and pick star-anise as a gift for Buddha.

DAINAGON.

Gladly will I go with you ; let us gather brushwood and pick bracken, and make an offering.

KENREIMONIN.

Though it is presumptuous to speak of him in comparison, Prince Shaka went forth from the palace of his royal father and climbed the steep path up Mount Dandoku, there to pick greens, draw water, and gather firewood ;

CHORUS.

> And by such labours
> Toilsome, striving hard,
> He wrought salvation fully,
> Serving thus the saints.
> " For Buddha's sake I gladly
> Go," she said, and took
> The basket willow-woven,
> Going deep and far
> Into the mountain forest,
> Into the mountain forest.

PART II.

MARINOKOJI.

> Under the green boughs,
> Over the mountain pathway,
> Journey we onward,
> Seeking the ling'ring cherries
> Late in their blooming.
>
> Brushing aside the lush grass,
> Heavy with dew-drops,
> Brushing the lush grass,
> Up to Ohara's hamlet
> Hurry we onward.

Having made haste, we have already arrived at Ohara. Coming to Ohara, and calling at Jakkoin, we find the summer grasses thickly growing within the dewy garden, and the willows waving low their pendent green. The floating water-weed upon the pond moves with the moving waves, like brocade laundered in the stream. The *yamabuki* blossoms bright along the way ; and, through thick folds of mountain mist, a cuckoo's note sounds welcome to the coming guest.

Hoo (*looking upon the banks of the pond*).

> Over the water,
> The cherries of the lakeside,
> Scattered, have fallen ;
> The ripples all are blooming,
> Their flowers are at their best.

CHORUS.

> Between the age-worn rocks
> Drops fall, drops fall
> With sound suggestive.
> The fence, vine-covered, green,
> The mountain's beetling brows of green,
> A picture make
> Too beautiful for brush
> To paint——!
>
> A hall stands yonder.
> Through its roof-tiles broken
> The mist burns incense ;
> Through its open doorways,
> Whence doors have fallen,
> Pours the moon her light eternal.
>
> Can such words describe
> A place like this ?
> A horror, dreadful !

MARINOKOJI.

This must, indeed, be her retreat. Over the eaves, vines and morning-glories clamber ; and the goosefoot blocks the door-way ; what a sight !

Well, I will call.

AWANONAISHI.

Who is it, please ?

MARINOKOJI.

It is Marinokoji.

AWANONAISHI.

What ! Why have you come to this deserted mountain ?

MARINOKOJI.

To visit our Lady's dwelling, Hoo has come thus far.

AWANONAISHI.

Our Lady is not in ; she has gone up yonder mountain to gather flowers.

MARINOKOJI TO HOO.

When I told her of your coming, she said our Lady was not in, but gone to gather flowers on the mountain. Please sit here awhile and wait for her return.

HOO.

But look, there is a nun !

Who may you be ?

AWANONAISHI.

No doubt you have forgotten me. This is what Shinzei's daughter, Awanonaishi, has become. Though I have such a miserable appearance, as a nun I care not at all, for I am one having no dream of the morrow.

HOO.

Where is our Lady, now ?

AWANONAISHI.

She has gone to the hill to gather flowers.

HOO.

And her companion ?

AWANONAISHI.

Dainagon. Please wait a little longer ; she will soon return.

*   *   *   *   *

KENREIMONIN.

> Yesterday has gone ;
> To-day as vainly endeth.
> Though dreams of future days come
> Not to me again,
> The time comes never when his
> Image fair I can
> Forget : my royal son.

> Though there is no other way
> To win salvation,
> The repetition of the name
> Divine—Amida—
> Brings rebirth in paradise
> To all, though evil;
> So pray I ever
> That His Majesty, my son,
> My sainted mother,
> All our family, may gain
> Great Buddhahood.
> I worship thee, Amida!

Hark, I hear voices near our cell!

DAINAGON.

Will you be pleased to rest a moment here?

AWANONAISHI.

Look, there comes our Lady down the hill-side, yonder.

HOO.

Which is our Lady, which Dainagon?

AWANONAISHI.

The one who bears upon her arm a basket filled with flowers is our Lady; she who carries brush and bracken bound is her attendant.

What do you think? Hoo has come!

KENREIMONIN.

> Being unable to put aside
> My love of life with its illusion,
> I sinned in being saved.
> I weep——
> I am ashamed to meet him.

CHORUS.

> Yet he is a man of faith
> Like to my own.
> Together may we walk the Way,
> Devout, I pray.

At the window where I offer
Daily prayer,
At the window where I offer
Daily prayer,
I've been hoping for Amida's
Light to greet me ;
At the door of brushwood lowly,
Where I offer
Daily prayer ten times repeated,
Have I waited
Angel visits from the sainted ;
And to-day, this very evening,
Unexpected,
Am I carried back to childhood—
Tears of memory !
Surely kindness, such as his is,
Will continue
To the end of future ages ;
And the fountain,
Called Obara,
Flowing on the pathway narrow
At Seriu,
Will reflect his image holy,
Not the moonlight.

What season is this in which he comes to visit me ?

KENREIMONIN.

The spring has vanished,
And the summer grown
To Kamo's festal season.
Mid summer forests,
With their leaves of green,
We long for tokens of the spring.

CHORUS.

White clouds that linger lowly
Adown the distant hills,

KENREIMONIN.

Can they be keepsakes precious
Of vanished blossoms ?

CHORUS.

At the end of the path which he has taken, aimlessly wandering through the thick summer weeds.

KENREIMONIN.

> Is this the place ?
> Is this the place ?
> The tranquil light of Jakko—
> Precious the shadow of that light divine !

CHORUS.

> On the pine branches
> Where bright light is playing, bloom

KENREIMONIN.

> Vines of wistaria ;
> And over the water
> Waves of wistaria,

CHORUS.

> As well for his visit,

KENREIMONIN.

> Seem long to have waited.

CHORUS.

> Belated cherry blossoms,
> When the leaves are green,
> Are far more precious, surely,
> Than buds that early bloom.
> These sights so rare he'll cherish
> Long within his heart.
> I'm thankful, oh, so thankful
> That he comes to-day,
> Although this hut of brushwood
> Seems unfit to shelter——
> I wonder, is it ? is it ?

KENREIMONIN.

> Ah ! no least thought of planning
> Led me here to dwell
> Within this mountain shelter.
> Never did I think
> In this secluded place to
> See the moon, as once
> From palace windows.

So I dreamed not ; but you have come to see me ; and I thank you, truly.

Hoo.

Of late one told me you had seen the span of life's six worlds. Strange was the story, for it is said that only saints and those who have attained great Buddhahood can have seen the span of life's six worlds.

KENREIMONIN.

'Tis so, indeed ; but I have seen them all with my own eyes.

> My life, a floating grass
> Unrooted in the shore,

CHORUS.

> A boat that is not tied
> Upon the river——

KENREIMONIN.

> To me the joys of heaven
> Are all unknown, unknown ;

CHORUS.

> And through the endless days
> And months when slow decay
> Cut loose the bonds that bound
> To things of earth and sense,

KENREIMONIN.

> While yet they were not all
> Forgotten wholly——

CHORUS.

> I wandered, groping where
> The cross-roads meet, the roads
> Of the six worlds.
>
> First and worst of all,
> When on the western sea-waves
> Tossed in boats that knew
> No destination, like were
> We to those in hell
> Where starve the hungry—all were
> Parched with thirst 'mid seas
> Of water—it was salty.
> Once the waves rose high;
> We thought the boats were turning.
> How we cried and screamed
> In agony, our voices
> Shrill like those of sinners damned
> In purging torture !

KENREIMONIN.

> On the land, where was
> A battle fiercely raging,

CHORUS.

> 'Twas as in that hell
> Where strife goes on unending ;
> And the sounds, the sounds
> Of horses, horrid, rose up
> As from purgatory.
> To see them suffer and to
> Hear those fearful sounds
> Was human anguish, truly.
> Sad, oh, sad indeed !

HOO.

> A strange experience !
> Tell me now about
> His Majesty's last moments.

KENREIMONIN.

> To tell the story of that
> Time makes me regret
> That I was rescued.

At Hayatomo, in Nagato, we were planning to go for a time to Tsukushi; but, Ogata proving false, we were obliged to enter the bay of Satsuma. Just then the tide set in; and we all thought the end had come.

> Noritsune, then,
> The head of Noto Province,
> Holding by his side
> The brothers Aki, bade them
> Follow him,
> And jumped into the sea-depths.
> Tonomori,
> Appointed new to office
> High, upon his head,
> As helmet, placed the anchor
> Heavy, grasped his bow,
> And, with his foster brother,
> Plunged beneath the wave.
> At that time Nidono,
> Dressed in grey—
> Her silken skirt about her
> Bound, full nobly said,
> " Though woman I, I will not
> Yield to hostile foes,
> But follow with my Lord."

Holding Antoku, her grandchild, by the hand, she led him to the side of the boat. He asked where they were going, and with tears she said :

> " The Land is full of rebels,
> Evil is the place ;
> Beneath the waves a happy
> Paradise awaits us ;
> Let us go."

> He was content, and turning
> Toward the east, he bade
> A last farewell to Great
> Amaterasu.

CHORUS.

> With faith in Buddha,
> Turned he to the west.

KENREIMONIN.

> Now I know, in truth,

CHORUS.

> There is a city waiting
> 'Neath the waves that flow
> Where deeply rolls the river,
> The river Mumoruso.

Composing thus his last poetic lines, he sank to depths unmeasured ; and I would have followed, had not a warrior of the Genji Clan saved me a prisoner for a useless life.

I weep with shame at sight of you.

For ever ! How can they bring their mournful parting to its close ? He may not linger ; and, at bidding, his palanquin is borne in haste, leaving Jakko in the distance.

KENREIMONIN.

Leaning by my brushwood door,

CHORUS.

She watches for a time ; then enters her lonely home, her lonely home.

CHAPTER VIII

KYOGEN

THE element of humour was conspicuous in the popular amusements from which patronage developed *Kagura* and *Noh*. It was never entirely excluded from even the most serious forms of Japanese dramatic art.

When, in ancient times, *Kagura* was performed at the Imperial Palace, impromptu comical plays were given by a wit or clown (*sai-no-o*) ; and, in entertainments of Court dancing, the stately and beautiful Chinese dances were frequently interspersed with light and comic dances from Korea. *Dengaku*, even under Shinto patronage, as played by Kwanami, was full of rude pranks ; and *Sarugaku* only gradually threw off its original *monkey* nature.

All early forms of dramatic art in Japan, however, were dependent upon Buddhist priests for literary preservation ; and the priests were loath to give the dignity of letters to any but the most stately and serious productions. Such comedy as was looked upon with favour was for the most part extemporaneous, and none of the early plays of humour are now extant. More than that, the forms originally devoted to humour became, under the pressure of serious-minded writers and players, purged from all elements of comedy in pure *Noh*.

Human nature, however, demands relaxation, and the attention cannot be held for long periods to a single emotional note. Masters of *Noh*, in proportion as they excluded the comic, were compelled to find a place for comedy as an interlude, thus giving relief from their more dignified productions, and incidentally deepening the effect produced by the *Noh* themselves.

L

Buddhism, as a religion, is ever ready to utilize all contributions, and, supported by psychologic necessity as over against the conservatism of literary art, gladly accepted the cast-off remnants of *Sarugaku*, at first in their original form of social comedy, and later as converted into valued instruments of popular instruction. The name *Kyogen*, however, signifying wild or crazy speech, in designation of comic interludes which early formed an inseparable part of every *Noh* programme, is in itself an expression of the semi-apologetic contempt in which plays of that character were accorded a place. They were of the earth earthy, and, as such, were thought to have little to contribute to the enrichment of Buddhist services, the goal of which was escape from the joys as well as the sorrows of earth. They were at first merely concessions to the frailty of human nature. They came to have a valued place, only second to that accorded *Noh* itself, and of even greater significance in relation to the common people.

To resume, *Sarugaku*, of original rude and comic character, gave rise to distinct but associated forms in *Noh* and *Kyogen*. In *Noh*, purged of its comic character, it became an austere medium of didactic narrative and spiritual edification, addressed to the cultured classes of society. In *Kyogen*, its rejected element survived as light social comedy, which Buddhism fostered as an attraction to its services, and, in certain instances, as a distinct contribution to its means of instruction among the common people.

The associated forms grew more and more distinct even as they became more closely associated, and certain distinguishing characteristics are readily noticeable. In *Noh* every element of beauty and of mystery is intensified, while in *Kyogen* the human elements of drama are given increasingly free expression. Actual names and titles are used in *Kyogen*, where in *Noh*, for the most part, formal designations, such as *Waki* and *Shite*, are employed. In *Noh*, priests are wise and noble, ascetics are powerful over all forces of evil, and women are beautiful and devoted even to madness ; in *Kyogen*, priests are depraved, ascetics are weak, and women are ugly and faithless. In *Noh*, actual life finds little expression ; in *Kyogen*, realism upon low levels finds free play. In *Kyogen*, the stilted, artificial language of *Noh* gives place to colloquial dialect in conversational prose, and the service of the *Chorus* is entirely dispensed with.

Among the themes deemed suitable for literary treatment in the ancient Orient, love occupied no important place. The reason for this lay in the dominating influence of Buddhism, with its doctrine of repression and its will to die rather than live. The necessary continuance of the race and family was one thing ; passion, or any feeling which might be called love, was quite another ; and love, forbidden the elevating, ennobling sanctions of religion, naturally proved worthy of social condemnation. Human attachment between men and women found no expression in *Noh* ; and in *Kyogen* it was a subject of mockery, through the moral weakness of degenerate priests, the buffoonery of country clowns, the plight of unsuspecting men, and the shrewdness of immoral women.

From the freedom accorded *Kyogen*, we might expect some genuine art form to have developed ; but comedy was kept strictly in its place as a non-literary subordinate, and found preservation only at the hand of those who in reality despised it. Hundreds of *Kyogen* are known to have existed at the time of its greatest popularity, but to them no author attached his name ; and most of them were lost, except as their stories were preserved in more serious versions, or as temples found them useful in holding the interest of the common people.

BUSU : A KYOGEN

Characters :
FEUDAL LORD, *Master of a House.*
TARO AND JIRO, *his House-boys.*

FEUDAL LORD.

I am the Feudal Lord of this place. To-day I am going out. There is something I want to say to Taro.

Taro boy, are you there ?

TARO.
Coming !

LORD.
Where are you ?

TARO.
Right here !

LORD.
Quick, for once ! Call Jiro too.

TARO.
Sure, I will.

Jiro boy, Master wants you.

JIRO.
Yes, right here !

LORD.
It's nothing very special that I want you for. I'm going out to-day. Take good care of the place.

TARO AND JIRO.
Yes, we will.

LORD.
Stay on the place.

TARO AND JIRO.

Of course !

LORD.

And be careful ! There's a *busu* [1] over there.

TARO AND JIRO.

Oh, then we can both go with you.

LORD.

Not at all ! There's a poison, which I call *busu*, over there. Be careful, for if even the wind, blowing from it, touches you, you'll be killed.

TARO AND JIRO.

Oh, we'll be careful ! (*Exit Lord.*)

TARO.

See here, Jiro boy ! We're never left alone together like this.

JIRO.

That's so ! When you go with him, I stay at home ; and when I go with him, you stay at home. We're never left alone together so nicely as this. It's as if we'd arranged it ourselves. Look out there !

TARO.

What's the matter ?

JIRO.

The wind is blowing from *busu*. Let's get away from here.

TARO.

I'm going to have a look at that *busu*.

JIRO.

Don't be foolish ! Let it alone !

---

[1] *Busu*, which serves as the title of the play, is a meaningless word by which the master wishes to awe the boys. They mistake it for *rusu*, which means watchman or guard.

TARO.

If the wind from that direction does not touch me, there's no danger. You just fan, please.

JIRO.

A'right !

TARO.

Fan, fan hard !

JIRO.

A'right ; be quick !

TARO.

I sha'n't make a slip. Now I'll untie the cord. As I untie the cord, you fan hard.

JIRO.

A'right !

TARO.

There, I've got the cover off ! I will take a look at that *busu*.

JIRO.

Had you better ?

TARO.

Hee-hee, I've seen it !

JIRO.

What's it like ?

TARO.

I don't know what it is. It looks sweet ; I'm going to taste it.

JIRO.

Don't be foolish. Let it alone !

TARO.

I believe I'm bewitched by that *busu*. I want to taste it so, and I'm going to eat some.

JIRO.

I won't let you while I'm here.

TARO.

>Shaking off detaining hands
>From sleeves that linger,
>Now again that *busu* strange
>I'm drawing nearer.

Yum, yum !

JIRO.

I say, Taro boy, what's the matter ?

TARO.

It's sugar !

JIRO.

What ! Sugar ?

TARO.

Sure thing !

JIRO.

Let me see it.

TARO.

Help yourself !

JIRO.

I will. Yum ! It is sugar, truly !

TARO.

He said the *busu* was poison because he did not want us to eat it.

JIRO.

Well, don't eat it all.

TARO.

Oh, I will leave you a little.

JIRO.

Don't take so much ; take a little at a time.

TARO AND JIRO.

Yum, it's sweet !

TARO.

Ho, now you've done a pretty thing ! Though Master said it was poison, you've eaten it all up ! I'll tell him just as soon as he gets back.

JIRO.

You opened it, though I told you not to.
I'll tell him that.

TARO.

Hee-hee, what a joke ! To cover it up, you'd better tear that picture scroll.

JIRO.

A'right, I will.

TARO.

Well done ! That's Master's pet picture, a picture of Kwannon by Priest Mokkei ; and you've torn it ! I'll tell him when he comes home.

JIRO.

I tore it because you told me to. I'll tell him that.

TARO.

Hee-hee, that's a joke too !

JIRO.

But what shall we do to cover this up ?

TARO.

We can cover it up if we break this big bowl.

JIRO.

Not that, no ! You want to get me into more trouble.

TARO.

I'll help you. Take hold on that side.

JIRO.

A'right !

TARO.

Gwaran !

JIRO.

Chin !

TARO.

Now, set up a howl when he comes back.

JIRO.

Will howling help us ?

LORD.

I am returning.

Hey, there ! I've come back !

TARO AND JIRO.

Boo-hoo ! Boo-hoo !

LORD.

Ah, what is the matter ?

TARO.

Jiro boy, you tell him.

JIRO.

No ; you please tell him yourself.

TARO.

Jiro boy and I were wrestling to keep awake that we might take good care of the house.   Jiro boy is very skilful, you know, and I tried to throw him by tripping him up.   Trying not to fall, he clutched that picture, and it—got—like—that——

LORD.

My precious Kwannon ; and you spoiled it like that !

JIRO.

And he threw me over that bowl, and it—broke—into—pieces——

LORD.

What, oh what shall I do with you !

TARO.

We thought you would surely kill us for breaking your precious things, and so we ate the *busu* to kill ourselves.   But we are not dead yet !

LORD.

Go, hang yourselves, this minute !

TARO.

Though a mouthful I've eaten,
Not yet have I died !

JIRO.

Though I've eaten two mouthfuls,
I cannot yet die !

TARO.

Even three or four mouthfuls,

JIRO.

Even five or six mouthfuls,

Taro and Jiro.

> Though more than ten mouthfuls we've eaten,
> Not yet have we died.
> How charmed are the lives which we cherish,
> How charmed are our lives !

Lord.

Confound those fellows !

Jiro.

Ha-a-a !

Taro.

What shall we do ?

Lord.

Are you still there ?

Taro and Jiro.

Excuse us, excuse us !

Lord.

Not much, not much !

Kyogen, as we have noted, became a recognized form of interlude for use in connection with the more stately *Noh*, but its power of popular attraction suggested an independent use in connection with Buddhist services. This use for purposes of instruction and propaganda is nowhere better illustrated than at the Mibu temple in an old part of Kyoto, where was once the centre of the city.

The Ritsu sect of Buddhism was first introduced in Japan between A.D. 749 and A.D. 758. Mibu was founded in 753 by Kakai Daishi, a Chinese priest, in accord with the order of Emperor Shomu (reign 724-748), as a Ritsu temple. This sect, like the Shingon, teaches the doctrine of *jiriki nembutsu*, according to which sinful humanity may hope for salvation only through worshipful deeds. In 991 the temple was re-established by Kaiken Daiso, for the worship of Emmei Jizo ; and the strict doctrine of *jiriki nembutsu* seems to have yielded to the doctrine of *tariki nembutsu*, according to which followers of the Jodo and Shin sects hope for salvation through worshipful faith in the merits of Amida Buddha. However that may be, the Jodo and Shin sects, with their doctrine of salvation through faith, made much progress and greatly undermined the influence of the sterner Pharisaic Ritsu during the fourteenth century. To meet this movement, and to make religious experience more easy for those who might be won at Mibu, Engaku Shonin, about the year 1300, introduced at Mibu the use of *Kyogen*.

The *Kyogen*, as at first presented, were probably ordinary plays, designed to attract the crowd and humorously to instruct in Buddhist ethics ; but a strange modification took place wherein the action accompanied by spoken dialogue gave way to pure pantomime of so dramatic a nature as to be understood readily by the most ignorant. This silent drama, this morality pantomime,[1] continues to the present time ; and annually, from April 21st to May 10th, presentations are given daily from a collection of some thirty plays. These plays are handed down in oral tradition from generation to generation of actors, who are from families within the parish. Some of the plays are evidently didactic, while others show little relation to Buddhist teachings. Some are to be found in general collections of *Kyogen*, and others are peculiar to Mibu ; but all are handled with great freedom and originality.

The usual character for *Kyogen* (狂言) signifies wild, excited, or foolish words ; but the character employed at

---

[1] The term morality is here used with freedom. A morality, according to Mackenzie in *The English Moralities*, " is a play, allegorical in structure, which has for its main object the teaching of some lesson for the guidance of life, and in which the principal characters are personified abstractions or highly conventionalized types." These *Mibu Kyogen* have as their apparent object the teaching of some lesson for the guidance of life, but their characters, though often highly universalized types, are by no means personified abstractions.

Mibu (敎言) signifies teaching word. The use of this peculiar title is significant of the didactic intent of the moralities; and the inclusion of plays unsuited to didactic purposes may be explained by the theory now held by the priest in charge, briefly, that the essential element is to be found not in the didactic quality, but in the sacramental nature of the acting.

Although Ritsu emphasizes personal effort, rather than faith in Amida, the service at Mibu is declared to have been modified by Engaku for the sake of the common people by the introduction of *Kyogen* as a *yuzunembutsu*, or praiseworthy act of worship, imparting its merit to others than those actually engaged therein. Such transferable merit, made philosophically possible by the Buddhist conception of the universe, can be acquired by an acted as well as by a spoken service; and all present, held by the entertainment, may share therein without effort. The purpose of the *Kyogen* thus becomes twofold, primarily to perform an effective sacramental service, and secondarily to inculcate Buddhist teachings for the encouragement of the good and the rebuke of the evil. The sacramental purpose is effected in particular by the nature of the acting, in which the movements of the actors form a continuous repetition of which is an abbreviation of the characters given on page 174, which signifies Jizo Bosatsu, the deity to whom the worship is addressed, and is thus an acted *nembutsu*, or service of worship.

Of recent years the emphasis upon the sacramental character of the service as a *yuzunembutsu* has led to deterioration and to the inclusion of elements in action which cater to popular taste and attract the vulgar, even though they inculcate no moral lesson in accord with Buddhist ethics. The character of these plays, as survivals of strict Buddhist Moralities, is in danger of being lost in their very subservience to a Buddhist philosophy, the priest in charge going

so far as to say that anything, even a modern scenario, might be used effectively, provided only that its presentation involved the essential movements of *yuzunembutsu*.

The plays at Mibu are presented upon the upper balcony of the temple. There is, of course, no curtain. Scenery is entirely lacking or limited to the simplest hints to the imagination, such as a signboard to represent a market, or a sliding screen, held in place by an attendant, to represent an inn. The characters are well costumed according to their parts in garments presented to the temple. Faces are masked, as in *Noh* ; and expression is limited to movements of the body and limbs. The folding fan is used to a great extent as an accessory. In spite of such limitations, the effect produced is unmistakable ; and this is due largely to a wonderful expressiveness of posture and of movement of body and limb.

A temporary platform, some thirty feet from the temple, is built up to a level with the balcony for the use of spectators ; and the ground-space between serves as a " pit," which swarms with children during the performance of the more popular and amusing plays.

Horaku Wari ranks among the most popular of the Mibu plays, at least with the children, who in great delight gather up the fragments of hundreds of thin, unbaked pottery plates which are broken over the temple railing in the grand finale. The didactic element in the play amounts to little or nothing.

HORAKU WARI [1]

THE BREAKING OF THE PLATES.

Characters :
A VILLAGE MAYOR.
A SELLER OF PLATES.
A SELLER OF DRUMS.

Enter the Village Mayor, dressed in long robes, wearing a sword and carrying a wooden signboard. He looks with pride over his growing village, and, because of the evident prosperity of the community, establishes a new market-place by setting up the signboard. He withdraws with evident satisfaction.

Enter the Drum-Seller, his wares typified by a small hand-drum suspended by a cord about his neck. He has heard of the new market-place, and is much pleased with the general location. Selecting what he judges to be the best position in the market for his wares, he lies down for a nap, as it is still scarcely more than midnight and he has travelled far.

Enter the Plate-Seller, his wares typified by an unbaked pottery plate suspended by a cord about his neck. He has heard of the new market-place and finds the new sign. He is much surprised that anyone should have arrived before him, and he determines to remove the drums and place his plates in the best position at the entrance to the market. This he effects by taking the drum from the neck of the sleeping merchant. At length the plate-merchant also rests from his labours.

When the drum-merchant awakes there is trouble that leads to violence, but this stops as the Mayor reappears.

An investigation takes place, and occupies much time. At last it is judged that he who carries the most honourable goods shall have the place of honour in the market. Neither can succeed, after many trials, in telling a story of superior tribute to his wares, and the judgment must, therefore, be reached through a trial of their serviceableness.

In this contest the drum-merchant, in a game of " do as I

[1] A variation of this *Kyogen* may be found in a collection of two hundred *Kyogen*, first published in four volumes (1688–1703), under the title *Kako Horaku* (Drums and Plates).

do," tries hard to make the plate-merchant do that which shall break his wares. The plate-merchant is very crafty and outwits his adversary at every turn, so that at last he seems to give up the contest. He withdraws, and plates by the hundred are arranged along the rail of the temple veranda. Unnoticed, the drum-merchant returns and hides below the rail. Watching his opportunity, he quickly overturns the entire stock, which breaks, as it falls, into a shower of pieces over the mob of children waiting below.

The Mayor then awards the signboard to the drum-merchant as assurance that he has won the right to the chief place in the new market. The plate-merchant is driven off in disgrace.

* * * * *

The didactic element in certain Mibu plays is more clearly Buddhistic. In *Dojoji*, for example, it is unmistakable. The *Dojoji* at Mibu seems closely related to a *Noh* of the same name, by Kwanami (1333–1384), a priest of Kasuga. The story was later utilized in a *Joruri* by Itcho Asada and Muneke Maruike, but the Mibu version resembles the *Noh* more nearly. Since Engaku himself came from Kasuga and antedated Kwanami by merely one generation, it is not impossible that both followed an earlier tradition. In any case, the Mibu version is, as far as may be judged from a silent presentation, a more forceful lesson in Buddhist ethics.

DOJOJI (MIBU VERSION)

The scene is laid in the temple of Dojo. Two attendant priestlings, suffering greatly from heat and exhaustion, bring in a heavy bell suspended from a pole. The bell is, in reality, a light frame some four or five feet high, covered with cloth ; to it the property man fastens a little cord which runs over a pulley on a beam in the top of the temple veranda.

After a most dramatic period of refreshment, one of the young men attempts to hoist the bell by means of the cord, while the other pushes. The bell slips back and injures the leg of the one who had been pushing. There is great excitement as they attend to the injured member. They find themselves quite

MIBU TEMPLE, KYOGEN

exhausted, and fan themselves violently, wiping off the perspiration with their towel head-bands. At last, changing places, they hoist the bell and secure it in place, then dance a most grotesque but graceful joy-dance.

The chief priest enters, an old man with a face like a death's-head. The young men prostrate themselves in courtesy, but indulge in insulting gestures the moment his back is turned. His attention is called to the bell, and the young men silently tell him how hard they have laboured. He examines the bell, and gives them his blessing together with instructions as to its care. As he goes out, the young men again indulge in insults and are almost caught in the act. In the abandonment of clownish delight they play tricks one upon the other.

At length a woman appears on the approach to the temple. They are greatly disturbed, for they have been warned by the priest that women are not to be allowed within the holy place. She tells them that she has come particularly to see the famous new bell of which she has heard, and begs for permission to enter and worship for only a moment. At first they refuse ; but at last, infatuated by her charms and persuaded by her eloquence, they allow her to enter. As she admires the bell, they marvel at her and at her wonderful garments. She offers to perform a holy dance before the bell in its honour, and for that purpose puts on a head-dress such as is worn by Shinto priests. She wears many beautiful garments, richly embroidered, and these, one by one, she slips from her shoulders as she dances, until some six or eight are hanging in festoons of gorgeous colour about her waist. The young men, who have never seen the like before, are enthralled and dance in grotesque imitation before her until they fall exhausted. As she continues to dance, she weaves over them a hypnotic spell. When they sleep soundly, she stops dancing, goes hurriedly to the bell, and pulls it down over her upon the floor.

The young men are awakened by the thunder of the falling bell and rush about in wild confusion. Convinced that it is not all a dream, they attempt to hoist the bell again to its place, but are horrified to discover that they cannot move it in the least. Surely it must be bewitched ! Each rebukes the other for what has happened, and urges him to call the priest. The priest comes, uncalled, and rates them soundly, ordering them to rehang the bell. They protest that it is bewitched, and beg

M

him to exorcise the evil spirit. At last, after much questioning, they confess : a woman !

The priest is in agony of soul that such a disaster should have occurred, and rebukes the young men for gross neglect of duty. He offers prayer, while the young men try to lift the bell. They fail repeatedly. All pray, the priest rolling his beads, the young men going through the same motions with their towels ; and the bell rises, drawn up by the property man, revealing a devil in most brilliant attire.

Now begins the awful conflict between righteousness and evil. At one moment the priest is able to drive the Devil to one side of the temple, and, again, waving his wand, the Devil drives the priest back. The young men try to support the priest with their prayers, but again and again in fright are forced to climb out upon the timbers of the temple roof, where they cling, trembling in every limb. The end, of course, is assured, and the priest at last drives the Devil from the temple, thus showing conclusively the power of prayer over even the forces of hell, which love to array themselves in the charms of womanhood.

*　　　*　　　*　　　*　　　*

Better than either *Horaku Wari* or *Dojoji*, in illustration of the peculiar nature of these *Mibu Kyogen*, is *Sai no Kawara* (The River of Fate), in which there are six characters.

SAI NO KAWARA

(THE RIVER OF FATE.)

Characters :

EMMA, *the Judge who passes sentence upon all who enter the realm beyond the river.*

A BLACK DEVIL, *Chief Assistant to the Judge.*

A RED DEVIL, *a Subordinate, a Clown.*

A RECORDER, *Keeper of the Records of Life.*

A SINNER (LIAR).

JIZO, *the God of Mercy.*

Enter Emma, the two Devils and the Recorder.

Emma sits on the judgment seat, the Recorder upon his left, the Black Devil upon his right. The Red Devil sits upon the floor. Emma announces that they are about to pass judgment, and orders the Black Devil to have the prisoner brought in. The Black Devil passes the order on to the Red Devil, who goes out and returns with a trembling sinner whose hands are securely fastened behind her back.

Emma asks the Recorder for the record of her life. He sets forth her sins and records them in his book. Kneeling before Emma he presents the record. Emma rises and (silently) reads aloud the record. Facing the audiences he then reads the charge and declares the penalty.

The Black Devil is ordered to proceed with punishment. He in turn orders the Red Devil to punish the woman; and the Red Devil begins to beat her. In this he is so unskilful that the Black Devil has to show him how it should be done. Thereupon the Red Devil becomes so efficient that Emma and the Recorder leave the scene.

Since the woman was a liar, her tongue must be pulled out. The Black Devil orders the Red Devil to do this; but, as the Red Devil is unable, he is obliged to do it himself, throwing the tongue—a piece of red cloth—into a basket. They then carry the woman and put her into a cauldron of water. Under this a fire is started by the Black Devil with a flint-stone, after the Red Devil has failed. Both fan the fire; and then test the water, which is found too hot to bear. Thereupon the victim is pulled out, boiled to a rag-doll. This the Devils begin to eat.

While they are eating Jizo enters and begs for the bones, which, after some objection, are given to him.

Jizo places the bones upon his fan, then lays them down tenderly and offers prayer. While he prays the dead arises (from where she had been hidden in the floor) weak and trembling, so that she cannot walk or stand alone. Jizo takes her by a supporting hand and leads her forth into Paradise.

*   *   *   *   *

At some temples ordinary spoken *Kyogen* are employed as popular attractions; and occasionally *Kyogen* are presented in entertainment apart from *Noh*, with which they are usually associated; but they have never broken from the stigma of literary inferiority on the one hand, or the grasp of temple patronage on the other, sufficiently to enjoy any free development into a form capable of satisfying the dramatic demands of a growing people. Again a hopeful lead has resulted in a finished form apparently incapable of further development ; and still again must we return to the amusements of the common people for a beginning which, under freer treatment, may develop further towards the modern drama.

CHAPTER IX

JORURI AND AYATSURI

THE literary element in all early librettos was kept strictly subordinate to a liturgic purpose. In *Kagura* we found no conscious incongruity when vulgar love-songs appeared in Shinto ceremonial, because those who effected and those who observed the union cared only for the music and the dance, which clothed the words with a significance quite independent of their literal or original meaning. *Utai* (*Noh* libretto), in spite of their beauty, are tenuous in plot and simple in structure, special compositions for a clearly defined purpose—that purpose being presentation in song and dance for religious or æsthetic satisfaction. Whatever may have been spontaneous in their antecedent forms was sternly brought into subjection to this purpose by a self-conscious art. It is evident that the writers of these *utai*, in seeking to express emotion, for example, sought not words whereby to give utterance, but an atmosphere through beauty of sound and magic of movement, together with an association of ideas not clearly expressed, or even consciously understood—an atmosphere designed to arouse appropriate feeling in those under their influence. The appeal was not primarily to the intellect or to the emotions through the intellect, but to deeper centres of being through those subtler channels of approach utilized among all peoples by those skilled in the exercise of religious influence. The effect likely to be produced by the words alone was entirely disregarded.

The *utai*, composed by men who, like Seami, were also actors, seem never to have been conceived apart from the music and the dance which give them interpretive utterance.

Devotees of *Noh*, except as they may have the text before them, seldom attempt to follow the words of the actors, but yield themselves to the magic of a unified art. The texts may be said to exist only in their presentation as *Noh* ; and therefore any presentation in mere words, such as has been attempted in previous chapters, is certain to prove unsatisfactory.

We have seen, thus far, nothing resembling a popular drama. Social song and dance, taken into patronage by shrines and temples, developed, with the addition of dialogue, to a high degree of art for devotional, didactic, and even sacramental purposes ; but further progress was checked by that very patronage, and those fragments which fell back into the unskilled use of the vulgar were doomed to deterioration. Even as *Kagura* had to be left at one side while a new and popular start was made for *Noh* and *Kyogen*, so these in turn have to be left as finished products, while from among the people new lines of development push forward, later to utilize the best that has been gained in earlier experience. *Kagura* remained an art-form addressed to the deity and to nobles upon earth ; *Noh* an entertainment for the warrior class, whose highest virtue, under Buddhist tutelage, was self-repression.

Yet the Japanese are no exception in their love of a story, and their early literature was not confined to social and ceremonial lyrics. In fact, the *Ko-ji-ki* itself is declared to have been put in writing from the oral report of Hiyedano-Are, " who never forgot anything that he had heard." He was apparently one of a hereditary body of *kataribe* (reciters), whose duty it was to recite before the emperors. We may naturally suppose that these *kataribe* had their counterpart among the common people long before the written word became common ; and the fact that no *Homeridæ*, no composer of a *Beowulf*, no story-teller voicing the legends and the aspirations of an entire people, arose is due, in part at least, to the absence among the early Japanese of any sense of popular unity or racial culture.

It is fascinating but useless to surmise what might have been, had no Chinese influence, with its written character, come at an early date, and by its overmastering superiority utterly crushed the movings of native instinct. As it was, travel diaries and *monogatari* (narratives, both historic and romantic) took conspicuous place in Japanese literature as early as the beginning of the tenth century. Some of these, like the *Genji Monogatari* of Murasaki Shikibu, were fore-runners of the modern novel with its portrayal of character in social life ; while others, like *Gempei Seisuiki*, lent them-selves to the service of public reciters for popular entertain-ment and instruction ; and it is to this latter class that we must turn for the literary material later utilized by actors and writers for the drama.

Gempei Seisuiki, by an unknown author of the early fourteenth century, is a history of the struggle of the Mina-moto (Gen) and Taira (Hei) clans from 1161 to 1185, when, as a result of the decisive naval battle off Dan-no-ura, Yoritomo, brother of Yoshitsune, general in command of the Minamoto forces, established his shogunate in control of all Japan. The account follows the facts of history with fair accuracy, merely adorning the recital with ornate detail and purely fictitious dialogue, and with oratory appropriate to the occasion.

Upon this story is based the more famous *Heike Mono-gatari*, which, of inferior literary value, is an attempt, through further elaboration, to popularize the heroic tales for public recital.

Kojima, a Buddhist priest of great learning who died in 1374, continued the historic narrative to the end of the reign of Go Murakami, 1367, in *Taiheiki*, The Record of Great Peace. This Record, while following the thread of history, is even more dependent upon the imagination than the

Heike Monogatari ; but, like the latter, it provided material for much later composition and a text for public recital.

The recital or reading of these two works became the art of a profession. Public readers with great dramatic skill made the stirring tales live again for a people who still for the most part could not read. Seated before low desks, marking time and emphasis with no other accompaniment than a fan, they read with such expression as to bring both tears and laughter, satisfying through vicarious heroism the drab lives of a degenerate age. Reciters of the *Heike Monogatari*, who were often blind, shaved their heads and accompanied their recitations with simple melodies upon the *biwa* (lute). They were popularly known as *biwa bozu* (priests of the lute).

During this period, and in close association with these public readings for the common people, *Joruri* had its origin. In *Sarugutsuwa*, published about 1658, there is an account which, while legendary, may be taken as expressing an essential truth, as does the story of Anglo-Saxon Cædmon. A reciter of *Heike Monogatari* in the era of Bunan (1444–1448), Uda by name, was blind. For this he grieved greatly and prayed for years to the *Yakushi Nyorai* (Healing Buddhas) that his eyes might be opened. Upon one occasion, after having prayed with great lamentation for twenty-one nights, he looked up at dawn and saw the pale moon above the western mountains. His prayers had been answered. In joyful thanksgiving he composed a story, *Yasuda Monogatari*, divided into twelve parts in imitation of the divisions in the classic *Heike Monogatari*, or, it may have been, in tribute to the twelve forms of the Healing Buddha. As the Healing Buddha dwelt in Joruri land, the Land of Bright Purity, he called his story *Joruri*. Of this story only the name remains to make a legend ; but sometime before 1485 there appeared *Junidan Soshi* (A Story-book in Twelve Parts), called *Joruri Monogatari*.

NINGYO SHIBAI STAGE, SHOWING A SCENE FROM " KAMIYA-JIHEI "

To the imagination of the audience, the men who manipulate the dolls are invisible. Koharu is represented as seated, O San as standing outside. For the story as given in *Kabuki*, see p. 297.

This *Joruri Monogatari*, now extant in various versions, all published later than 1646, is a romantic recital based upon a supposed experience of Yoshitsune (1159–1189), younger brother of Yoritomo of the Minamoto (Gen) Clan, telling how in his journey he fell in love with a girl called Joruri-hime, from whose name this type of story may have been called.

Both the author and the date of the *Junidan Soshi* are unknown ; but it is reasonable to place its composition in the last half of the fifteenth century, during the period when Yoshitsune was a most popular hero in semi-historical sketches and in patriotic songs.

The chanting of *Monogatari* had already become popular in Kyoto ; but, although Uda is said to have introduced his *Joruri* there, this story of Yoshitsune failed of success in that city. In the region of Yedo, however, where were many descendants of the Minamoto family, it spread rapidly through the recital of blind readers called *Zato*.

The chanting of *Joruri*, like that of the earlier *Monogatari*, became a fashion ; and other stories, both old and new, came to be included in the readers' repertoire during the next century. The use of the *samisen* in accompaniment of *Joruri* seems to have become general before the end of the sixteenth century ; and at about the same time Menukiya Chogoro and a doll-maker named Hitta began to use puppets in their presentation of *Joruri*. This great innovation won immediate popularity ; and the chanted story took on new life, as an appeal to the eye gave greater dramatic effectiveness.

For somewhat over one hundred years *Joruri* held its place and name as a popular entertainment of recital ; but with the introduction of puppets and their immediate great favour the name *Joruri* became a designation of the libretto, and the entertainment came to be called *Ayatsuri* (manipulation), the skilful handling of another, as of a cat's paw.

The stories as stories are still *Joruri* ; the plays are *Ayatsuri*, or, in recent times, *Ningyo Shibai* (doll theatres). The reader continued to hold his position of first importance. He was the real *puller of the strings*, using others as subordinates, who in turn manipulated the puppets. His name gave designation to the hall or theatre ; and his subordinates, however skilful, seldom gained public recognition.

In 1597 *Ayatsuri* was presented before the great Hideyoshi by a famous reader, Satsuma-no-jo. Satsuma's son, Joun, studied *Joruri*, reading under Sawazumi, who was a master of the art before the introduction of the puppets ; and at the beginning of the Kanei Era (1624–1643) went to Yedo. Under his direction puppets of wood, more easily managed, took the place of earthenware dolls ; and doll-costuming became very elaborate.

In *Ayatsuri*, as in *Joruri* proper, different schools arose, distinguished by the type of their libretto—some being so violent as to cause the destruction of their puppets in a single presentation. The most violent type may be illustrated by *Kimpira Monogatari*, which is no longer extant as a *Joruri*, but merely as a legend of animal ferocity displayed by one who had been reared by mountain beasts. The difficulty of presenting such stories with the use of puppets, and the temper of the time which found little pleasure in such violence, prevented the success of this type. Historic or semi-historic tales of heroism and loyalty on the part of *samurai* were most in popular favour.

Although *Ayatsuri*, beginning in the Kyoto region, seems to have made its first great advance in Yedo, the natural tendency of dramatic art to find Kyoto Society more congenial soon brought the best readers to that city ; and among their pupils Harima (1631–1685) should be mentioned for his mastery of technique and for his originality. Readers were still to a considerable extent the composers of their *Joruri*, taking their material freely from old sources. In style of composition Harima is said to have left much to be desired, but his voice was excellent and his compass great, so that he became a favourite, especially in the presentation of travel description and the pathos of battle. By him, about 1660, *Ayatsuri* was made a regular entertainment in Osaka, where it has flourished up to the present time.

Uji Kaga, also known as Kadayu,[1] was perhaps more influenced by the effeminate taste of the Kyoto region. Under him the *Joruri* of historical event, with its brutal loyalty, so popular at *samurai* headquarters in Yedo, gradually gave place to more sentimental tales of love and double suicide. He was trained in the refinements of *Noh*, and brought his great power of poetic interpretation into the reading of *Joruri*, establishing what might be termed a second type or school of *Joruri* reading.

In the meantime Gorobei, a farmer of Tennoji, near Osaka, had become much interested in the *Joruri* of Harima, and studied its presentation under a follower of the Harima school. He developed great skill, particularly in rendering battle scenes and parts demanding virile power. In 1677 Kadayu and Gorobei together read *Saigyo Monogatari*, a story of the life of Priest Saigyo, Gorobei acting as assistant for the more stirring scenes, which apparently were prepared especially for his rendering. Thus the two types of reading came into co-operation to the improvement of both ; and what gave promise of distinct development were united.

Gorobei later took the name Takemoto Gidayu, and in 1685 began independent performances at Dotombori, in

[1] *Dayu*, modified from *Tayu*, signifies the fifth grade in social rank. In older times, when a player of any sort attained such perfection of skill as to attract the attention of the nobility and secure an invitation to play before the Court, he was, for the occasion, given social standing of the fifth grade in order to permit of his entrance to the Court. Although the rank was merely temporary, one who had received it was for ever honoured ; and the habit arose of incorporating the term within the personal name, as in the case before us.

Osaka. His assistants became famous for their skill in handling the puppets ; and his own name, Gidayu, became the popular synonym for Joruri reciter. Harima, his earlier model, endeavoured in 1686 to run opposition performances, but found it impossible to compete with the younger man, who, in addition to the skilful handling of the dolls, began to present new Joruri by Chikamatsu, who had already become noted as a writer for the Kabuki stage.

Of Chikamatsu, Japan's great playwright of the late seventeenth century, little is known apart from what can be gleaned from his own writings. Many places claim the honour of his birth ; but the following more or less legendary account of his family and early life may be taken as sufficiently trustworthy.

According to the Junibungo by Tsukagoe, 1894, he was born of a samurai family, of the name of Sugimori, in 1653, at Hagi, on the west coast of Japan. He studied for the priesthood at Chikamatsu Temple, in Karatsu ; and from the name of that temple later took his own pen-name. Of his parents nothing is known ; but a brother was head-priest at Sokokuji in Kyoto ; and, for that reason it may be, the youth went to Kyoto, when he left Chikamatsu in anger because of temple discipline inflicted upon another. In Kyoto he entered the service of a family of high rank ; but became restless and, leaving the employ of the nobility, turned his attention to the entertainment of the common people—in 1677 writing his first play for the Kabuki theatre.

In 1689 Chikamatsu went to Osaka, and from the next year gave himself entirely to writing for Gidayu, withdrawing his interest from Kabuki, and seeking to produce plays adapted to the possibilities of the doll-stage and designed to develop those possibilities to their utmost.

Takemoto Gidayu lived until 1714, but retired from the management of his theatre in 1705, being succeeded by Takeda Izumo, who followed closely the traditions of the great master and retained the name *Takemoto* as the designation of his theatre—a tribute continued now for over two hundred years. Under the joint efforts of Takemoto Gidayu and Chikamatsu, *Ayatsuri* gained its highest development ; but this development was of necessity limited by the possibilities of the puppet stage, and could not keep pace with the progress of *Kabuki*, where human actors were coming into prominence as interpreters.

CHAPTER X

THE SOGA REVENGE

A STORY FOR PUPPET DRAMATIZATION BY CHIKAMATSU, 1718

THE SOGA REVENGE

ACT I

Persons Represented :
NORIYORI, *younger brother of Shogun Yoritomo, retired as a Priest of Shuzenji.*
KAJIWARA-KAGETAKA ⎫
YAWATA-SABURO ⎬ *partisans of Suketsune.*
HANGAE-SHIGETOMO ⎭
INUBOMARU, *son of Suketsune.*
ONIO, *follower of the Soga.*
NINOMIYA-YASUKIYO, *brother-in-law of the Soga.*
ASAHINA, *son of Yoshinori-Tomoe.*
LADY YORITOMO, *wife of the Shogun.*
SUKETSUNE-AKOYA, *wife of Suketsune.*
YOSHINORI-TOMOE, *wife of Yoshinori, an officer.*
HONDA-TOKONATSU, *wife of Honda.*
YOSHIYUKI-NAKAHARA, *a Lady-in-Waiting.*
SERVANTS AND ATTENDANTS.

Prelude.—A Chinese king once called his followers *faithful dogs* ; but one who wisely planned he called a *man*, since by the trapper's fire 'tis men who guide the hunt, while faithful dogs run down and kill the game.

SCENE I. *Residence of the Shogun at Kamakura.*

YORITOMO, the Shogun, was encamped for hunting at the foot of Mount Fuji. At Kamakura, where shogunate authority rose more supreme than Fuji in its height, the Tiger Gate was opened at half-past four in the morning of the 28th of May, in the fourth year of Kenkyu (1193). In the General's absence salutations for the day were to be received by Lady Yoritomo. She entered the reception-hall, and received in audience of salutation for that day the ladies : wives of Ministers Wada, Hatakeyama,

Chiba, and Kasusa ; wives of Captains Kudo, Kajiwara, Utsunomiya, Dohi, and Sasaki ; wives of the nobility ; wives of the most immediate hereditary retainers—all of worthy birth, who sat in order of their husbands' rank.

Her rich, embroidered sleeves so brightly shone in light from lofty candle-stands that the golden painting of old Taketori's daughter on the wall paled into dimness.

Well pleased, Lady Yoritomo in greeting said : " My noble ladies all, it surely is because of our great General's might that, even in his absence at Mount Fuji for the hunt, Kamakura remains in peace for the lad, Yoriie, for your honoured selves, and me. In respect to those whose game, surpassing praise, has here been sent, let us listen to the reading of the official record of the hunt."

At her command Nakahara, Yoshiyuki's wife, read the list fluently, translating as she read official language into that of common speech.

" First on the list—a mighty stag, with hair for brush-work good, by Otomo-Ichiboshi, a youth of fifteen years, was shot ; he well deserves reward. Second, a doe at distance great by Chichibu was slain ; and, as the arrow cut is small, its spotted hide a garment for the General will make. A wild boar next, its ribs thrice deeply cut by strokes of Natta-Tadatsune's sword—the highest honour of the hunt to that brave hunter falls.

" A lusty stag,
    From grazing startled,
    In pride of youth with angry roar,
    Charged Nakanuma-Goro.
    Its horns, torn in two fragments from its head,
    Bear witness to its taking by hand unaided !

N

" Adroitly
Dohi-no-yataro crushed
The neck of a wolf,
That o'er a cliff had fallen,
With one kick
That like an iron hammer-stroke descended ;
And like iron hammer-strokes
Were the blows of that wild bear,
Which, fiercer far than wolf or tiger,
Fell 'fore Mirenaga's men—
His white neck gleaming
Like the hornèd moon,
In light of which two rabbits,
Running o'er the waves of pampas grass,
Were speared by Koyama
Who mounted rode the field.

" Without a scar,
The bony forehead of a wild boar broke
Beneath the impact
Yoichi's blunted arrow gave.
Breathless, died a fox,
Hard pressed for miles
By Rokuyata,
Who ran and ran with speed of mountain hawk ;
And this again is worthy praise—
An unarmed capture.

" Kodama-no-taro,
Hurling his spear aloft,
Brought down a wild goose,
With broken wing.
A flying deer,
Shot through the neck,
Rewarded Saburo's aim.

> And Takenoshita on his sword
> The charging boar received
> Too close at hand !

" Usami-no-saemon,
  Kawagoe-Taro,
  Soma-no-kotaro,
  Yuke-no-tomoshige,
  Tsuchiya, Hirayama,
  Chiba, Utsunomiya,
  All deserve honourable mention.

" In addition there is a stag, claimed as his own both by Kudo-Suketsune and by Honda-Jiro, of Chichibu's train : claimed by them both for it bears two arrows—that of Kudo in its side, that of Honda in its breast.   Though the game seems six-tenths Honda's, the dispute is not settled yet ; and so do the arrows remain as they struck ; and so is the record thus writ in conclusion.

" (*Signed*) WADA-YOSHINORI,
           " *Clerk of the Hunt.*"

When she had finished reading the ladies were pleased, and whispered each of her husband's skill as if it were her own ; but Akoya, Suketsune's wife, drew near and boldly said : " That record is an offence to the ear.   The fact that a Honda of Chichibu's train, of humble rank, would contest the spoil with my husband, Suketsune, is full outrageous, without the false declaration that the game seemed six-tenths his.   'Tis Yoshinori's partiality.   In the record, that will stand throughout all time, I pray thee have it written that Suketsune, and that he alone, killed the deer."

No sooner had she ceased than Tomoe, Yoshinori's wife, came to her side and said :

" Indeed, Akoya, though Honda be a retainer in Chichibu's train, he is a Genji of Musashi. His exploits in battle far surpass those of Suketsune ; and in this present hunt he has received, by our Lord's direct command, commission as night-guard. He is accorded place as Yoritomo's follower ; and his wife has here been granted audience by our Lady. Whom should he fear ? Before whom silent keep, when wronged unjustly ? ' Yoshinori's partiality ! ' Why, Mrs. Kudo, 'twas your word ; that's putting it too strongly."

Reddening with anger, Akoya retorted :

" Though he were a king's grandson in olden days he's but a servant now. Once you were Lady Tomoe, wife of a great general ; but, that he might have big, husky children, Yoshinori took you ; and now you are but as the rest of us. There's no use in talking of Honda's family, since now he does not know his place. Suketsune's arrow has his sign in gold upon it—Kudo-Saemon-Suketsune ; but Honda's arrow is one in common use, bearing not even a family name. Disgraceful, for one ignorant of the rules of the hunting-field, to claim the deer ! Make a new entry, or strike out Honda's name. I will not cease to speak till it is done," she said, insisting with vehement gesture.

Tokonatsu, Honda's wife, from her humble seat at the end of the line, laughingly cried :

" I say, Madame Akoya, one may speak of rudeness in matters of precedence on horseback, the order of seats in a room, or the lift of the wine-cups ; but you, I suppose, would run, turning your back on the enemy, rather than rudely to fight with a foe of superior rank in the battle. Your impertinent criticism, based on no knowledge of knighthood, is merely ridiculous."

AKOYA.

That which you say is rude, beyond question.

TOKONATSU.

No ; 'tis you who are rude, reflecting thus on the General.

So, like the twanging of bows, strident contended the women.

Rising from her seat, Lady Yoritomo exclaimed, in voice that commanded : " Silence them, ladies ! A dispute which even ministers of State could not determine needs no comment from women. It is well that Noriyori, Yoritomo's younger brother, is now a priest in retirement here in Kamakura. Hither will we invite him ; and to his impartial judgment leave this, that there may be no enmity. Tomoe, give orders that this be done."

Akoya, springing forward, sought to clasp Lady Yoritomo's skirt, exclaiming, " Impartially to judge between Kudo-Saemon-Suketsune and that low creature, Honda, spiteful woman ! "

But Tokonatsu held her fast, demanding from whose lips came the words *low creature*.

AKOYA.

From mine ! From a daimyo's lady, who holds as vassal Omi-Yawata and many a Honda's equal. Is it strange that I should call him *low* ?

TOKONATSU.

Ho, daimyo's lady ! I'll make an end of you.

(*They claw with blood-stained nails. Like wind-blown flowers, the women fight.*)

Tomoe rose to her full height, and, seizing Akoya beneath her strong left arm, tossed both her legs aloft with loud " Yo, ho ! " Painted brows and ornate head-dress were disordered ; tears fell, and faint grew the breath of her nostrils.

Tomoe.

How sweet a body ! How pleasant to embrace ! With good reason, the apple of Suketsune's eye ! But it is not nice to speak so rudely in the presence of our Lady. I will send for a carriage and a horse to go with it. If you will insist upon having your own wilful way, insist to Suketsune upon his return. 'Mid the private billing and cooing of lovers there's no limit to wild wantonness, wilful ; but, if you persist before others, you will be treated like this. Does it hurt you ? Oh, does it ? You will have a hard time, indeed.

Tightening her grasp upon Akoya, she seized Tokonatsu's left hand and hoisted her under her free arm, saying, " I am lop-sided with the weight as it is. Sorry, Tokonatsu, to use you thus as a balance ! "

Two faces, pale, with tumbled hair, with Tomoe's face

between them, made *Tomoe*  truly.[1]

Six strokes upon the courtyard drum proclaimed the opening of the gates ; and slowly morning dawned ; and slowly morning dawned ; and slowly morning dawned.

Scene II. *Upon the Road in Kamakura.*

Noriyori, second son of that same Minamoto Family of the banner white, had become a priest at Shuzenji to remove all suspicion of intrigue against Yoritomo. He took the name Genyu ; but, though he dyed his garments black, and lived in ways austere and plain, the people felt for him respect, profound and passionate.

In answer to the summons, now he took a common palanquin and set forth attended by one servant only. His

[1] The character which may be read *Tomoe.*

sandals and his bamboo staff might well have to a mounte-
bank belonged.

From the Castle Square came Kajiwara-Kagetaka,
paunched like Hotei, god of luck, in a palanquin with
doors flung wide. Five mounted spearmen rode before.
Noriyori's bearers drew aside for Kajiwara, whose attendants
asked if he would descend to greet the princely priest. With
gruff voice questioning the use of courtesy to a mere prince
retired to monkish life, Kagetaka stuck out his head.

KAGETAKA.

Is it Prince Priest ? You are on the way, I suppose, to
Lady Yoritomo's to settle the question at issue between
Kudo and Honda. Those in charge during the General's
absence, big and little, will be there with me. This quarrel
over a deer between Suketsune, leader of the hunt, and
Honda, a lowly retainer, is like a dispute between a paper
lantern and a temple-bell. If you give judgment against
Suketsune, causing him in the least to be vanquished, it
will go hard with you. Go on !

The palanquin was hurried forward by his eight bare-
footed carriers ; and the prancing horses led the way,
scattering dust upon roadside travellers—troublesome gnats
—shoo, shoo.

It was outrageously discourteous.

A young man of about twenty came out from an open
well ; and, throwing aside the low hat which disguised him,
bowed with hands to the ground. Seeing him, the Prince
Priest addressed him with courteous gesture—" Retainer
or free-lance, if your salutation is in my honour, pass on,
pass on." But the youth bowed the more, crying, " Sir !
Sir ! " with tears that would not be hidden. Marvelling
at his tears, the Prince Priest descended from his palanquin
and drew near.

NORIYORI.

Who are you ? Why do you weep ? Answer me.

Lifting his tear-stained face, the youth replied : " Your
pardon, Sir ! Is not the world, indeed, a world of shame ?
Your Highness, our General Yoritomo's brother, was, with
Kurohogan, deputed to attack Heike's great leader in command of fifty thousand horse ; and you took Ode in Ichi-
no-tani and the woods of Ikuta by assault. Your exploits
and your kinship with Yoritomo should place you high
above all challenge throughout our sixty provinces. Well
I understand your resentment at being spurned by Kagetaka,
Kajiwara's youngest son. My masters, also, are sons of
one who gained fame at Sagami and at Izu, and, through
a turn of fate, lost their father by a kinsman's hand and saw
his estate become an enemy's harvest field. They have
become soldiers of fortune, masterless men, whose once
bright swords are rusty now, shelterless, friendless, despised,
and rejected. I weep ; my tears I cannot restrain as I think
of you, and from shame since we are like withered trees that
know not when, if ever, they may bloom. Pardon my
unsought words of explanation." Again he burst into
tears ; and to him with low voice the priest replied :
"You are, then, a follower of the Soga. How hard
have been the years of waiting ! Suketsune is a villain, who,
veiling his insincerity 'neath service sincere, has become
powerful, and, exulting in his lord's favour, has debauched
the Kamakura soldiery. How humiliating that you have
not been able to slay him. If this priest were but the
Noriyori of other days, surely he would give aid. Vexa-
tious ! "

YOUTH.

Since I am known, there is no need of further conceal-
ment. I am a follower of the Soga, Onio by name. Thinking

this hunt might afford good opportunity, the brothers have stealthily been on the watch ; and, yesterday morning, when our enemy, Suketsune, saw a deer that was passing upon a hillside, and fitting arrow to his bow, ran after it, Goro-Tokimune from behind a thicket shot an arrow in haste at his heart. The arrow struck the animal's breast, merely grazing his enemy's hat. Suketsune's arrow also hit the body of the deer ; and quickly the animal died.

Tokimune's great strength is well known ; and his arrow was large, long-feathered, and entirely unmarked. An inquiry was to be made concerning that arrow, when Honda-Jiro-Chikatsune, a petty officer in the service of Chichibu, declared that he was the first who had shot, and, obscuring the inquiry in a quarrel with Suketsune over the game, saved Tokimune from great peril. If they should fail in this time of the hunt, when, like the century plant, will the fortunes of Soga bloom ?
Oh, please understand—

He checked himself suddenly, and wept, bowing low.

Then said Noriyori, with tears—

" Sad, indeed, such noble knights should be lost to the world! "

And, taking from his garments two wooden checks, continued—

" These checks, countersigned by Hoji-Tokimasa and Oe-Hiromoto, will give you entrance to the very presence of Yoritomo. Suketsune is on his guard, making Yoritomo his shield ; and it is said that he never goes far from the General. These passes I will lend to the brothers. Fearlessly go, and bravely revenge, even under the shadow of Yoritomo, wiping off all old scores. Take care, though. Be secret, be secret ! "

With that, Noriyori continued his journey, leaving

Onio trying in vain to check tears of gratitude such as he had no words to express. Again and again the youth bowed low in reverent obeisance, then himself turned away.

SCENE III. *The Palace of the Shogun in Kamakura.*

In the great hall of Kita-no-maru were gathered all the knights, both great and small, waiting for the coming of the Priest, for through Tomoe an order had been given that the impartial judgment of Noriyori should be sought to end the quarrel between Kudo and Honda. The body of the deer had been placed on the veranda near.

Kajiwara-Kagetaka with Inubo-maru, only son of Suketsune, made his way into the hall, accompanied by Yawata-Saburo.

Saburo, making a grimace, exclaimed :
" What a mighty big arrow ! Look here, my lord Inubo, if such a little fellow as Honda had shot this arrow, it would not have flown six feet. In days of old, Tori-no-umi-yasaburo alone could have shot that arrow ; and, to-day, Asari-no-yoichi. If he had shot it, there would be his mark upon it. Now, well I know why the arrow bears no name. A starving beggar, Soga-Tokimune, a distant relative of my lord Suketsune, must have slipped in to steal from the hunting field, for the people are getting tired of his begging and cheating, his asking for this and for that. Yoshinori's examination was right careless.
" If the wisdom of the Kajiwara family does not settle this question, it will not justly be settled."
Being thus flattered, Kagetaka spoke, saying :
" There's nothing difficult in this. If Honda be made to shoot the arrow again, the secret will out. I will take and retain the arrow."

But when he went to draw forth the arrow, Tomoe called
out :

"Hold, Kagewara! As soon as ever your fingers touch
that arrow, I will rip your arms off."

And she threw back her sleeves and tucked up her skirt
till her knees showed, white as snow amid plum-blossoms
red, sturdy as rocks though swathed in silk.

Thinking it no use to contend, Kagetaka retorted :

"Oh well, it all will be settled when we have heard Noriyori's opinion, I suppose! Women and headless stone
Buddhas should mind their own business; they are things
of no use"; and with this, he retired to the room of
reception.

Asahina, who at his words could not restrain himself,
rushed into the hall with a boxwood club from the guard-
room ; but his mother sprang upon him ; and grasping the
club by the handle, cried :

"You fool! Don't you know that this is the General's
Palace? And that you are a son of Tomoe, Tomoe ordered
to stop the row and hush it up quickly? Whom would you
strike with that club?"

ASAHINA.

Those who called Soga-Tokimune a beggar and cheat,
who said that my father's, that Yoshinori's examination
was careless. I will break their heads. Look out, or you
will get hurt !

And he tried to wrench the club from her grasp.

TOMOE.

To break their heads, I need not your help, you brat.
Headstrong! Would you be pinched like a dough-ball?

and lifting her leg, she broke the club over her knee.

ASAHINA.

Kajiwara ! Yawata ! Both will I give a sound thrashing.

When his mother grappled with him, he tried to get free ;
then in turn seized her ; and locked were they, each with
the other.

> Not like a mother, that mother ;
> Not like a son, that son ;
> Wet with sweat was his beard ;
> Blown by the wind was her hair.

ASAHINA.

My mother's belly, whence I slipped forth, now is a
tower above my own.

And he held her three feet aloft. Tomoe, then, standing
with legs braced apart, lifted her son. Asahina had not the
guts wherewith to do aught against his mother's great
strength ; and in turn each lifted the other. It was as
when the spirited carp beateth its fins in vain against the
dashing spray of the falls.

Suddenly springing to one side, she lifted the huge man
and flung him down with a bang. The fall of the temple-
bell at Gion would make a sound like that. The whole
palace seemed to tremble. Sitting upon him, as with
grimace he strove vainly to rise, Tomoe lectured him
roundly.

" What a hateful, rough fellow you are ! What a lot of
bother you cause me ! With foolishness headstrong, you
take the part of the Soga, and get a bump for your trouble.
A *samurai's* strength is not that of body alone. He must
excel in wisdom as well as in courage. Again and again
you get into trouble, striving with others, and care not at
all for the arts that strengthen the mind. How can you

hope thus to honour the name of your father ? Now will you study your lessons, learning to write ? " And over and over she kneaded his flesh as a woman kneadeth the dough-ball.

ASAHINA.

Ouch, ouch ! I will learn, I will learn to write.

TOMOE.

Will you learn to read ?

ASAHINA.

I will learn, I will learn to read. Ouch !

TOMOE.

If you do not obey your mother, you will catch it again.

ASAHINA.

Ouch, ouch !

TOMOE.

Do not forget how the dough-ball feels, do not forget

Pinching him yet again, she picked him up, and said : " Stay quietly in your place in the watchman's lodge. If you are rude and come into the hall, no matter what happens, I will punish you again. Why don't you stop glaring ? Shall I burn you with moxa ? "

Cowed thus in spirit, he withdrew to the next room ; a whiskered man afraid of the moxa. But his mother's warning was moxa, indeed, strong to cure the fever of his rash impatience.

Soon the guard at the gate announced the arrival of Noriyori ; and forth to greet him went Kajiwara, Inubo, and Yawata.

(Enter NORIYORI.)

Studying the deer for a season, Noriyori smiled and said :
" Man's vulgar greed accounts for strife over land and
treasure, Tomoe ; but this dispute concerns a point of skill,
professional. Confucius surely would commend it as
worthy men of honour. This must take rank with the strife
of princes over precedence, over skill in poetic composition,
over the supreme excellence of spring or autumn scenery.
How vital, yet refined ! I am reminded of a story, old.

" Long, long years ago, in the Province of Yamato, there
was a female mountain, Ama-no-kagu, and two male mountains, Unebi and Miminashi. The two male mountains fell in
love with the charming figure of Mount Kagu, and quarrelled
because of her. Night after night, mountains and valleys
roared and shook. Unebi said : ' I will make her my wife ! '
' No,' retorted Miminashi, ' that I will do.' The deity of
Abo, living in Izumo, wished to mediate and took ship.
Hearing of this, the two male mountains became reconciled ;
and the deity of Abo stopped at Harima. Nakano-Oe's
poem concerning this is contained in the Manyoshu ; and,
even to this day, perhaps from this story of Kagu, we call
a beautiful woman a mountain.

" To mediation even senseless mountains were not
obdurate. Much less will Kudo and Honda complain of
reconciliation. Make this dispute the beginning of their
friendship ; and all, both high and low, will be at peace.
Harmony is the basis of the Genji rule and of the welfare
of the State."

Thus adorning wisdom with grace, he gave his counsel
shrewdly. Tomoe nodded her approval. The vassals
and the guard in adjoining rooms heard and were satisfied.

Kajiwara, alone unsmiling, said :

" This will not do, this will not do. First of all, that
large arrow is quite unsuited to the strength of Honda's arm.

Again, it is a practice arrow, *Go*, an arrow of fate. According to an honoured custom, such an arrow may be used in vengeance against a father's foe ; but there is no precedent for its use in shooting deer. Let examination, then, be made of him who shot the arrow."

Seeing the priest's hesitation, Inubo and Yawata sought further to silence him through ridicule, questioning:

" Did Honda, perchance, seek vengeance on the deer for a father slain ? Do you think it may be so ? "

Too impatient to restrain himself, Asahina pushed half-way in from the next room. Whereat his mother, glaring, muttered, " The feel of the dough-ball, and of moxa burning ! " At her look, he shrank back, his face remarkable in its emotional control.

But Noriyori, without a moment's hesitation, continued, " Knowing a hundred things, you know not one thoroughly. You know that a practice arrow is called *Go* ; and supposing that word to mean *fate*, you have judged the arrow one to be used in avenging a parent. Several things you have badly confused. Since we are accustomed to use such an arrow in training, and since its flight is sure, we call it an arrow of *Go*, meaning *action*. It is the custom for warriors of rank who serve at the palace to place such an arrow among those in their quivers. With it they may shoot bird or beast, as well as the foe of a father. Though I wear the garb of a priest, I was born in the house of a soldier ; and I know the laws which govern the use of the bow and its arrows. To talk of an investigation is useless, insulting." He spoke with evident traces of anger.

YAWATA.

Oh, but we have already heard that the Soga are lying in wait for Suketsune, our master, the foe of their father. What harm can there be in making assurance more sure ?

NORIYORI.

Is that so ? For that reason, I wager, Suketsune takes excellent care not to wander from Yoritomo afar. The Soga have no wings ! By what means could they come near our General ? Little's the need of your worry.

Yet ere he had finished, Kajiwara broke in, interrupting : " Oh, yes, indeed ! There are many who, jealous of Suketsune's advancement and taking sides with the Soga, would give them passes admitting to His Excellency's presence. You, yourself, have received two such passes, if you have not surrendered them. To us show them now, right now."

NORIYORI.

Shall I produce them at your insulting bidding, saying, " Here they are, Sir Kajiwara—passes of great worth " ? I will not produce them ; no, I will not.

KAGETAKA.

Indeed, it is rather suspicious—your refusal to show them to us. Ah ! Surely you've given them to the Soga Brothers yourself. Right is my guess ! Sir Priest, oily and eel-like, you shall not escape us.

So with insulting language assailed he the Priest who risked his life in excitement of anger ; while Tomoe, not knowing the cause of the trouble, anxiously waited.

NORIYORI.

What would you say, Kajiwara, if the priest had indeed lost the passes which he had been given ?

KAJIWARA.

The Soga Brothers are sons of old Ito, you traitor. Harakiri at best, harakiri !

NORIYORI.

And do you not know that Noriyori, at his harakiri, takes with him to death a companion ?

KAJIWARA.

An insult ! Whom, for a companion ?

NORIYORI.

Kajiwara-Kagetaka will I take.

Thus saying, he drew from his robe a blade, ice-thin and gleaming, mere twelve inches long, and cleft with its stroke but the top of Kajiwara's ceremonial head-dress. Springing back to avoid the blow, he kicked down the fragile paper partition and fled, with Inubo. Noriyori struck down Yawata with a blow on the shoulder and, catching him as he fell back groaning, three times pierced his breast.

Sitting on the dead body, he paused and breathed deeply. The guards and other knights were in confusion at the noise of the struggle ; but Tomoe, raising her voice, commanded : " Be not excited ! The Princely Priest has killed Yawata-Saburo. Run to our Lady's apartment and make report. Let no one enter this room without orders."

Her figure in the entrance was commanding, as became Koso's widow, Yoshinori's wife.

Meanwhile Noriyori slipped down his garments and, through teeth firm set, muttered :

" How mortifying to have failed to kill Kajiwara because the blade was short ! No amends were needed, had I killed fifty, yea, one hundred, like Yawata there ; but, for the passes not to be found upon me, I shall indeed have to cut this body through. To lay down one's life for the valiant Soga Brothers—bliss for the warrior, now a recluse priest ! Lead me, O thou great Amida ! "

Praying, he thrust the blade into his side and drew it across ; then turning the weapon, seized its haft in his

o

mouth. The cut was deep, complete and, like a dream in May's brief hours of darkness, his life of four-and-twenty years was ended.

Icho-Gozen, Shigetada's wife, came running in, sent by Lady Yoritomo, and summoned Hangae-Shigetomo and Ninomiya-Yasukiyo, saying :

" Hangae, take charge of the dead ! Ninomiya, run to Fuji's Hunting Field, and tell the General that Noriyori has slain himself and that the Soga Brothers are supposed to have slipped into the Field. Tell him, that they may be on their guard. Get there by daylight's eighth hour (2 p.m.). If late, the fault thou shalt atone. Important the office ; at once, get thee gone ! "

NINOMIYA.
All that you say, I will do.

He started to run ; but Hangae stopped him by grasping tightly the end of his sword, saying :

" Wait, Ninomiya, you are brother-in-law to the Soga, and dare not carry unaltered a message fraught with such danger. Change your commission for mine, and take thou care of the dead, while I go forth to the Field."

With this, he started ; but Ninomiya grasped his sword, and laughed aloud, saying :

" And you are brother-in-law to Suketsune's own wife ! Because of favour to him, you suspect me. 'Tis like you, quite like you ! The bond of kinship is one thing ; that of loyalty to our General, another. Your doubts I resolve ! "

Pulling Hangae down beside him, he reached for an ink-stone and quickly, in three lines and a half, drafted a writ of divorcement. Then from his short sword he took the metal bar-pin and rolled it tight in the letter. Calling a servant, he said :

" Back to our quarters, go ; and there tell the woman that this ends our union for life here and hereafter. I am a courier to the Hunting Field, a stranger to the Soga Brothers, Ninomiya-Taro."

Again he started ; but Hangae, holding by his garments, stopped him, saying :

" Your prompt act of deception deceives me not. I, Hangae-Shiro, will beg them to send me. I will not let you go."

NINOMIYA.

Damn it ! I'm in haste ! 'Tis almost eight (5th hour) ; and fifty miles to run ere two is work for courier swift. When I would borrow devil wings, you hold me, to my shame and death atoning ! You should be slain ; but both have been assigned important duties. Damnation on damnation ! I spare your life ; but you shall let me go.

However hard he struggled to get free, pushing and turning, he could effect nothing, so firmly did the stronger Hangae cling. From the next room, impatient at the sight, Asahina crept forward with clenched teeth ; but suddenly withdrew, fearing his mother. Forth and back he swayed, with staring eyes, impatient, till Tomoe, seeing his fixed gaze, called out :

" Come, Asahina, come and join the fight. Fight, now I say, fight ! "

ASAHINA.

Trust me !

Thus exclaiming, in he bounded, crying :

" Thank God for a mother's permission ! " And going to Hangae, twisted his arms o'er his head.

ASAHINA.

Go at once, Ninomiya !

NINOMIYA.

Duty demands it. No thanks can I speak.

And off he ran quickly.

HANGAE.

Since now I have let Ninomiya escape, there is no reason to hold me. Let me go, I say, Asahina.

ASAHINA.

Ninomiya's time is limited. The time to let you go is also fixed, you good-for-nothing rice-box, you cracked rice-tub. You're so light, you must be empty. 'Tis time to feed you. Take my fist for a ball of rice.

Just then the temple-bell sounded the hour through the hazy air. "Dong!" He struck Hangae's head. "Dong!" Again he struck; three, four, five, counting the hours upon the head with blows that rang. For every hour throughout the day, he struck. The skull broke in; the bones were crushed. Throwing the body into the yard, Asahina said:

"When I think of Kajiwara, with his face like a temple-bell ready for striking, how I regret that I did not thrash him as well! However, though he escape this time, my grudge is a hundred times that of the relentless crocodile. Think not I shall ever spare."

> Asahina stamped,
> As beat the waves along the shore
> Where, over shallows,
> Surges roll from off the sea of Being
> Wherein our days are numbered;
> And quickly, side by side,
> Like lover waves that rise and fall,
> Together mother and son
> Withdrew from the chamber.

ACT II

Persons Represented :
   NINOMIYA-YASUKIYO, *Brother-in-law to the Soga.*
   ZENJIBO, *a Priest, brother to the Soga.*
   SHIRASAKI-HACHIHEIJI, *Servant to Ninomiya.*
   KAJIWARA-KAGETAKA ⎱ *Partisans of Suketsune.*
   OMI-KOTODA   ⎰
   HEAD PRIEST OF FUJISAWA.
   RETAINERS, SERVANT, PRIESTS.
   WIFE OF NINOMIYA, *Sister to the Soga.*
   WOMEN ATTENDANTS.

SCENE I. *Home of Ninomiya.*

CLEAR as hallowed shrines, spotless without, within, was the sky on the twenty-eighth of May. In the absence of her lord, the wife of Ninomiya-Yasukiyo, as became a soldier's spouse, took his place in the day's devotion, cleansing heart and hand with purifying water, and taking from its case the pictured scroll, a drawing of Holy Fudo. Saying " It is May, the Festival of Fudo," she hung the scroll in the place of honour on the alcove wall ; and maidens brought wine and cakes like mirrors, round and flat.

With clear conscience, confident of Buddha's care, Ninomiya's wife, sister of the Soga Brothers, in silence prays :

" May Fudo give success unto my husband, in high commission during the General's absence, and protect him from all danger and misfortune. Especially I beseech Thee for my brothers, for Sukenari and for Goro-Tokimune, who, when a child called Ichiman-Hakoo, confused Fudo with Kudo and, absorbed in thoughts of vengeance, sought to destroy thy Holy Image. Sacrilegious deed ! May

Fudo help them to vengeance on their father's foe Kudo-
Saemon-Suketsune."

Surely, her sincere, ardent prayer must be granted.

Shirasaki-Hachiheiji, coming in haste, entered her room
without waiting permission ; prostrated himself all out of
breath, saying :

" From the master, a message important. Excuse my
entrance, neglectful of custom ! "

In surprise the woman asked, " What is the message ?
I am eager to hear it. What is it ? "

HACHIHEIJI.

All service for my lord is duty ; but this, my present task,
is hard, indeed.

He handed her the letter with the signet-bar. Opening
it, she burst into weeping ; and, lifting her tear-stained face,
exclaimed :

" Have I not but now prayed for your health and success ?
Our words at the time of your leaving ! Were they but
empty breath ?   As a brute, heartless ! "

Rolling, unrolling the message, she read and she cried.
Putting her face to the paper, she threw herself down, and
sobbed brokenly. Her maidens and servants attending
could but sigh, looking one at another, understanding
nought of her sorrow.   Then in impatience, she questioned :

" Why, Hachiheiji, did not your master confide the
cause of divorcement ?   Do you not know ?   Speak out."

HACHIHEIJI.

I do not know all that has happened ; but, because Kajiwara declared that Noriyori had conspired with the Soga
against Yoritomo, that noble priest has made harakiri ;
and my lord was commanded to bear the news to the Field.
He was told to reach there by daylight's eighth hour.   Then
was there quarrel with Hangae ; and I was told to give you

this note of divorcement, the bar as a proof of its power.
Nothing more do I know.

Not letting him go, the woman continued :
" Enough, enough !   Had Yasukiyo already set forth for
the Field at Mount Fuji ? "

HACHIHEIJI.

No, by the portal still was he striving ; but by now he
well may have started.

At these words, she rose to her full height, and, tucking
her skirt up, tightened her sash, saying :
" Those who are quick, follow with halberd, "
and started.
Her attendants clung to her, crying :
" Not to your mother's !   'Tis but natural that you
should wish to unburden your heart ; but much it is better
to wait ; and, on your lord's coming, seek his forgiveness."
Freeing herself from those who would hold her, she—
" Abandoned, unwarned, 'tis the fate of a woman !   Not
of myself am I thinking ; but if I release him now, I fear
greater grief in the future.   Such is my haste, I cannot
stand idle.   Hachiheiji, take good care of the place in my
absence.   Girls, take good care."
And choosing one from her maidens, she set forth,
halberd held high o'er her shoulder.

SCENE II.   *Zenjibo's Tea-House at Fujisawa.*

The temple-bell booms down the air,
Daylight's fourth hour sounding ;
In glassy waters, here and there,
Lies reflected, Fuji.
Its very snows seem gleaming hot
Over summer travel.

The saddle-horses, men on foot,
All for rain are asking.
The gathering clouds,
Cool breezes blowing,
To weary travellers bring
Boon beyond all blessing.

Beside the weary road, with rushes screened,
O'er-canopied with cryptomeria-trees,
Near to a water-mill, moved by a stream
That sings in crystal clearness, night and day,
Beneath a willow shade, where water falls
Like pearls dropped forth from out a bamboo pipe,
And men are like to pause and rest awhile,
There is a tea-house with a sign on which
Is writ :
" Original and best in all the land."

Before it swings a curtain, Chinese, silk,
Displaying ice from Himuro afar ;
Set forth on green leaf-doilies, neat and clean,
Tin plates look cool. The God who cares for leaves,
Himself could feel no disapproval here.

The master of the tea-house is Zenjibo, who, having
secretly learned his brothers' plan of seeking vengeance in
connection with the hunt at Fuji's base, left his temple at
Kugami and came forth as one skilled in the business which
makes needless doctor's drugs, in hope to aid his brothers or
to gather up their scattered bones. Disguised beneath a
wig, he has been conducting this tea-house for now ten days.
Couriers from those on guard about the Hunting Field,
Kamakura tradesmen on their daily trips to Oiso, and
travellers, out and back, rest here. Among them, Omi-
Kotoda, Suketsune's man, on his way back to Kamakura,

stops and calls : " Here, there, Keeper ! Bring me some water."

ZENJIBO.

Certainly ; won't you try our gelatine, just for luck ? It cools one off, stops thirst, and a bowl of it will surely cure the headache on the morning after. General Yoritomo, at the lunch when all the daimyo, great and small, were served, enjoyed our jelly, and addressed me, saying : " I am astonished at its sweetness. It's first-class. Better get many helpers in your business and hunt the pennies from the passers-by." I have made a mountain model before the house ; and, with the help of dolls moved by that water-wheel, I will show you scenes from the Hunting Field. Now they are beginning," he said in showman style, beating time with his hands.

" Yoritomo's favourite dish that day was jelly, under the cool, green leaves. With a good appetite, he took one or two trays of it. Goromaru, who of his attendants sat with him, was served from a red-patterned Chinese plate. The company ate eighty-five *mon* worth of jelly to cool their heated bodies. A forty-eight-inch water-tub, and a ladle eighteen inches long ! As I served hurriedly, they ate eagerly, round, white chop-sticks in hand, just drinking it down ! Sir Chichibu took it with an order of vegetable soup and fancy citron blossoms. For the whole Wada family, ninety-three dishes, the charge for jelly and other things was three hundred and eighty-four *mon*. Chiba, Koyama, and Utsunomiya, all disliked mustard, but used sugar and bean-flour instead ; flour, flour, flour, piling it up in their surprised gluttony.

Against the plates and *sake*-cups of metal fine, their chop-sticks made a merry sound ; and the wide field was covered over with serving trays. Among the three thousand beaters of the hunt were some who ate largely and then emptied slender purses, begging pardon for the balance due me ! "

Telling of his own blunders and other funny tales, he fussed about with his dolls, which, moved by the water, drew the attention of people, while his tongue ran on like a mill-clapper. Stopping a moment to catch his breath, he looked up and down the road and then cried :

" Look ! Look there ! There comes a palanquin with out-runners tugging at the rope."

KOTODA.

Sorry for the rider ; he must be jolted to pieces.

ZENJIBO.

Must be in an awful hurry. How he flies ! How he flies !

Before he had finished speaking, the palanquin, like a boat before the wind or a wheel down a hill, came up and stopped in front of the tea-house with a *yo-heave-ho*. The door was opened by one of the bearers ; and the rider came grandly forth, wrapping his body in folds of white.

" Look here, Keeper ! has a palanquin or horse in hot haste passed from Kamakura to Fuji's Field to-day ? Out with it, don't try to deceive me.

ZENJIBO.

Good gracious me ! What have I to gain or lose ? Why should I keep it from you, if I had seen anyone ? In haste, hot or cold, this morning there has come no other palanquin than this of yours.

GUEST.

Good ! Give me a drink of water.

Turning to him, Kotoda gazed at his face, and exclaimed,
" Why, Kajiwara-Kagetaka ! "

KAGETAKA.

And you are Omi-Kotoda, are you not ?   'Tis well we
are met.   There's something which I would say unto you.
Come nearer.

When Kagetaka drew Kotoda aside, Zenjibo knew that
they were hostile retainers ; and hoping to overhear their
talk, came out shoving his jelly, as though in fun, under
their very noses.

" What are you up to ? "

Frightened at Kagetaka's eyes, glaring like saucers, he
dropped his dish ; and the bean-flour got all mixed up
with the sand at his feet.   Crying, " Your pardon," he
vanished.

KAGETAKA.

Is there anything wrong at the Field ?   Where are you
going ?

KOTODA.

We have only just learned that the stag, over which
Suketsune, our master, and Honda have quarrelled, has been
taken to Kamakura ; and I have been asked to find out the
gossip.   So am I bound for the city.

Then Kagetaka, interrupting :
" Because of that very stag, good luck has come to Suketsune.   Upon my accusation, Noriyori has paid with his
life ; and my purpose now is to charge the Soga with
treason and have them beheaded.   To Ninomiya-Taro
fate is unfriendly.   To the Hunting Field was he sent to
report the case to the General.   He was to arrive by daylight's eighth hour.   Though he's divorced his wife and

severed all ties with the Soga, surely he will not venture 'gainst them to bear a charge to the General. So would I steal a march, and tell a tale that is different. So am I hurrying on to the Hunting Field at Mount Fuji. Well for my plan it is, that not yet Ninomiya has passed.

Go up to yonder temple and tell Fujisawa's head priest that Kudo and Kajiwara request as a favour, richly rewarded, that he on the bell will strike eight at the hour of nine.[1] Coax him to do it, and keep a sharp look-out below, that, on the coming of one borne in haste, he may strike ; for then I've a plan for quick action. Should the priest refuse, tie him up to a post and yourself sound the bell. My attendants take with you and go."

He entered the tea-house.

Omi looked up at the temple buildings, high on the hill-top where but few ascend, and called his men. The few who climb that pathway use roots for foothold. Big stones are there ; and where the reddish clay is wet with dew, feet slip and rough rocks bar the way. So Omi climbed, pushed and pulled by coolies strong. At last before the temple gate he paused to breathe.

" Ah ! I see the grove of pines at Nioho and Seiken's temple. There goes a fishing-boat. It's cool and pleasant here. The road below is like a thread, and from this height the people there seem small," he said, not thinking that he himself looked small to those below.

An attendant led him to the high priest's quarters ; and the priest came forth to greet him ; but when Omi-Kotoda courteously made his request, the priest could not understand.

PRIEST.

I cannot think that Kudo and Kajiwara would ask for such a thing. In Kamakura, the officers and others tell

---

[1] Will strike the hour of 2 p.m. when it should be 1 p.m.

the time by the bell at Tsurugaoka ; and this temple-bell tells the time to labourers and tradespeople for fifty miles around. We are given the temple estate in return for this. To change the time in secret and deceive the people would be a sin, a downright sin, a downright sin ! I will not do it.

While yet he spoke, Omi sprang upon him and dragged him to the ground.

KOTODA.

You will not grant the request of Kudo and Kajiwara, your great masters ? Tie up all the priests, my men.

And at his bidding, they seized and roped the priests together.

KOTODA.

Don't let them cry aloud! Lock them all up within.

And they marched them off to the inner part of the temple.

A gale of summer wind along the tree-tops ; and a cloud of dust along the road ! The one approaching straight as an arrow is Ninomiya's wife, who, on reading her husband's brief letter of divorce, had been blinded with tears. Tying her tear-wet kerchief round her head, taking her halberd, white of handle, 'neath her arm, she ran along the hot sand road like fire, burning to tell her husband the secret sorrows of her heart. Her maid can scarce keep pace with her, and, panting, cries :
" Madam, please rest awhile. All is not lost while yet you live. My eyes are swimming in my head, and I am out of breath." Then caught they sight of Kagetaka's palan-quin.

WOMAN.

Oh, there's my husband !

And coming up, cried out : " Taro ! Yasukiyo ! This morning from one pillow you and I heard the bells of dawn and the song of waking birds. For what reason have you cast me off ? For a woman to be divorced is as great a shame as for a man to turn his back upon his foe. Though with a razor I should seek to shave this off, the shame would cling. Was it because some evil men of your associates declared that I was sister to those Soga Brothers, social outcasts, sons of one who felt the anger of his lord, that you divorced me ? Whate'er the reason, I want the answer straight from you."

While there she stood with halberd in her hand, Kaji-wara-Kagetaka slowly rose from off a bench within the tea-house, and going to her, grasped the handle of her halberd, saying : " Thinking this to be your husband's palanquin, you have betrayed yourself, ill-fated woman. Do you not recognize Kajiwara-Heiji-Kagetaka ? " As he spoke his servants crowded round.

WOMAN.

Alas, a grievous error !

Though greatly frightened, she assumed boldness ; and jerking the halberd from his grasp, held herself right soldierly.

KAGETAKA.

Woman, look here ! Whom do you mean by *evil men* of his associates ? Come, now, name them. Every man who has aught to do with the Soga is a foe to those who still hold social standing. Ninomiya, I fear, may not tell aright the message this day entrusted to his care ; so am I hastening. You intrude, detaining one on urgent errand bound. I spare you not.

And with drawn swords, he and his men stood threateningly.

WOMAN.

Then, Kajiwara, you who would take the wind of my husband's sail, feel the point of my halberd.

And she swung it round. The maid, following her mistress's example, drew the sword from her sash ; and together they faced the throng. Brave, but yet women !

ZENJIBO.

A hand let me take ! The very thing. I'm skilful in service !

Putting handfuls of white pepper, hot, hot mustard, and still hotter red pepper into the water-bucket and mixing it well with vinegar, he spatters it well over the crowding servants, using the spoon as a weapon. From the left side, swift, an arrow of red pepper ! from the right, another of the hot mixture ! They sneeze and strangle. They weep scalding tears. Their throats are burning. Though they struggle to defend themselves, they can open neither mouths nor eyes. Filled like sauce-dishes with the burning sauce, they run. Zenjibo follows them shouting, " Not one will I spare, not one ! "

WOMAN.

From the direction of Nakamura, 'mid a cloud of dust, swift as an arrow, my husband, Yasukiyo, comes riding ! Now, life or death ! Stop the horse !

Like a flash of light she ran and caught the trappings. Her maid grasped the cord of the saddle ; but, in spite of their efforts, the horse dragged them on some twenty yards. Though dragged, they clung, and halted the galloping steed. 'Twas as if they had grown to him.

Yasukiyo angrily cried : " I'm a courier, I ! Fifty miles in six hours ! If I fail, I'm for ever disgraced ! I'm quick to feel honour and shame. ,The disgrace ! "

He was about to ride on, when she stopped him, grasping the stirrup.

WOMAN.

How brutal you are, Ninomiya ! Are men only quick to feel honour and shame ? There's no greater shame for a woman than to receive a writ of divorcement. In vain I depended upon you, than iron shield stronger, to guard my brothers from danger. But since you have divorced me, I no longer can ask you a favour. Poor boys ! Won by the kindness with which you received me, me a Soga ill-fated, I have served you, body and spirit. Care you no more for my service ? Have you to-day, for the first time, seen the fate that hangs over the Soga ? Would you now injure my brothers ? Now do you wish to forsake them ? Though I am merely a woman, yet am I Kawazu's daughter ; and from your hand will receive no writ of unrighteous divorcement.

Against the cloth of the saddle she threw herself, clinging in anguish. Pathetic, that grief and devotion !

Though in a hurry, Yasukiyo dismounted and threw himself down at the foot of a tree.

" Though to the woman, divorced, I ought not to speak ; yet, for the sake of our former relation, ye may hear me. This morning, at Kitanoura, trouble arose because of your brothers. It caused Noriyori to commit harakiri, and threw Kamakura into confusion. For reasons well-grounded, I fear the Soga lives are in danger because of an inquiry pending ; and, just when it seemed that my heart would burst with the longing to settle the matter in secret by telling the real facts in the case to those high in position, our

Lady gave me an order to report the affair to the General by daylight's eighth hour. I received the order with gladness, for that was most what I wanted ; but when I set forth, Hangae-Shiro protested and stopped me, declaring any allied to the Soga unfit for the errand. While with him I debated, I thought of a method ; and there, in the presence of all, wrote out the writ of divorcement. My reason—to remove all suspicion that I, estranged from relations with Soga, might in mere kindness be free to assist them in every endeavour. By the vow of married love unbroken, I had no other reason. If still so much you wish to stay united as on the public road to make a scene, we will remain as heretofore through this world and the next ; but so, I cannot, as related, serve your brothers truly. For them and for the mother old, whatever happens, I can do nothing. Blame me not for this."

He spoke and moved away.

WOMAN.

One moment, stay ! I never dreamed the writ to be a loyal soldier's kindness. Terror-stricken at the letter, I only wept and roared in anger, thinking our relations broken would mean to Sukenari and to Tokinari the loss of vital aid, their very arms dissevered. To escape suspicion by breaking all connection, that you might stand with them in loyal kindness ! How can I thank you ? Tears of gratitude will flow. For my brothers' sake, indeed, divorce me, putting any shame you please upon me. Again, divorce me.

YASUKIYO.

Confound it ! You bandy words. Would you have me late, and pay atoning death ?

WOMAN.

With lips which speak such heartless words, can you not say *divorced* ? ('Tis woman's weakness thus to value

P

marriage ties, though she must thousand pardons beg. What
evil lot to Soga men and women has been given !)

She sobbed ; and at the sight, her maid dropped on her
garments rough the big, round tears.

YASUKIYO (*in pity*).
You have understood aright. This is a token (*giving her
a pledge*) that from this day you are to me a stranger.

He turned abruptly from the pain of parting ; but as he
started, through the air above his head the bell struck *one*.
Upspringing, on bending fingers tense, he counted—three,
four, five, six, seven, eight ! No more ! "How did I fail
to hear the bell at nine ? Did I forget the saying that
clouds of idleness muffle the strokes of the bell ? 'Tis still
a distance to the Hunting Field. My strife with Hangae
will have been in vain, if I am late. My life is spent ! My
doom, with that of Soga, at once is sealed. Grief and
disgrace ! "
Grasping the ground with clenching hands, he scarce
kept back the tears.
Kajiwara-Kagetaka, with some fifty footmen wearing his
livery, ran up. "Attend, Ninomiya ! Courier com-
missioned ! The hour is passed ; your fealty broken !
Great is your crime ! Those who have charge in our
General's absence have sat in judgment and thus have
decreed : you may commit harakiri. Your head shall be
borne to Fuji's Field. I am ordered to attend. Perform
the deed ! "

YASUKIYO.
Wherein I fail, I am prepared. As I need borrow none
other life, I need borrow none other's hand to take my own.
Nor will I trouble you to bear my head. Before the

General's presence will I atone, and for his approval present my head. I will not trouble you.

So saying, he set forth.

KAGETAKA.
Halt! Halt! Halt! I say! Coward, who by his own hand dares not die! Fellows, attack and kill!

FOOTMEN.
We will.

They made an uproar; and his wife, following Ninomiya, was about to strike in his defence, when Zenjibo, who all-unnoticed had climbed the temple hill, now shouted from the cliff whereon Fujisawa's temple stands, " Do nothing rash! The hour was wrong!"

Kajiwara's men upon the height broke into shouts: " Confound the fellow! He has untied the priest and all the rest. Throw him down! Crush him!"

Seizing one who sprang upon him, Zenjibo, with a cry, lifted him upon his shoulder and hurled him from the ledge. 'Twas one of Kajiwara's footmen in livery dressed that rolled, and rolling fell at Ninomiya's feet.

" So that was it!" thought Yasukiyo, still standing dazed and looking up.

Zenjibo grappled with the next who came; and they, tumbling, fell; but the footman, heels over head, flying from the top, struck on his head and straightway died.

" Shall we yield to such as you?" gasped Kotoda, black with rage, as he clung to Zenjibo, who, borrowing strength from the four gods who every pathway guard, now with him grappled. Rolling over and over, now up, now down, they fight; crashing off the edge of the hill, they plunge half down the slope, then pausing, breathe awhile in strife with grip unloosened.   Down on the plain Yasukiyo and the woman stood waiting motionless.

At Zenjibo's cry, "Ready!" again they strain ; once, twice they roll together, with a shock as of an earthquake, to Kajiwara's feet.   At once Zenjibo, springing up, bestrides his fallen foe.   Frightened at this, and thinking it ill longer to stay, Kagetaka runs off, not once turning back, Ninomiya on the point of following.

ZENJIBO.

A moment, one moment wait! You're on important business bound.   Let him go on his way.   Sister, your brother, I.   In childhood called Onbo.   A priest in Kugami's temple, now I'm known as Zenjibo.   My story I will tell some future day.   But now, Kajiwara planned to have the bell at Fujisawa strike eight instead of nine that so Yasukiyo might die atoning death for fault supposed. Though yonder cloud now hides the sun, not yet westward hath it turned.   Hasten at once to Fuji's Hunting Field.

Ninomiya with reviving joy exclaimed : "Omi is a criminal, having changed the hour.   By virtue of my right within the law, I here behead him.   This branch from off the tree hateful to Soga I give in parting "; and to them he handed the severed head, and rode away.   The two watched him and wept at the parting.

> From between the rain-filled clouds,
> Sweetly ringing, one,
> Two, the bell was heard ; three, four,
> Five, six, seven, eight, nine !
> Courage it gave to the rider, who
> Quickened his steed at the sound.

Although no love-sick girl,
She shed such tears as those which flow
At sound of morning bell
To cruel parting calling ;
And pledged her lover bliss
Again at eventide—
Her brother leaving.

ACT III

Persons Represented :

KUDO-SUKETSUNE, *Foe of the Soga.*
YAWATA-SHIRO, *Servant to Suketsune.*
SOGA-SUKENARI, also called JURO.
SOGA-TOKIMUNE, also called GORO.
KOSHIRO, *Half-brother to the Soga.*
DOSABURO, *Follower of the Soga.*
MADAME SOGA, *the Mother.*
TORA ⎫
SHOSHO ⎬ *Public Entertainers.*
KAMEGIKU ⎭
SERVANTS AND ATTENDANTS.

SCENE I. *Fuji's Hunting-Field.*

OVER fields and mountains, where the young stags roam,
the nobles hunted, each attended by his servant train.

" 'Tis little use to quarrel about a stag in such a motley
crowd of hunters," thought Kudo-Suketsune, camped upon
a sightly hill-side, while his beaters ran down deer and
monkeys. Near him, by the wine and food outspread,
sat Kamegiku, Kisegawa's dancing-girl.

SUKETSUNE.

Ho, all you fellows ! A pretty girl is watching. Catch
a pig or deer by hand. Kamegiku will bind it with a hair.[1]
Do your best ; try hard ! A prize I'll give.

BEATERS.

We'll do our best. We'll capture one by hand.

---

[1] A woman's hair will bind an elephant. (Proverb.)

Some boors themselves, like clowns, chased boars, and
failed ; some, gored by stags, wailed loudly ; one grappled
with a bear and headlong tumbled ; others were scratched
by monkeys old and ran, their faces red with shame, than
monkey-faces redder. All day they laboured ; and their
shouting rang. 'Twas fun ; and only fun, what time they
failed to capture any.

Taking a cup to Kamegiku, Suketsune said :

" Dancing-girls and harlots many are guests at various
daimyo camps ; but you're a lucky girl to be my guest. To
carouse with a boar-hunt for accompaniment is a delight
even Lady Yoritomo cannot enjoy. But you do not yield
in answer to Suketsune, who loves you so ; you don't, you
know you don't " ; and nearer drew.

KAMEGIKU.

" You quite mistake ! A man of mere pretence, no
heart within : that's you. Each night you leave Kamegiku
all alone, and sleep within the General's inner camp. I
never see your sleeping face ; and yet you say you love me !
Of course, entrance to your lady in Kamakura is closely
barred ! You carry with you, I suppose, her guardian
letters ; but on the hunting-field this Kamegiku'll break
the barriers through," she said, and slipped her hand into
his bosom.

SUKETSUNE.

You are unjust. I bear no letters from a jealous wife.
A trouble faces me. Ah well, the whole I will confess.
Surely you must have heard it from Tora at Oiso or from
Shosho at Keoizaka. It is rumoured that Soga-Juro and
Goro have mingled with the throng upon the hunting-
field, and are looking for me, their father's foe. My life is
not so worthless as to be thrown to them ; and so, to guard
against surprise, I go not far from the General, sleeping at

night in the next room to his. I am under great restraint. Naturally, I snore ; and, if I try to check the snores, they block my throat, and so I cannot breathe. Suppose I must learn to snore through my ears !

But the women, left at home in Kamakura, with care and clever wit, have cajoled a vagabond, called Koshiro, half-brother to the Soga, and with a bribe have sent him to Madame Soga's as a spy. Deceived by love for one born of her flesh, she nothing hides from him ; and, thanks to the women's clever plan, through Koshiro's treachery we have been informed of all that happens, even to the chop-sticks' falling, in the Soga home. Still better luck than this—their mother has become severely ill, and for her sons has sent that she may see them once before she dies. This also has been reported. Juro and Goro are very filial fellows. Upon the summons they must have started home ere now. Suketsune is protected by the Gods and Buddhas blest ! Having driven away the gods of plague, I feel as free as Musashi's open plain. Here lies great Fuji's hunting-field ; and from to-night, where'er I sleep, the world is safe for me.

But Kamegiku did not welcome news like that of those two men who were allied with Tora and with Shosho, friends of hers.

From among the beaters, Yawata-Shiro, Yawata-Saburo's younger brother, came forth, dragging a mighty stag with rough rope bound, and said : " A thieving stag, with bald spot on its back ! A crowd, we captured it as it was creeping through the palings." Down before Suketsune he threw it ; and it looked much like a man wrapped up in deer-skin. Beneath the head Kamegiku saw a face familiar—that of Dosaburo, a follower of the Soga. At once her eyes grew wet with tears, and much she longed to sink into the ground.

Suketsune, with keen eyes, of course :

" Buo of Shu caught a wise man called Taikobo at the Ihin Hunt ; Confucius captured a giraffe at the hunting in Ro ; Kudo-Suketsune at Fuji-Field caught a four-legged creature called Dosaburo, Onio's younger brother, a servant of the Soga. Surely of Buo and Confucius I am a peer !

" Beast, some secret reason must be yours that, wrapped in deer-skin, you have tried to steal in through the palings, when you know the penalty if caught. Speak up, confess ! If you lie, beware a punishment befitting thieves. At once, out with it ! "

Showing no fear, or the least hesitation, Dosaburo :

" I, who thus lowly would mask as a beast, wearing a deer-skin, stand not in fear of punishment vile ; but to be reckoned a thief I cannot endure, not for my own sake alone, but yet for my masters'. The truth I will tell you.

" Sukenari and Tokimune have been upon this hunting-field, mingling with the servants of the friendly nobles, to watch the hunt. At home their aged mother has suddenly been taken ill. The end, we fear, is near. She longs to see the brothers once again before she dies, and to receive from them water at the gates of death. Last night, after midnight, I left the Soga home, and ran, unmindful, over hill and stream. I was afraid the watchmen would not admit me with such a face of fear ; and wrapped myself in what the hunters who had killed the deer had thrown aside. The moment that I passed the paling I was caught. I might have known in such a throng of hunters. I was caught.

" Oh, Madame, you have feeling, and you many know. If you can, please tell them, and let a dying mother see her children, have her last request. This do, for mercy's sake.

" For myself, I've failed in duty ! " and he wept.

SUKETSUNE.

His story that the old woman in her illness wished to send for them may be quite true. The rumours fit, as two parts of a seal. There's something else ; but let him bleat before the General.

The servants were taking him away, when Tokimune— how he came to know, I wonder—dashed down the hillside ; and, seizing five or six of the beaters, tossed them as balls afar, then tore the ropes and skin from off Dosaburo, kicked Yawata-Shiro down and stamped upon him, shouting as a tempest shakes the trees, " Great skill, indeed, to take a man in deer-skin for a deer ! I, Soga-Tokimune, here find a deer, in form a man ! A deer, indeed ! Juro, hasten here ! "

And at his call Sukenari came running in, exclaiming, " A rare chance for us both to meet you thus ! " and on his sword he laid his hand.

" Let them not strike our master, or escape," cried Suketsune's servants, crowding round ; but Dosaburo, pushing through the throng, implored :

" Oh, masters, be not rash in haste ! Your lives entrust to me this day. I have a message fraught with meaning now for all your years. Your aged mother, there at home, grew ill the night before the last. Worse and worse, until each moment seemed the end. She knew her life was ebbing fast, and she prepared.

" ' I wish to see the children once again, to say a last good-bye. Come to me at once, Tokimune ; leave all things, Sukenari. If you disobey me now, I will disown you through all eternity.'

" Before her weakening voice had ceased I had started."

Hearing this, the brothers felt their warrior-courage flee. They looked one upon the other, and seemed as men who dream.

DOSABURO.

This is no time for hesitation. That rascal, Koshiro, is taking care of her; he's with her all the time. If your filial piety prove less marked than his, she will for ever mourn, in heaven uncomfortable. Make peace with Suketsune, and come home, come home.

Suketsune was much relieved when Dosaburo urged them to go home; and, seeing their nerveless hands, made tall talk, boastfully:

"Come now, young men, it is not clear whether your father, Kawazu, was killed by Matano-Goro or by an arrow shot astray; and yet for me you lie in wait, for me—your father's foe unproven. As you please, I make no craven self-defence. Strike! Kill! You are not, then, such men as I have heard. You dare not? Men of Soga!"

Unable to endure such words, Tokimune cried:

"Be careful, Suketsune!"

But Sukenari checked him as he sprang, exclaiming:

"How have you received the tidings from our mother? Are you crazy, Tokimune?"

TOKIMUNE.

Never, though torn in pieces, can I, craven, bear to leave my foe unanswered at his challenge; give way, Sukenari.

SUKENARI.

So soon have you forgotten, Tokimune, our prayer from childhood, that as brothers we might our parents please—a mother here, a father yonder, all honour, all shame disregarding?

TOKIMUNE.

'Tis true! How we are thwarted! Balked! A thousand pities, Sukenari.

SUKENARI.

With you I grieve, my brother. Such is the fate of the Soga.

With tears, clenched teeth, and trembling rage they grasped their swords, plunging them into their scabbards so that all the metal trimmings seemed to scatter.

Kamegiku watched with bated breath. She was not frightened, for with good and bad alike from childhood she had been familiar ; then she stood :

" Sirs, I say, why do ye colour so ? Ye seem o'ercome with shame. Ye are not like experienced blades who oft frequent our quarters, demimonde. Is this disgrace ? Impertinent and useless my words may be ; but I cannot have Tora and Shosho, friends so dear, think that Kamegiku, happening to be present, looked on, ignoring. His life a soldier risks for duty. A woman hers no less for love. I mean there comes a time when one, with foul intent, would make us drink. In such a case the choice is crapulence or duty. We must not drunken be. Yet will he urge, presuming on our helplessness. We seem to yield ; but then with mighty effort of control, such as subdues a thousand horses wild, must we convey our shame to basis of heroic deeds. By feigning drunkenness we throw men off their guard and easily escape. If unexpectedly, at early dawn, we're ta'en, and made by force to drink, our arms entwined, our necks pressed back, our mouths with *sake* filled, the last cup poured, we yield completely. This we call passion's way through wine. Yet, knowing all, I do confess that three days and nights at Yamashita, at Wada's banquet great, with Asahina's wine I was by force compelled to break my vow."

She ended with a laugh of no disgrace that courage gave. Her way was that of one who knew the world.

At her words the brothers felt depression take its flight ;
and to Suketsune said :

" About our mother's suffering we are much concerned.
To see you, yet again, we shall have pleasure."

SUKETSUNE.

One moment, one moment ! By your filial faithfulness
I am impressed. A distant relative am I, and cannot feel
myself to her indifferent. The public road is long ; and
you would better take for haste the shorter mountain trail.
In aid, I'll make a parting gift : my favourite horses, brought
to the hunting-field, a pair, Devil and Saint, one white, one
black. Hither bring them ; bring them here at once.

A servant answered, and the steeds were brought. Tall,
big-jointed, brawny, tough of mouth, untamed, untrained,
they each a saddle wore and double reins. At heads up-
tossed six servants reeled. Pawing and gnashing they
threatened all. Their gleaming eyes, through tousled
forelocks glaring, made them seem unhorned demons surely.

One to the other, in a glance, the brothers spoke :
" Surely he plans that they shall throw and kill us ; yet to
decline the challenge were a greater shame."

And to Suketsune, bowing low :

" What horses fine ! and can it be you give us such as
those ! We, *ronin*, lacking mounts and grooms attendant,
perforce must borrow for this ride."

Approaching Devil, the white horse, Sukenari fain would
mount, but could not. A hand upon the saddle, a bound,
in front up-rearing, behind out-kicking. Stamping and
striking, the brute neighed loudly and showed no sign of
yielding.

" A dilemma ! Faced by a foe, called by a dying mother !
The crisis of a lifetime ! Ye God of arms, ye Patron
Gods of Tsuruga, of all this region round, Kamakata

Gongen, adored at both Hakone Shrines, Bakwa Ryuo,
Ujakuo, Sajakuo, divine in birth, I worship bring. Monju
Bosatsu of the lion-steed, may thy wand became my whip ;
thy cord, O Fudo, be my rein ! "

Over and over, repeating prayers for Fudo's care, he
grasped the bridle at the bit, and without trouble mounted
the horse, which now held down its head and stood un-
moving. The power of Buddha and the Gods be praised !

Delighted, Tokimune cried:

" A serpent bridling, I would gladly ride."

But when he approached Saint, the black horse, and tried
to grasp the bit, it reared, sprang back, and raised a cloud of
dust. Whereat the youth ran to the horse and kicked its
side so hard it seemed to break. Wild as it was, the beast
flinched and staggered, then stood as Tokimune drew near
and mounted.

The brothers rose in their stirrups and, bringing their
horses side to side, one moment waited. Foiled, Suketsune looked at them, amazed in mouth-open wonder.
Sukenari was in spirits, Tokimune much excited.

SUKENARI.

Here, Dosaburo, convey our thanks to Lords Chichibu
and Wada, and to others whose favour we have shared.
Tokimune, let us go !

TOKIMUNE.

Yes, let us go !

Touched with the whip, the horses quickly started.
Quickly the hour of noon, the hour of the horse, sped by ;
and quickly moved the sun. The temple-bell struck the
hour of mid-afternoon, and with its sound prophetic
seemed to tell a future fair for them.

SCENE II. *The Soga Home.*

Zephyrs, called into being by a tolling bell, oft tempt to fall the cherry blossoms from a tree so old—its spring of youth so passed that waiting for a coming spring seems long and useless.

Within her humble home through twenty years and more, her husband dead, had their mother lived in anxious poverty. She had not realized that to hasten the quick growth to manhood of her children, poor and in obscurity, meant hastening, for her, old age and death. As a pine-tree breaks with weight of snow, she suddenly grew ill, and lay 'twixt life and death. Into the straw-thatched cottage, 'mid poverty like his who never found such pleasures as even the Chinese sage enjoyed, the wind blew through holes in the thin paper walls ; and each breath, as she turned in her sleep, seemed final.

Then came Tora of Oiso and Shosho of Keoizaka to visit her, inquiring for her health in the absence of her sons upon the hunting-field ; and in her condition they could not leave her. They stayed and did their best to care for her. They could not otherwise, because they feared the care of strangers might trouble her.

Dosaburo had been sent to Fuji's Hunting-Field. The Ninomiyas had been summoned ; but from them no answer came beyond the news that both from early morning had been out. No one else was there but Koshiro. Listening to her breathing from behind the screen, Koshiro impatiently exclaimed : " Have they not yet returned, Sukenari and Tokimune? How slow they are ! " Going to the door and looking southwards, he moved about nervously.

" Young women, though I am indeed her son, I am only a half-brother to Sukenari and Tokimune. Because of absence I have had but little intercourse with her. I have but just come home. A show of filial faithfulness on my part, as boasting over them would not be fair, or meet approval. Though you may not know her well, you do not deny that you are her sons' betrothed. She, though old, is a woman ; and women for a woman are best nurses. Please attend her, and most of all give comfort as she lies near death."

At his words the women cried : " Alas, is there no hope ? " They felt depressed and helpless. Drawing near to the screened bedside and bending low, they murmured : " Your sons will soon return. Pray only for thy happiness in the life to come. Forget not the prayer, ' Namu Amidha Butsu—I worship thee, great Buddha, and to Thee commit my ways.' " Their voices broke in tears.

'Mid painful breathing she replied :

" The sick bed of a woman old ! Prayer I have not forgotten. When one renounces the worries of this life and prays wholeheartedly, prayer for saving light at death is ten times repeated, and invocation to the welcoming saints who gather at the pillow is graciously received. But as for me, I stray from dark behind to dark before, bound by ties of human love for children dear. Sukenari is dearer than the welcome of the Triune Buddha, and Tokimune sweeter far than five-and-twenty Bosatsu. Can there have been some accident ? I feel so lost ! How late they are ! "

Her resolution weakened ; and she seemed forgetful of herself, even as a pheasant in the field that worries for its young.

Toro and Shosho were more impatient than on those evenings when, night after night, they waited for the coming of the brothers. Their hearts were in the sky ; and in the sky the sun began to sink.

TOGETHER.

Listen ! the bell strikes seven (4 p.m.). Why are they so late ?

They ran outside. Once out, they worried about affairs within : once within, they were no more at ease. Often they went out and in. Whenever the bell rang.

*   *   *   *   *

The gift unkind proved kindness ! Driven by the spur of their riders' faithfulness, the horses quickly ran the six and one-half miles of steep, rough mountain road. Dismounting, the brothers went directly to the house.

TORA AND SHOSHO.

They have come ! There is but little hope of her recovery. The end may come even while we speak.

It seemed their hearts would break with grief.

BROTHERS.

O Koshiro ! we are grateful to you for your tender care.

With this greeting and a bow, they entered the house and went quietly to the hanging paper-screens, beneath which their mother lay.

" Sukenari has come. Tokimune has come."

" How are you feeling now ? Why have they given you no medicine ? Here is something of wonderous power, given us by Lord Hojo. Out of pity for us, please take it ; and live if but for one more day, mother." Hardly they restrained their sobs.

MOTHER.

What is it ? Have the boys come back ? Come here ! Come here !

She grasped their hands firmly from beneath the screen. Her clasp was strong, unusual for one at the point of death.

" Toro and Shosho, take this screen away and let the light in."

Q

Young Women.

Yes, yes, certainly.

She was so impatient that she could hardly wait even while they answered. They tried to untie the cords ; but the strings were short and much entangled. The more nervous they became, the worse the strings got snarled.

" Provoking ! " Pushing the screen aside, she came out, her face quite natural, the usual look in her eyes, and her breathing as regular as ever. Those about her were more agitated than she.

Yet were there tears of anger in her eyes as she said :

" Now, boys, what's the use of Hojo's wondrous medicine? Your mother's illness was a trick to call you back. Even those who feel no ties of blood come at once, laying all things aside, when they hear of the mortal illness of friend or neighbour. That's mere humanity, a human instinct, no rare thing. Do you think it filial piety peculiar that you have come at once on news of a mother's dying ? Surely you would not have returned, had I summoned you on any other pretext, especially since, as I understand, you went to the hunting-field plotting to kill Kudo-Suketsune. It was only a few days ago that I received you back under my roof, lifting the ban of your banishment. Often and often I have talked with you of this, with one argument after another. There is no need of saying the same things over and over again. You have not, I hope, forgotten. Did your elder brother persuade you ? Or were you, though younger, the leader ? I can't in the least understand Sukenari's changeless expression. I see that you have not wavered at all in your purpose.

" Suketsune is now a lord over territory, a master of hundreds of horsemen. Can he be slain by boys like unto you ? Whom could you blame if you were murdered in

stealth by one of his minions, you who have no attendants ?
Of course, Lord Kawaza, your father, was the bravest
man in the region, and lord of two provinces ; and yet on
his way home from the hunting at Okuno he could not
escape from an ill-aimed arrow and so lost his life. When
I think of your father's death and the days of old, I cannot
help foolish fear for you off at the huntings. I, your mother,
am at least one of your parents. Take pity a little on me.
This illness of mine was an honest deceit. Think you there
is no disease except of the body ? There are treatments
and cures for diseases caused by the weather, the rain and
the wind, and for diseases caused by a curse ; but for the
disease caused by the darkening of parental love there is no
medicine, though you send to the most skilled doctor of
China or Chosen, or look through countless volumes of
medicinal lore. My two children should be my medicine.
Those two are the cause of my illness. 'Tis better, as with
venom from the poisonous bird, to kill me straight, than,
morning and evening, day and night, to give me pain and to
be the cause of my illness. Kill me at once, my children ! "
and on the floor she cast herself down and wept.

All four, exclaiming " How sacrilegious !" burst into
tears, their heads bowed to the floor. No wonder even
ignorant and unfeeling Koshiro wept out of helplessness.

Sukenari, unable to dry his sleeves for falling tears,
sobbed : " Your teaching and your loving anger ! I grieve
that I have pained your heart even for a time. It is our
duty to risk our lives against our father's foe ; but it is wrong
to risk our lives thereby displeasing you, our mother. As
for me, I am resolved and abjure revenge entirely. How
is it, Tokimune ? "

To his question Tokimune, reluctantly, with sullen look,
replied, " Since he, with whose fate I vowed to cast my own,
has changed his purpose, alone I cannot be insane." His
voice was harsh, unfeeling.

MOTHER.

There, there, there is your mother's devil of disease. I cast you off, even as before.

YOUNG WOMEN.

" A wicked way of speaking, Tokimune ! If you yield at all, why can't you answer kindly, saying, ' I will obey your bidding,' or words like those?" They urged ; but his expression changed not.

SUKENARI.

Cause of your mother's death ! Have you not learned the lesson of her former dismissal ?

Frightened at his rebuking look, Tokimune said :
" To take the oath upon the sword, as soldiers should, is better far than so much talking."
And the brothers, drawing their swords, were about to strike in sacred asseveration when their mother, clinging to their arms, prevented, saying, " A noble pledge ! A noble pledge ! Young men, with life before them, must not take that vow. Since now I see your willingness, I feel at ease. I am happy, happy ! Now have you two, my children, become your mother's medicine. To have made you *samurai*, indeed, has cured my pain."
Her face, wreathed in smiles of joy, was very touching.
" Young men, in general, with no family ties of their own, are careless and value life but as the dust of the earth. Though you have alliance with Tora and Shosho, until I recognize them as my daughters it cannot be thought of as marriage. I have heard that it is written in the book of etiquette that children should consult their parents when they marry. To-night, right here, exchange your nuptial cups and celebrate your wedding.
(Taking two dress robes from a chest by the bedside.)

" These robes I have kept for this great occasion : a wedding, an event of a lifetime. As bridegrooms, put them on at once, and make that room there, though small, the palatial hall of your marriage. Let your feast with joy be enriched ; and, bringing the wine-cask, the gift of your sister, Ninomiya, in imagination let the ceremonial ribbon be bowed. I this night will lie in front of our family altar, where is enshrined our guardian Buddha, and there, before your father's memorial tablet, will I hear the voice of your festal rejoicing.

" Koshiro, you have many places to visit. Suppose you go for to-night and come back again on the morrow. The day is already declining ; go now, before you are sent for.

" Sukenari, you lead the way, and enter the room with your bride."

SUKENARI.

Yes, gladly.

But he seemed afraid to rise ; and Tora, noticing his blushes, put her arm through his, saying :

" How childish ! Do we need a mother's urging ? Only remember the nights when you strove with others for the right to have my company, and come along."

Tokimune, seeing them move off arm-in-arm, said under his breath : " How very unconcerned ! I cannot do it so ; I feel too shy." And with bowed head he huddled on the mat.

SHOSHO.

You must not let your mother think your love for me, since I am younger than his bride, is less than his for Tora. Do come on.

But when she sought to lead him out—

TOKIMUNE.

No, I cannot, no !

SHOSHO.

You must not say no.

TOKIMUNE.

But mother is watching !

SHOSHO.

No matter ! See, she is looking in the other direction.

TOKIMUNE.

No, no !

SHOSHO.

No more NO !

And she dragged him into the chamber as the evening bell struck six.

A cloudy sky ; a moonless night. Koshiro peeped into the room and found them exchanging cups by the bright light of a big rush, lighted in honour of the occasion ; and, strangely inappropriately as it proved, they were in celebration singing of their marriage long to endure and of generations to spring like seedling pines by sheltering rocks—

The whispered murmurs of the seashore pines,
Like jewels hidden deep from passing eye.

All had turned out as he wished. It was fine. If the brothers were more or less than human, even so they would now be unable to stand alone, but become mere carpet-knights, fettered by love of wife and mother ; and as for Suketsune, his fears had been exorcised for life.

" I will go at once and make report of this. What will
the guerdon be ? An allowance ? If they offer money—
A business life is far too troublesome. I will ask for coin
of gold, gold coins, gold coins ! " he whispered, sucking his
coin-shaped tongue.

Instead of sensuous perfume, smoke that in a mountain
home drives off mosquitoes ! Two thin nets of paper
screening, side by side, domestic ; and upon the floor, mere
mats of straw, reversible, life's stark sincerity.

On the couch in their Royal palace the Chinese Emperor,
Bu, and his bride compared their marriage bond to the ties
of life unending, of the millenary crane.

How strong—a mother's prayer, in love outpoured !

Though fearful of offending, Tokimune questioned :
" How is it with my hope, long-cherished ? How can I
pass the night in pleasures vain ? " Having made Shosho
sleep, the wine-cups empty, he came from out the net
quietly, lest the rustle of the paper might waken Sukenari.
With care he gathered up the skirts of his garment, and with
his mother's gift, a treasured keepsake, neath his arm, in
cautious stealth crept like a fox avoiding some hidden snare.
They had not conferred ; but to Sukenari came the same
thought, and, having made Tora sleep with wine, he
reasoned : " My mother in this life would be offended ;
but my life is for this night alone." Putting on his robe,
he stole out on tiptoe, wondering who the figure in the
shade might be.
Neither recognized the other. Stealthily they drew near
and met.
" Tokimune ! "
" Sukenari ! "

SUKENARI.

Hush ! Have you resolved to do the thing this night ?

TOKIMUNE.

I surely have. How well our hearts agree ! In but a moment now we shall have gained our hope, long cherished.

SUKENARI.

Yet will it grieve our mother. Poor mother ! In sleep upon her pillow, she must now be dreaming happy dreams. Her sorrow upon waking ! My heart aches as though it felt her sorrow now.

Looking toward the inner room, the brothers sobbed. Then, choking back the tears—

SUKENARI.

I had in mind to write my will and leave some keepsakes ; but though we fly, 'twill be past midnight when we reach Fuji's Field, and there may be difficulties unforeseen. A comfort in her sorrow, I will write, though but a line.

TOKIMUNE.

Good !

Drawing the ink-stone nearer, they were in too great haste to hunt for paper, but began to write upon the net that with which they would have their mother dry her tears. Gathering memories as men gather seaweed, memories of twenty years since first they had been given her breasts, sorrows and joys, they wrote. Their hearts were too full for complete expression. Sukenari's writing ran to memories of Tora's love. Tokimune's brush swept on to write of Hakone priests and of his gratitude for that mother-love which had received him back and allowed them thus to make their mark as men, avenging their father's death upon their foe eternal. And, for the rest, the brothers wrote as one—that they would wear the robes which she had given unto death, and that it would be to them as though she were herself accompanying them to the world beyond to greet their father's spirit ; that she should look upon the garments old which they had left as treasured tokens ; to give to Ninomiya their bows and quivers ; to their sister the poems and the Hokke Scriptures on the desk, which Tokimune for eight long years had kept and read ; to Zenjibo their amulet cases, with the request that he should read prayers for the safe passage of the dead for them, according to the promise of the Gods and Buddhas ; to Tora and to Shosho their hair, with the request that they should pray for them to Great Amidha times as many as were the hairs they stroked, nor forgetting but embracing the fragrance of their pillows ; to Onio and Dosaburo saddle and stirrups, with the command that they faithfully should serve the mother in her children's stead. This was their only command ; and they added the date : " In the Dark of the Twenty-eighth of May, in the Fourth Year of Kenkyu." Though the sky was heavy, their hearts grew light. Then they added their names, " Sukenari, Tokimune," using their seals. Casting the brushes aside, they wept silently.

" The sorrow of parting is endless ; surely the short night must already have passed. Let us be going, Tokimune."

Sukenari went out first ; but when Tokimune stepped out after him, his weight broke the veranda of the old house, and down he fell upon the ground. By the noise of his falling, the clatter of the falling screens and the rustling of the paper nets, the young women were awakened.

TORA.

Why, Sukenari is not here !

SHOSHO.

Neither is Tokimune here !

" Are they out in front ?   Are they in the inner room ? "
they called excitedly.

TOKIMUNE.

It will be hard if we are discovered.

SUKENARI.

Let them pass by, and we can then slip out.

Nodding one to the other, they hid themselves behind the
hedge of shrubs and pampas-grass in the neglected garden.
" Look, the writing on the net ! They are gone to throw
their lives away. We have but just exchanged the cups of
marriage, and shall we thus so soon be separated ? We
will not allow it. Think of mother's sorrow, of her anger.
Let us catch up with them and urge their quick return.
If in that we fail, we can at least die with them."
Tightening their sashes and tucking up their skirts, they
were leaving the house, when forth from the inner room
came the mother, a brush-broom in her hands, striking
about so violently that her arms seemed waves and the very
broom to break. " What, women faint-hearted ! " Calling
them cowards, she struck them again and again. " At
the Quarters, indeed, ye may ebb and flow as the tide ;
but here ye are *samurai* women and wives. Bear your own
part in revenge against the foe of your husbands, seeing
and sending them off, though you must hide it from mother.
So are you women, indeed, and wives worthy of bowmen.
" Though I lay down, I could not sleep. I wept as I
heard them writing behind me. Imagine how a mother
endured it."
Dropping the broom. she threw herself down and wept.
Behind the fence in the garden the brothers : " How

changed her mind since last evening ! How can she have changed ? "

They dared not move, but clung to the wet, broken hedge, sobbing noiselessly like cicadas through the night hours.

Likewise the women : " Just but a moment ago she rebuked them, declaring revenge to be evil ; now she reproaches us roundly for seeking to stop them. Surely her senses in all the confusion have left her. Still, if we must, our hearts' deep devotion we'll render." They faltered.

Closed were her eyes, and her lips moved not, though her heart strove to speak, till, at last :

" I am ashamed of having struck you with the broom. 'Tis only natural that you, who know not of days that are past, should think this all strange. When the brothers were children, but five and three years of age, they gained the conviction that it was for them a disgrace to have had their father slain. That feeling never has changed, saving to deepen as older they grew.

" Will the purpose of a bowman be broken, though a mother seek to restrain ? I knew it well ; and so I called them home, surprising and alarming the poor boys with my pretended illness unto death. I opposed their plans. Why ? I shame to tell you. Koshiro, whom I once brought to birth, their wicked half-brother, blinded by avarice, awed by Suketsune's power, joined himself to our enemy and became his slave. Recently he returned home. Like a dog he has smelled out everything, important, unimportant, and reported it to Suketsune. Because of his reports, so I have heard, Suketsune takes great care that no chance be given to attack him.

" With intent that Koshiro should know, I pretended illness and called my children home, to scold them cruelly. What Koshiro knows, Suketsune knows ; and now is off his guard ; and they may kill him easily. Mother-love planned all ; but how I taxed my brain !

" Even when a little lad, called Ichiman, Sukenari was precocious and very cautious. Tokimune, even in his babyhood, while yet called Hakoo, was self-willed and over-hasty. I sent him to Hakone temple with intent to keep him safe till fully grown in strength of arm and to lull suspicion ; but he rebelled and became a warrior. I disowned him for that deed, and banished him, until a brief few days ago, with purpose still to break the vigilance of Suketsune's guard. This, too, was all for love.

" For children who in filial piety risk life there is the consciousness of duty done ; but for a mother who sends her children forth to fall in battle, what comfort is there ? A cruel fate, indeed, I have been given. Love may hope for their safety ; no mother-heart can desire their death. Though there may be faithless children who mourn not the death of their parents, no mother, none but I, regards not the death of her children. When I go down the road to meet my husband in the future world, what reason can I give for sending such young boys along the path before me ?"

While she lamented till all her tears to the last drop were shed, her very heart poured forth, Tora and Shosho choked with grief.

The brothers were melted to the heart by her mother-love. So great their grief, they knew not what to do. Kneeling to worship, they wept ; weeping, they knelt in contrition, adoring. The broken fence, that lay a barrier between such love, will rot away beneath their tears.

MOTHER.

My boys, my boys ! Hindered, as they think, by a mother's foolishness, they must by now be hurrying on their way. But if their hearts' desire be here fulfilled, there will be greater peace in all the years.

I made a priestly scarf and robe for Hakoo, and swore to Buddha that he should be a priest. And, not to break that vow, I myself took orders as a nun, and wear that robe and scarf. Look here, my daughters !

Slipping off her outer summer robe, she showed the scarf and priestly garb of black.

With deep inhalation, all clasped their hands ; and the murmured prayers of the four, in garden and home, were like the promises four of Buddha the blest. Most reverential !

MOTHER.

For a parent to say Mass for children who have gone before is unnatural and brings a curse upon the children, I have heard. I took Hakoo's place, and so from this day I am Priest Hakoo. Sukenari is my elder brother, and Tokimune is my parent. Come, Tora and Shosho, it is the hour of evening prayer. We will pray for the Buddhahood of our parent Tokimune and elder brother Sukenari. To the temple let us go.

In tears she beckoned them. The brothers saw them go, and breathed a last farewell. Sad with pangs of parting, they also started towards the fields where deer abound. Their hurrying footsteps faltered. Though they paused, the hedges now hid their mother's figure ; and the evening bell surprised their ears, hushing the murmurs of her voice. The bell proclaimed that all is vanity—a truth they had not grasped before, but now significant. The mother heard it, and understood its application to her children's lives. The mother and her sons in tears heard the same sound at the parting of the ways. With tears, as with the dew, their sleeves were wet.

ACT IV

Persons Represented :

SOGA-SUKENARI.

SOGA-TOKIMUNE.

NINOMIYA-YASUKIYO, *Brother-in-law of the Soga.*

HONDA-CHIKATSUNE, *Officer of Prince Chichibu and Friend to the Soga.*

NITTA-TADATSUNE, *Warrior and Friend to the Soga.*

TOKUTAKE, *Keeper of the Horse, under Yoritomo.*

ANZAI-YASHICHIRO ⎱
SHINKAI-ARASHIRO ⎰ *Retainers of Suketsune.*

MADAME SOGA.

TORA, *Wife of Sukenari.*

SHOSHO, *Wife of Tokimune.*

KAMEGIKU, *an Entertainer.*

WARRIORS, ENTERTAINERS, AND CARRIERS.

SCENE I. *On the Way to Fuji Field.*

DEER that long for mates
In the end become brushes
Wherewith to write love-letters.

The old woman, whose life no longer seems worth living, has determined to make the same encircling plain whereon her children fall the place wherein to put her own dead body. She has started, leaving it entirely to the horse to find the way. The horse is young. Those with it are an old, old mother and two youthful brides.

Stirrups, unfitted to her feet, yet prove a help upon the journey dark. Sadly and alone the women move forward with but a candle-lantern small, lighting at their feet, for guidance in the dark. So dark the night that, though they strive to see what cometh next, Mount Fuji's towering form cannot be traced. They long to change the darkness of the night for moonlight that on the fifteenth shineth.

The stars are twinkling, twinkling ; and look, those lights that come and go. Can they be fireflies ? No, but they may be the souls of the departed brothers. To catch, to hold them fast, they try ; but in the night-wind, which blows their light-held skirts about, they flickering fade. 'Tis but the fox-fire which comes and goes.

From up above the clouds a cry ! and yet again a cry ! " Where are you going ? Wait a moment ! If you are a bird, upon the holy way which spirits traverse, put a barrier on the mountain path of death and stop my children who are speeding on ahead."

The road we travel is familiar to our thought. The mountain wind blows down upon the left from Chichibu. Is that the murmur of the pines we hear, or of the waves that roll along the shore ? If it were day, we could see if this were Niho or Kiyoni temple. The faint notes of a distant bell quicken our heart-beats. The hamlet of the jewel-swamp, where dewdrops glitter bright, and Umesawa, where amid the plum-trees it is dusk, we pass ; and passing these, to Mariko we come, where horses rear in protest at the flood. Here at the cross-roads the horse has stopped. Why, though we strike and urge, will he not move ? Alas ! can he not know our impetuous desire ? Know it he must. We lash his white flanks with whips of falling tears, but all in vain. The horse is not to blame. This branch road leads to Oiso. Many an evening with this horse the brothers took this road to visit sweethearts there. He knows the road ; but, poor horse, to-night he does not know his rider, and the way is different. When, in memory of the boys, we turn his head towards Oiso, again, indeed, he goes on as before ; but when we turn him back, he halts. For whom is he waiting ? Our husbands ! My children ! His masters ! The dear horse, like ourselves, grieves separation.

As they weep, clinging to the front rings of the saddle,

the horse in sympathy bends his ears and droops. Women and horse together weep. Their tears would cloud the skies.

" Do not mourn." Encouraging the horse, they cross Ashikara, where strong winds blow and dewdrops scatter. Hakone, darkly outlined, now appears. The road they take is like the river-bed at the last crossing where old and young continually do cry :

> Our sins are heavy,
> Our delusions deep ;
> Where lies the way of spiritual awakening ?
> Repent ! repent ! repent ! repent !
> Where lies the way of spiritual awakening ?
> Repent ! repent ! repent ! repent !

Dyed in colour, and bewitched by fragrance, we have failed to garner seed of future life ; and now what can be done upon the darkness of the way ?

> Shine brightly, holy light of Mishima,
> And enlighten our understanding !

As they pass the shrine's enclosure, the mother clasps her hands and prays, silently repeating prayers by hundreds, by thousands in her heart, as she hurries her horse forward.

An old pine-tree unkindly casts its shade o'er early blooming cherries and a grafted plum. How feel the women in their bloom of youth ? To them it surely seems the month when all the gods the shrines desert. When will they cease, the rains of May ? With tears like showers, they wet the bridle reins ; and though wrung out, there is no time in which to dry.

Lest they should be too far behind, they had not dared delay for hats or taken staves, but started in the clothing which they wore ; and truly life's daily garb is but a traveller's suit which weareth thin.

They now approach the great encircling plain. The pine groves thicken, that they cannot see the stars ; and o'er the ground the water from the swamp flows murmuringly. Wild thorns their garments tear ; their sandals bite their feet along the stony way where sticks and stumps are many. An inch ahead is pitchy black, and, in the lantern small, the little candle lights their way but dimly. They fear the horse may stumble. "The hunting-field is near ; from here we'll lead you by the hand. Walk slowly."

They stagger all, as from the horse they help the mother down.

MOTHER.

My daughters, even though on horseback, I have weary grown. With your fatigue I sympathize. What time now is it ? My thoughts were busy that I did not count the bell, if it struck four (10) or midnight. The night seems growing late. From the hunting-field do you hear any sound ? Who will tell us of the boys, alive or dead ? We are so helpless !

She dare not venture on.

THE YOUNGER WOMEN.

Yes ; but there is a woman, Kamegiku of Kisegawa, who is like a younger sister. Suketsune likes her, and has called her to the hunting-field. We begged her to keep watch over the brothers. Though she is young, she is a woman of noble character ; and faithful is she by nature. I think she knows what she is doing ; but I wish we could see Kamegiku.

While they are talking, lights appear and disappear behind the grass. They shine along the way.

R

The Younger Women.

What is happening ? I'm afraid. Shall we go and see what it is ? But we cannot leave her alone ! There, there !

While they watch with anxious eyes, the lights gradually draw near, and the laughter of men and women is heard.

" Oh, there is no danger, there is no danger ! They are all carriers from the Quarters. I see, they are entertainers called to the camp who are now going back. I wonder if Kamegiku is among them. Let us wait here and ask them. Mother, you stay here awhile," they said, hiding her in the deep grass and snuffing the candle in the little lantern.

Not knowing that the women are waiting, the girls from the Quarters chatter away, and some of them sing. Beautiful are their voices !

> Dark was the night of May,
>   Three years ago,
> When on the homeward way
>   From Shigetatsu,
> Someone, a little girl
>   It may have been,
> Said that to capture the
>   Fireflies would be
> Fun for the riders all.
>
> To-night the breezes blow,
> As pleasantly as then
> They cooled the fevered brows
> With wine o'erheated.
> The bearers lightly swing
> Their laden palanquins ;
> And yonder fireflies flit
> Above the shallow stream.

CARRIERS.

Step over!

The riders in the palanquins are known each by her lantern's crest. There comes the crest of Iwasaki; the flying crane of Ibaraki-no-Samon; the tortoise-shell of Wachizaiya-no-Hanasaki, the conductor of all; daiichi; daiman; daikichi; ori-eboshi; tate-eboshi; white ichimonji; black ichimonji; Sendaiya-no-Michinobu's sparrow on the bamboo; luck-bringing water-nuts covered with dew, the crest of the procurers; and the plum-cups' wide-open eyes; two lanterns side by side, the well-known crests of Morohoshi and Takahashi of Yamato—their hearts, indeed, ride in one palanquin. Palanquin after palanquin, they pass. Tora and Shosho, in impatience, let them go; and on they go without a word.

Behind them comes a lantern with a crest of maple leaves flying, wind-driven in the storm; beyond all question, the crest of Kamegiku.

THE YOUNG WOMEN.

Oh, Kamegiku! 'tis Tora and Shosho. There's something we want to ask you. Stop, just a minute.

KAMEGIKU.

Bearers, halt!

Though in haste, they put their burdens down amid the summer grass.

KAMEGIKU.

How much I've wanted to see you!

THE YOUNG WOMEN.

So have we; and how about the brothers?

KAMEGIKU.

How unlucky they are! They have just gone home because of their mother's illness; and Suketsune, because of

Koshiro's secret messages and the like, is off his guard. He said that he would stretch his limbs about the camp hereafter, and planned to hold high carnival throughout the hunt. I thought it would be a good chance for the boys, and vowed that I would help them to fulfil their cherished dream. But this afternoon, about the eighth hour (2 p.m.), a man called Ninomiya came, a messenger from Kamakura on errand urgent. 'Tis said that Noriyori, great Yoritomo's younger brother, has killed himself; and in the reason, I have heard, the Soga Brothers are involved. Confusion, you can well imagine, reigns in all the camps. 'Tis like the ending of a dance.

So great Yoritomo is starting for Kamakura to-night at the eighth hour (2 a.m.). However, if it rains even three drops, his going will be put off till the fifth hour (8 a.m.) to-morrow; but, rain or shine, the advance carriers are ordered to start at the eighth hour. Packing and all, what a confusion! The women, like me, called to the camps are suddenly sent back to the Quarters. Just look at my appearance. But I could just take those boys in my arms, unlucky fellows! I'm sorry for their mother, with whom I am not acquainted; and I can only weep at thought of you two girls. But don't worry! I also am out of luck. If I could have stayed at the Field a few days longer I would have reaped a fortune. Take heart; nothing can be done just now. I must go on—in a few days!

Giving thus the main points of the story, in a manner unfinished and reckless, she ordered her palanquin to hasten away.

Unable to keep still any longer, the mother tumbles out of her hiding.

" I have heard her words, Kamegiku's, if that is her name. How grieved you must be! Think of my sorrow! All that I have said and done turns out amiss. Must I still live on to see the fate of my children ? Long life, many sorrows ! Farewell, my daughters ! "

She drew her guardian sword, holding its point towards her.

" Thee I adore, Eternal Buddha ! "

Ere the Buddha's name is spoken they spring upon her and take away the sword.

" Unthinking mother ! Would we hesitate, do you suppose, if to cast our lives away would help the brothers ? They cannot now fulfil their hearts' desire ; and if they shall have caused their honoured mother's death, never will their fortune change, since upon your sons would fall the charge of filial impiety."

MOTHER (*bursting into tears*).

To wish to die rather than to hear such grievous things may seem as though I did not care for them ; but stand once in my place. 'Twas for the children's sake I feigned my illness ; and all my plans, made in mother-love, have turned out to their ruin.

If it does not rain the General's departure will be at the eighth hour (2 a.m.), so I think I heard. There'll not be time enough for them to turn around. When the camps are all astir, if they go near and are found out and captured, as if thieves, then must they suffer indignities still greater, at the mere thought of which I tremble. Even if I do not kill myself, surely I shall die.

Rain is the only thing which can prevent the General's departure. Look ! The stars are shining. There's not a trace of cloud. How can it rain ? And, if it does not rain, how can their hopes be realized ? The rainy season begins in May. To-morrow it is June ! This evening is the last ! Why does not the rain of May begin to fall ? Do the

seasons fail, the sun and moon make error ? As fate is
merciless to me, a mother, 'gainst heaven I rebel. Look
not ; but let me die. Give back the sword.

The while she clung to them they held her arms and
wildly looked one at the other. All were weeping.

TORA.

Shosho, what think you ? If it rains, the General will
not start until the fifth hour of morning. By that time,
surely, the brothers can have accomplished their will. It is
the rain alone which honours or defames their name. There
was a woman once who turned to stone with longing for her
husband. Though I am but a humble girl, of life unstable,
is my faith less than that of others ? Never ! There is no
saying that the gods of heaven and earth, of sea and air,
refuse their aid to women such as I. My mind I have made
up ; and I will pray the heavens for rain, though life be
forfeit. How say you ?

SHOSHO.

That is what I too would do. The ways of death are one.
Come, let us make haste.

They are inspired ; the mother also. " Great in mind and
in spirit, will not the heavens hear ? I too will pray ! "
With hearts of faith they tie the summer grass in pendent
wands, and, closing their eyes to all without, within, unite in
prayer.
" To Thee, Great Deity of Mishima, we pray ! Noin,
priest of Kosobe, it is said, composed a verse in supplication :

> Dam the water of the Heavenly Stream,
> And for the rice-fields pour,
> If indeed Thou art the God
> From heaven that cometh down.

" One-Komachi's prayer for rain is well known. She composed a poem, protesting to the Goddess of the Sun which shines o'er all the sunrise land, wherein as well the name of the treasured Rain-Child is adored. Her prayer was granted, and the rain fell. One-Komachi was a woman ! So, too, are we ; and, though we write no poems in finished form, our hearts sincere compose. So grant our prayer, we beseech Thee, and send down the answering rain.

" We worship Thee, Thou Buddhas many of Fumombon, Ye Dragon Gods of the Southern Seas and of the earth below. From out these praying women, press the blood, and, changing it to rain-drops, grant our husbands' longing, comfort a mother's heart.

" The mercy of Bosatsu is a great cloud, covering all things with sweet dew, and pouring forth the rain. If one prays, though in the midst of sin, the hosts of evil, all, are put to flight."

Tora and Shosho bite their fingers, and wet their sleeves with blood, as well as flowing tears, spattering it through the air as, all perspiring, they stand on toes, up-reaching, and smite their frenzied heads. They worship heaven and earth, and pray from hearts sincere.

Have mercy on sincerity !

The answer of the gods is not delayed. Quickly the clear sky turns black and lightning flashes through the air. Clouds cover Mount Ashitaka. Invited by the rain of tears, the rain of heaven begins to fall, with pattering sound as though bamboo sticks were falling. Their joy and gratitude ! Unmindful of the wet, they worship and adore. Confident of the success of the brothers, they hasten towards the hunting-field, sheltering the mother with their sleeves.

So till this day the rain that falls upon the last of May is known as Tora's tears, the night rain of Shosho.

SCENE II. *Within the Camp.*

The hunt at the foot of far-famed Fuji was ordered to be stopped because of the confusion at Kamakura, and Yoritomo's departure was announced to take place shortly ; but because of the rain it was postponed, and the noises of the camp grew still, the watch-fires along the pathways dimly burning.

> For men in slumber,
> Pillowed on their hands and worn
> With labour lengthened,
> Bells at midnight, tolling low
> The short night hours,
> Broken dreams to dreams united.

Thinking that now the time had come, the Soga Brothers dismissed to their home-town the faithful Onio twain, and started towards the camp. Dressed in summer silk, embroidered with autumn grasses in a field, his mother's gift, wearing a flowing robe in plover-pattern with its sleeves bound back, his bamboo-braided hat by strings tied tightly, and over all a servant's rainproof, blue, Sukenari led the way by camps torch-lighted.

In under-dress of lined white silk, with circled cranes embroidered, his mother's gift, wearing a flowing robe of butterfly design, a sword, red-handled, in his belt, upon his shoulder an heirloom of the Minamoto Clan, a sword—Offend-me-not—Hakone's priest the giver, and over all a waterproof of paper, oiled, Tokimune, tying the cords of his hat, followed his brother.

SUKENARI.

Brother, if we do not kill our foe this night, but useless render all our mother's love, our lives will not be worth the living. I speak not of the shame of faithlessness, the gossip clustering round our deeds. As if a gift from heaven, the rain began to fall ; the General's leaving was put off ; the noises of their packing on the hunting-field have stilled ; and here are passes whereby, 'tis said, we may freely go even to the General's quarters ! To kill Suketsune now lies well within our power.

Many dancing-girls may be about the camps. Be careful not to injure them, a sin to add. Rain is but a common thing ; yet this night's rain seems deeply meaningful. If mother hears that we are killed in strife, how she will grieve, although her heart is brave !

TOKIMUNE.

Truly, as you say, Suketsune is a bird in a cage, a fish in a net. How can we fail ? I have courage to meet the king of hostile devils ; but the rain to-night falls on me and soaks my inmost soul. It makes me sad.

When we have fought our fight it may be that we die, apart. The cup of parting drink with me.

From his belt he took a cup, and, holding it to catch the rain-drops, offered it to Sukenari.

SUKENARI.

Man pledges seven times and is born an elder brother, six times he vows and becomes a younger brother. Though I die and live again repeatedly, I will not cut the bond between us twain.

He drank it all and handed back the cup to Tokimune, who held it high above his head in reverence, saying :

" An elder brother is as one's parent ; so my mother's parting-cup must be included here. Can heavenly dew or hermit's holy cup than this be sweeter ?"

He takes and drinks ; he takes and drinks the falling rain. They know not that they drink the blood and tears that flow from love, the love of wife and mother, the blood for children and for husbands shed.

At last the May rain ceases ; the sky clears ; the Northern Measure shines. Anzai-Yashichiro and Shimbai-Arashiro, in travelling costume clad, come forth, saying to a servant,
"The rain has ceased. The General starts at the fifth morning hour (8 a.m.). The carriers must at once prepare to start."
Bidding the servant announce the order, they pass on.
With looks which say, " 'Mid the confusion of the hour let us slip in and do the deed," the brothers hurry by.

ANZAI.

Here ! who are those fellows sneaking about the camp without permission ? Horse-thieves ! Robbers ! Catch them !

As he bellows Sukenari calmly says : " Be not disturbed. We are messengers on secret errand sent to Suketsune from Kamakura. Forfeit not your feudal holdings by questioning our affairs. If still in doubt, look here ! " and from the cord about his neck he holds forth the pass.
Surprised, the two their words of challenge change :
" Excuse our rudeness, for we knew you not, we pray. Let not Suketsune know that Shimbai and Anzai challenged you. We beg your favour. To reach his camp, turn to the left at the next corner, and at the end you will see a large encampment. Freely pass ! "
With courtesy, excessively polite, they calmly turn aside, not knowing they have shown an enemy the way to Suketsune's camp.
As from the jaws of death the brothers have escaped in the might of those passes ; and in their hearts they thank Noriyori. 'Tis dangerous, indeed, to draw near the

General's quarters. In camps on either side people are shouting :

" The order has been given for the vanguard to start. Get ready the raincoats. Look out for your pocket-money ! Horses ! Saddles ! "

The brothers are consumed in anxiety :

" Like this it must be in Suketsune's camp. Have our lives been spared unto this day for naught ? Does the stopping of the rain portend that we are now forsaken of the gods, our fortune at its end ? "

They stand with tightened fists and hard-clenched teeth, gazing into nothingness, when Honda-Chikatsune, Chichibu's chief retainer, on night-guard, in armour lightly clad, seeing them, draws near, and to their questioning challenge whispers :

> " For boats that are drifting,
> Tossed by the waves,
> Here is a coast-line familiar."

Sukenari, delighted at the voice, answers :

" For Prince Chichibu's great kindness and your friendship, now and ever, we've had no chance to speak our gratitude ; and you must think us graceless. This night we had determined to fulfil our purposes long cherished ; but now the rain has ceased, and in the camp is preparation for departure. Though we fear that we may fail in this confusion, we are resolved to fight our way unto our foe, and there our bodies, slain in fight, expose. Prevent us not, we pray ; but to Prince Chichibu convey our thanks eternal."

Honda in their ears whispered :

" Fear not ; Suketsune is to follow the General's horse in the morning ; and so all in his camp are now sleeping. This way ! This way ! Quietly ! " and he led them on. How great their joy at finding thus a guide upon the way !

HONDA.

Here is Suketsune's sleeping-place. Here do your will and wipe away the shame of life's disgrace.

BROTHERS.

Though through five hundred lives we give our bodies to be burned, your kindness we cannot repay. These passes from Noriyori, secretly received, we can in no way now return to him, since he is dead. If on our bodies they are found, false men will say he was a traitor, siding with the Soga, descendants of that Ito who incurred the anger of his lord. It would disgrace his name with falsehood after death, and ill requite his goodness. We give them you in charge," and unto Honda handed the two passes.

HONDA.

'Tis true! Trust them to me. Lord Chichibu will make it right. Neither will he neglect your mother, old. Longer would I stay, but ignorance must feign for my position and the honour of a bowman," and to the outer camp he turned away.

" Is there need to hesitate ? This, Honda told us, is the camp." Throwing off their raincoats, jumping the wicket, vaulting the railing as though treading on air to heaven on high, the brothers, unchallenged, entered the chamber of slumber. A soldier on night-duty, asleep in the next room, roused at the sound of their footsteps, and ran out calling, " Thieves ! "

One in the camp, at the sound of his voice, took up the cry, shouting " Thieves ! " Another, " The General is starting ! " Shout followed shout ; the sound of the drum and the bell, that gives forth the signals : clang, clang ! dub-a-dub ! And one rushed into the camp in confusion saying, " Confound it ! The starting will fall, for the rain has again been postponed." And over and over the sound of the voice, the sound of the rain's rushing patter, the sound of the men's hurried footfalls, running now this way, now that.

In the meantime the brothers, as they had planned, killed Suketsune, and ran out through the gate. Great was the joy in their hearts as boldly they stood there quenching their thirst with the rain-water wrung from their sleeves.

SUKENARI.

How elated I feel, Tokimune! Compared with the long years of waiting, the killing was easy. With sheer joy I was hasty ; and now, indeed, have forgotten whether we gave Suketsune the ceremonial stroke in departing.

TOKIMUNE.

'Tis no matter, since we have slain him.

SUKENARI.

Not thus may we leave him. When his body is later examined they may say that we killed him, but, losing our presence of mind, failed in not giving the ceremonial blow. That would for ever disgrace us ; think you not so, Toki-mune ?

TOKIMUNE.

It is so.

And with a nod Tokimune, fearing no foe, proudly walked back to the chamber. Stamping his feet on the flooring, kicking the *shoji* aside and knocking over the screening, he seated himself astride the fallen Suketsune, and as follows addressed him :

" Give ear, Suketsune ! It is on tides of emotion that one becomes hostile or friendly. After your sins of body and soul, the six-rooted, all have been purged, we hope that you may attain the shore of unchanging reality." Drawing the sword from his sash, the short sword, he continued : " This is the sword with the red wooden handle you gave me when first at Hakone I saw you. You were its owner of yore, and so know the taste of its iron. To you I now will return it: accept." And from the right ear to the left he cut, making one opening. " On one lotus leaf in Paradise may we be born, Great Amidha, I pray," and, having prayed, he went where Sukenari waited. None dared question him.

SUKENARI.

Now, if we wish to escape we can do so ; but life lived in hiding is life not worth living. To flee, though one step, is disgraceful to bow and to arrow ; and above all, in return for the kindness of Priest Noriyori, who for our sake gave his life, we must follow.

Let us then, who owe no man allegiance, try unblunted swords with those of the noblest of Nippon, and die bravely striving.

TOKIMUNE.

Agreed !

Both with voices loud :
" Soga Sukenari and Soga Tokimune, sons of Kawazu-Saburo, grandsons of Ito-Sukechika, resident in the province of Izu, have killed Kudo-Suketsune, their father's mortal foe. Are there no bowmen brave under General Yoritomo ? Here, a challenge ! "

They called and waited. It was dark, and the rain fell pouring down.

From the camps the cry arose : " A night attack ! "

Three, or even five, to one bow or sword are clinging, fighting for it, shouting, " It is mine, it is mine ! " Some urge sleepy horses, whipping hard, impatient at their slowness.   Slipping on weapons, tripping over helmets, mistaking gauntlets for greaves, sandals for hats, they riot on. In loud tones Tokutake of the stables cries, " We cannot see white or black.   Get torches ! "   From every side upon the ground they throw quivers, raincoats, hats, umbrellas, brooms ; and fires are lighted till the darkness of the encircling plain flees as before a hundred morning suns.

From out the clamour men force their way and introduce themselves to fight the Soga Brothers, who with a brushwood fence behind them advance by turn, announcing each his name, and showering sparks like rain, defeating each newcomer.

Some with hands cut off retreat ; and some with wounds in face or shoulder, hip or thigh ; while some are cut to instant death ; but the brothers receive no slightest wound ; and Tokimune, full of youthful fire, on presses towards the General's tent as if to put an end unto all sons of men within the camp.

Sukenari was resting to regain his breath behind the brushwood fence ; the fires in all the camps had been put out by falling rain ; when from the shadows, wherein it was too dark to see east or west, a warrior, perhaps scarce forty years of age, dressed in red-threaded armour, came, bearing two swords : one short—two feet in length ; one long—three feet six inches, double-edged :

" Nitta-Tadatsune, who at the General's order some years ago entered Mount Fuji's cave and made a name known to the depths of hell, who at this hunt hath killed a boar, than tiger stronger of strength, who shines in fame unrivalled over all the land, am I.   How needlessly pretentious are ye, men of Soga ! The foe ye sought was Suketsune—he alone. Why, therefore, from their branches hack some fifty, some hundred leaf-like warriors ?   If ye wish capture by the hand of Nitta, and the shame of foul imprisonment, prepare ! " he challenged.

SUKENARI.

Indeed, you seem a goodly match for me. Though you be Nitta, it cannot yet be said that you are victor. To fight with me may be far different from fighting demons in the hell of Fuji's man-cave or the boar. Feel Sukenari's arm of might !

And sprang at Nitta.

NITTA.

Rash youth, there's no help !

Swords flashing like stars in the rain-swept sky, they clashed in fury. It was a battle drawn, without a victor.

Dressed in armour gay there came a warrior, with harsh voice, shouting :

" What beastly arrogance to steal my name ! Thirst ye for fame ? Nitta-Tadatsune of Izu am I ! I will meet ye in battle."

Sukenari, springing back :

" Wide are the sixty-odd provinces ; yet are there not, under our Lord Yoritomo, warriors other than Nitta ? How needlessly pretentious to kill one or two frail, masterless men ! There is a Nitta, and here is another. You, with two forms that are one, I will not spare either."

Renewed his assault.

" What, do you call yourself Nitta, though coming later than I ! You at least shall not kill Sukenari."

As the one sought to shield Sukenari the other passed under his arm ; as the other sought to attack, the one defended the youth. For one Sukenari, there were two Nittas ; and they fought in confusion. The Nitta behind Sukenari covertly parried the blows of the other, who openly struck ; but in vain, for Sukenari had his right thigh cut to the knee, a left leg alone his support. Twice—yes, thrice he struck ;

but the wound foiled his skill and weakened his strength, so that backwards he fell o'er his buttocks.

SUKENARI.

Tokimune, my brother, where are you ? I, Sukenari, am conquered. For you on the mountain of death I am waiting. 'Tis all. Come, behead me. Fear not !

NITTA.

If the name of your assailant is not known, troubled in the Land of Shades, you have my pity. I will show the face of Nitta, and compel the thief who falsely bears my name now to unmask.

" Bring out a light ! "

As he loudly called, Tadatsune's servants a lantern brought. Nitta stood facing Nitta.

NITTA.

Why, Ninomiya ! So 'twas you who called yourself Great Nitta ! Shameful deed ! When rabbits are slain foxes grieve, they say. Once you were a lowly relative ; but now, fearing to be involved in punishment, you wish to prove by killing Sukenari that you are none of his. A plan most excellent ! Your conduct I admired when first I heard that you had put aside your wife that you might help the brothers as a stranger could ; but now I question, Was that divorcement given for your own sake ? Deep wisdom surely !

Wondering at the shout of Nitta's name, I came upon you unexpectedly ; but much I grieve to have cut down so fine a youth."

NINOMIYA.

Fools sneer at wise men, as the saying goes. When one would measure wisdom by his ignorance, 'tis ignorance alone that's brought to light. If Ninomiya wished to kill

S

his brothers, why did he wait until this day ? Recalling your great fame, and wishing to overawe them, I took your name, intending, in the sight of heaven, to shelter them and at the proper time to bring them forth. With this in mind, I met him boldly ; but he would not flinch, and I was powerless.

You sought fame, but feared ; and, making Ninomiya's boasting words your aid, fought to his death. A windfall ! A mere hand-out ! A warrior, surely, who regards the right would say that he is sorry to have struck down so fine a youth. For a man, as for a hunter to boast of riding a boar, it is too good ! Too good !

No sooner had he finished than Nitta cried :
" Indeed, a fellow who would kill his brother may not appreciate a warrior's grace ; but you may cut the head and win renown."

NINOMIYA.
Yasukiyo is not a man to win renown from the deeds of others. Cut it off yourself and take the credit.

NITTA.
No, Ninomiya, 'tis yours to strike.

NINOMIYA.
No, Nitta, strike !

NITTA.
Ninomiya, you shall strike.

NINOMIYA.
Ah, Ninomiya has no sword wherewith to kill his brother. If you can strike with this, then strike I say.

And down he threw the sword wherewith he had fought with Sukenari. Tadatsune took it up, and by the lantern-light discovered that from root to tip it had been beaten flat as with a stone and changed to something like a hammer.

NITTA.

M'm! Were you pretending all the time to cut with this? Noble and kind! Bowman without peer! Forgive my slanderous words, Sir Ninomiya.

NINOMIYA.

And I—forgive my words of insult, Sir Nitta. Tokimune and Sukenari, who had in you so kind a friend . . .

NITTA.

Youths who had in you a relative so true . . .

NINOMIYA.

Have borne nor fruit nor blossom in their lives.

NITTA.

But were, indeed, unfortunate.

The two could not restrain their tears, which wet their armour sleeves.

Sukenari, raising himself with ebbing strength :

" Sir Ninomiya, who, though now a relative, wert formerly unknown, and Sir Nitta, unrelated, your kindness I shall not forget through births and deaths five hundred. How fortunate is Sukenari to have been struck down by you. Behead me quickly, quickly, I implore."

Blinded by their tears, the two looked down unheeding, when from the direction of the General's camp the cry was heard :

" Soga-Tokimune broke in near the General's quarters ; but was apprehended by Gosho-Goromaru. The camp is safe ! "

Sukenari, hearing the cry :

" Hark ! Tokimune has been captured, has he not ? He will be anxious over Sukenari's end. Behead me quickly, and make him glad with news that his brother's hour was calm, I pray you, Lord Nitta. Great Amidha, I Thee adore ! " and, extending his head, he closed his eyes.

NITTA.

As by name you have called me, I will obey. Be now at peace !

Drawing his sword, he walked behind Sukenari ; and when again he raised it Sukenari's head fell before it.

From afar the bell of dawn struck eight. The notes of birds, the voices of men !

In the flowing robe of plover pattern they wrapped his head. In vain they tried to check their tears. Famed Mount Fuji for the Soga Brothers had become Mount Kaikei, mount of vengeance.

Though their bodies lie buried at its foot their fame is blown by the winds of Miho's pines through all the provinces ; and the story old is told to wake from slumber the people of this present age.

ACT V

Persons Represented :

SHOGUN YORITOMO.
SOGA-TOKIMUNE.
OE-HIROMOTO, *Officer.*
ASAHINA, *Son of Yoshinori-Tomoe.*
GOSHO-GOROMARU, *Keeper.*
KAJIWARA-KAGETAKA, *Partisan of Suketsune.*
KOSHIRO, *Half-brother of the Soga.*
CHICHIBU ⎫
HOJO   ⎬ *Daimyo.*
WADA   ⎪
OKAZAKI ⎭
OFFICERS AND RETAINERS.
MADAME SOGA.
TORA, *Widow of Sukenari.*
SHOSHO, *Wife of Tokimune.*

SCENE I. *The Shogun's Camp at Mount Fuji.*

THREE hundred and sixty times, in annual round, the sun moves on three thousand six hundred times, bearing to General Yoritomo enduring fame.

At the twelfth hour (end) of the twenty-eighth day of May, in the fourth year of Kenkyu (1193), the hunt ended. By the eighth hour (2 a.m.), in the morning of the twenty-ninth, Kajiwara-Kagetaka and Asahina-Yoshihide had both arrived to act as escort. All the company who were to accompany the General to Kamakura assembled ; and Yoritomo entered the Hall of Audience. Chichibu, Hojo, Wada, and Okazaki, equipped for the journey, were in attendance.

Oe-Hiromoto, chief officer of the Province of Inaba, brought in reports, written petitions and depositions, saying, " Here is the file of various petitions and reports from the guard covering the time of the hunt. Will you deign to examine them upon your return, or will you receive them this morning ? "

To his words the General replied : " Upon my return to Kamakura there will be questions a-many, piled up in my absence. Now will I settle the problems that are concerned with the hunt. You may read, Hiromoto."

So at his order he read, one after another :

The Report of Takeshita-Magoemon and Yasuda-Saburo concerning retainers who suffered on the twenty-eighth of May, when the Soga Brothers broke into the Camp.

One, Tairaku-Heimanojo : deeply wounded in the cheek.
    (*Note.*—The wound, being on the right cheek, must have been received in flight.)
One, Aikyo-Saburo : wounded in two places, back of left arm and right shoulder.
One, Anzai-Yashichiro : deeply wounded in the right side, entrails cut in pieces ; slight hope of recovery.
One, Usuki-Hachiro : head broken, killed on the spot.
One, Shinkai-Shiro : pierced in the left eye with the sharp point of a bamboo when he tried to escape, breaking the bamboo fence. Admitted it was his own fault.

As he would have continued, Yoritomo interrupted, exclaiming : " Stop, stop ! There's no sense in my hearing all this. Though the Soga Brothers were devils, there were but two. These were deservedly beaten. Though some had given wounds in return, it would not redound to their credit unless they had taken or slain the two brothers. 'Tis as though one should leave, for critics unborn, the shame of his general."

Tearing the paper in shreds, he threw it aside to be burned. His wrath was worthy a general.

Opening the next, Hiromoto continued :

" Nitta-Tadatsune, of the Province of Izu, respectfully presents salutation.

" Ninomiya-Yasukiyo, out of loyalty, disdained relation with Soga, divorcing his wife ; but in sympathy with Sukenari's feelings, assumed my name and o'ercame him. Happening upon them, I beheaded Sukenari. My merit upon this occasion was wholly due to Ninomiya's great valour. I beg that this be recognized.

" Signed and dated."

Yoritomo was greatly pleased : " He failed not, what time he came, a messenger urgent from Kamakura ; and now, again, repeatedly wonderful deeds ! No law putteth a curse on the families of those who have killed neither parents nor masters. Let him continue to live in peace with his wife, and freely take care of their mother. Have this reported in judgment.

" This is not the first time that Nitta-Tadatsune has done nobly. Such is his greatness of heart that he gives credit to others. Worthy of praise he is, truly. In Kamakura his reward shall be given. Next, next ! "

" Most humbly I crave your indulgence ! Of Fujisawa temple in charge, your lowly servant is priest : Zuia by name. At noon this day one called Omi-Kotoda came to the temple and bade me strike eight instead of nine by order of Kajiwara-Kagetaka. When I told him I could not, he bound me, with the other priests of the temple. He himself struck the bell, confusing the time in the region. Fearing your later rebuke, respectfully now I report.

" Signed and dated."

Then cried the General in anger :

" Not from this letter alone have I learned this outrageous

behaviour ; last night to my ears came of this the report of my agents in secret. Heard have I also that Noriyori's opponent in death was this same Kagetaka. In Kamakura he shall be strictly examined. Till then, unto Wada-Yoshinori in charge I commit him."

Before he had finished Kagetaka attempted an answer : "There were many reasons—— " But as he began to speak Asahina-Yoshihide threw him down with a twist.

" If you have something to say, say it later. From this day you are put in charge of my father. Much I regret that I could not thump your face when a guest at Hangae's breakfast."

Striking him four or five times, he handed him bound to a keeper.

Hiromoto, taking up another, continued :

" Kyo-Koshiro, half-brother of the Soga, most humbly reports : ' I had heard of Sukenari's plan, of Tokimune's. Though I often reasoned with them, they gave me no heed, at last putting the Hunting Field into confusion. I am filled with amaze at their scorn of governmental authority, and have taken in capture three of their evil confederates— their useless old mother, with Tora of Oiso and Shosho of Kehaizaka, two harlots.

" ' If you are pleased to take note that I was not of their party, and reward me accordingly, eternally I shall be grateful.' "

The General flushed with anger : " A despicable petition, that from Koshiro ! Insolently he judged our age incapable of just examination. He could not render help unto the brothers, but became a spy for Suketsune, worming his way into their mother's intentions. Of this is Yoritomo ignorant ? Beyond excuse ! Of him let an example be made. From the mother and the two women remove the ropes quickly. Officers of arrest, go and seize him."

As in obedience to his command they started, Asahina came forward : " Why officers of arrest ? Give me the order, I beg you."

YORITOMO.
Then go !

ASAHINA.
I am grateful !

He started, and then turned back : " If he protests, shall I end him and throw him away ? "

YORITOMO.
No, no ! I would question him. There's no sense in killing him, no sense.

Asahina agreed and departed, but again returned, saying : " Then may I break his bones, almost to killing ? "

YORITOMO.
Well, as to that, do as you please.

ASAHINA.
" Oh, thank you ! 'Twill be most amusing," and out he went, dancing with joy.

Yoritomo continued : " If the day grows late, we shall have to postpone till the morrow our return to Kamakura, and that would be hard for the guards by the way. I will hear the rest of the cases at Kamukura. Now bring in Tokimune ; with him I would speak for a moment."
Gosho-Goromaru, who had been waiting in the next room, came in, leading Tokimune by a rope, and as a prisoner placed him, saying with serious air : " When the brothers played havoc in the camp, this one broke in near the

General's quarters ; but, when the guard was in danger, I without difficulty caught him."

Tokimune boldly then challenged :

" Why thus these words, all unasked for ? There is something that I, Tokimune, would say. Give attention ! " And, looking up at the General, he saluted : " Your pardon, sir ; but I am sure you think it not wrong or barbaric that one born a bowman should seek the foe of his father. The reason for which I'm now called in question is my having burst into the General's camp, I suppose. I did not intend it ; but those whom I met by the way were all dummies, though they ran with good speed. None were there strong to withstand me. I thought there might be on night-duty in the camp of the General genuine warriors, and, wishing to die by the hand of those who had merit, I forcibly entered. The officers all were as ghosts, warriors of unreal merit.

" When, at the General's coming, the voice of young Ichihoshi protesting : ' Though the Soga Brothers were demons, it were a shame on the name—Minamoto—for you to lift hand against them ; let me, a commoner, do it ' —when, as I say, these words reached my ears, I was moved by the grace of the speaker, by wisdom worthy Otomo's eldest, and wished to die by his hand. Just at the moment this Goromaru, shielding his head with a mantle, sprang forth, crying, ' I've caught you ! ' As the dress of his hair had the feel of a boy's, I said in my mind, ' 'Tis indeed Ichihoshi,' and gladly submitted to binding. Now I regret it a thousand times over. Had I known it was you, I'd have kicked you to death. But now there's no use in complaining. Kindly behead me at once," he said coolly.

Goromaru, hearing his words : " What ! Medicine to quicken the birth of a baby that's born ! Brag not, you boaster ! When by my hand you were captured, you struggled to free yourself, mightily barking with loud, roaring voice ; yet, holding you helpless, I roped you. Have you forgotten ? Offer a prayer as a boast," he insulted.

Tokimune, with laughter :
" The rope with which I allowed myself to be bound you say that you put on by main strength ! Your mouth is bigger than all the rest of your body. I must die in any case, and it may be a foolish contention ; but I cannot willingly let the General believe that Tokimune would lie, or have the Princes condemn me. In proof that I was not bound by your strength, behold ! " And, rousing to action each nerve and sinew, he squared his shoulders with a yell, while the rope on his body and arms burst asunder more easily than rush slashed by a sturdy youngster of three. Springing upon Goromaru, he knocked him down and sat upon him, saying :
" Now, if it's true that you caught me last night, rope me again in the presence of these." With this he pressed Goromaru's backbone so hard with his knees that the fellow seemed flat as a pancake, unable to speak, able only to weep tears like rain, like oil that is pressed from the oil-press.

Just then Asahina ran in, holding Koshiro by the neck like a kitten, and put him down near the Shogun.

Yoritomo, looking upon him, declared :
" A villain indeed to turn from your mother and brothers and side with the foe. As Suketsune's no more of this world, follow him on to the next and there serve him. Let him go, I dismiss him ! "

But at the words Tokimune, bowing low :
" Just, O Lord, is your judgment, and Sukenari, who has passed on ahead, will surely be grateful ; yet is this fellow a brother, though not a son of our father ; and I cannot in silence inhuman see him condemned to

destruction. Spare, I beseech you, his life," he said with unfaltering firmness.

YORITOMO.

For Tokimune's sake I spare you. Shave his head and send him forth !

" I will," said Asahina ; " but a razor would be disgraced, as would a sword, upon you. Suffer, instead, Yoshihide's hand-blade," and, winding his hand in Koshiro's hair, he gave a quick jerk.

KOSHIRO.

Ouch ! ouch !

ASAHINA.

Oh, it must indeed hurt you ! One pull is worth a mass said by a thousand priests. A second pull makes one the butt of ten thousand in laughter. I am plucking the feathers of a bird ; I am plucking the petals of poppies. There now, bald-head ! Sun-baked ! Bowl-pate ! You, Temple-jack ! " And with laughter he drove him forth.

Tokimune, picking up Goromaru, threw him off some twenty feet, saying : " I have no more to say, no further business in this world. Come now and bind me."

As he waited, with arms behind him, servants, rope in hand, drew near.

" Wait ! " ordered Yoritomo. " Brothers, without peer in Nihon, though I would save the one, he will not save himself, e'en at my bidding, since his senior, Sukenari, has passed on before. What joy was mine when I struck off the head of Shoji-no-Osada, my father Yoshitomo's foe ! His head was worth to me far more than hundreds—yea, than thousands slain from out the Taira Clan. This day's joy for them would make all future days seem tasteless.

And we must uphold the laws of the land. Take him to
Hawk Hill, and there let him leave this life. Yet is he a
match for thousands. That servants should bind him
would dim, indeed, the lustre of his warrior name. I,
Yoritomo, I myself will bind him."

And the General himself jumped down, and, drawing
from his armour the tasselled crimson cord, said :

" In Yoritomo's right hand are the thirty-three provinces
of the west, and in his left hand are the thirty-three
provinces of the east ; with the might of these sixty odd
provinces I put rope upon you. Be not offended ! "

Before his voice had ceased, Tokimune burst into tears,
crying loudly : " Princes and Nobles, high and low, gathered
here, if Tokimune, a creature more worthless than a drop
in the ocean, to which our great main island may be compared, had not taken vengeance on his father's foe, how could
he now hear these gracious words, and suffer binding from
Japan's great General, from Yoritomo's hand ? How glad
the holy spirit of Kawasu, my father ! How glad my brother,
who has passed on before ! Alas ! I would that I again
could be born to die in battle before my General's steed for
this his kindness ! Buddha Triune, have mercy upon me ! "

He wept, and all the warriors gathered there were moved
to tears. Even Asahina, who could outwit the devil, cried :
" I envy you, Tokimune ! Great is your fortune ! Praised
be our mighty lord ! "

He sobbed and sobbed ; joy mingled with his tears most
naturally.

Wada, Chichibu, Chiba, and Kazusa : " All who here
have spirits true, put hands unto the rope and prove your
nobleness ! The General is about to start ! "

At the noise of their shouting, Tora and Shosho, who
were waiting by the gate, ran in with the aged mother and
prostrated themselves before the General. They clung to
Tokimune, crying for joy.

Outside the gate the horses neighed. The gate of the camp opened. It was daylight's seventh hour (4 a.m.). To Kamakura, in its seven valleys, Yoritomo returned in safety.

> The twelve hours of that day !
> The twelve hours of that day !
> The twelve hours of that day !
> The twelve hours of that day !

Those hours increase to years, a hundred, yea, a thousand ; and the deathless might of the Minamoto House will surely keep the land safe for its people.

CHAPTER XI

KABUKI

DURING the period of the Ashikaga Shogunate (1338-1573), Kyoto was the centre of luxury and effeminate culture among the wealthy, and of increasingly licentious revelry among high and low alike. The first half of this era, known as the Muromachi Period (1338-1443), was characterized by an influx of Chinese influence, an increase of education among the priesthood, and of such gentle arts as *Cha-no-yu* (tea ceremony), *Ko-awase* (incense judging), and *Ikebana* (flower arrangement), among the leisured. *Noh*, also, during this period was brought to its perfection and exercised a refining influence over the military class in particular. None of these apparently noble arts, however, was able to check the social evils which grew up, especially during the later years of that Shogunate (1444-1573), in part because of the strict isolation of the sexes demanded by Buddhist ethics and Buddhism's failure to bring matters of sex under the ennobling sanctions of religion.

While the upper classes found their recognized amusements in cultured ways on the one hand, and their secret delights in the immoral practices of exclusively male society upon the other, the great mass of the people were entertaining themselves upon the dry river-beds or in vacant lots within the city with popular *Dengaku*, *Sarugaku*, and other sports of rude promiscuity, wherein not infrequently men of rank also found relaxation.

Into the arena of popular sport, somewhere about the end of the sixteenth century, when England's Shakespeare was in his prime, came a dancing-girl, known to us as *Okuni* of *Izumo*. She seems to have been the daughter of an iron-worker, and a skilled *Maiko* in the service of the shrine at Izumo, which, though Shinto, was at the time in the charge of a Buddhist priest. Her presence in Kyoto is traditionally explained by the supposition that she may have been on a tour seeking contributions for the shrine. However that may have been, she met with such welcome in Kyoto that she remained, to be identified with a new dramatic movement rising from the midst of the common people.

Okuni's *Kagura* seems to have been a form of Buddhist *nembutsu*, a dance of worship in praise of Amida ; but her reception on the Kyoto river-beds may well have been due more to her physical beauty and grace of movement than to any appeal in the interests of religion. Here, in any case, about 1596, she was seen by Sanzaburo, who from Nagoya had been sent by his family to be trained for the priesthood in the Kennin Temple, one of the then famous Five Temples, in Kyoto.

This youth of a military family had no fondness for the austerities of religion, but led a life of social freedom, and was popularly known for excellence in social arts, including the *Kyogen* of *Noh*. He was attracted by Okuni, but found her graceful dancing too restrained to satisfy his taste. Apparently without difficulty, he influenced her to greater abandon, and taught her to dance the popular songs of the day to music of his own composition. This was *Kabuki*, a slang designation of the time later to be dignified by the use of written characters signifying the art of song and dance.

Two trained players thus broke from the bonds of dramatic custom, and, seizing upon material nearest to the popular mind, made another beginning which is now to be traced through developing forms unto the modern legitimate drama of Japan.

A few of Okuni's *Kagura* are extant, and the following *Tenshi Wago Mae* (Dance of Heaven and Earth Affinity)

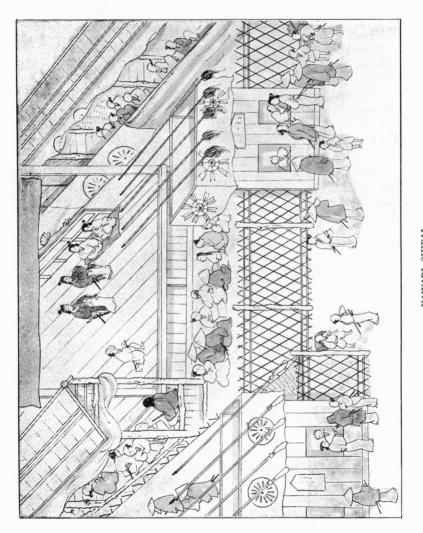

KAWARI SHIBAI

The Birthplace of Kabuki

is significant in its blending of Buddhist repression with
nature myths from Shinto, capable of most spiritual as well
as most carnal interpretation. Interpreted spiritually, we
cannot but be impressed with the beauty of its conception ;
but in an historic study we need to remind ourselves that
the carnal interpretation was most apparent in old Japan,
where, under Buddhist influence, all love meant passion
of illusion.

HEAVEN AND EARTH AFFINITY

With great endeavour
Expending from the heart,
No god soever
The work that I have finished
Can fail to mark as worthy.

The god of power
Enshrines within my being :
My very breathings,
That come and go, are shrines,
The outer and the inner.

With sounds of music
Ringing, I splash the water
So clear and shining,
Over my shoulders pouring,
Over my shoulders pouring.

Ocean eternal !
Drops from the creative spear
Had there been none,
I should not have been born—
Born to a life of illusion.

If from the spear-point
Dew-drops in falling had not
Hardened to mountains,
Naught would there be like to love,
Vanity all and illusion.

T

Like to the falling
Drops from the spear-point divine,
Newly created,
Man's life becomes but a dew,
Dew that a breath drieth up.

Gone are the worries,
Troubles of olden days,
All, all forgotten ;
While in their place flows great joy,
Joy that o'erwhelms with its bounty.

Kabuki—The Art of Song and Dance—was first called *Onna Kabuki*, Okuni being a woman (*onna*) ; although, as her religious chants gave place to popular folk-songs, she wore the garments of men and acted the part of one who frequented tea-houses and sported with their inmates. She soon gathered about her a group of players, women, children, and men in the garb of women, Sanzaburo himself presenting *Kyogen* as interludes.

Titles only remain of songs which might illustrate this transitional period more fully than do the *Kagura*. One was the *Crow Dance*, of which we know nothing beyond the fact that wings were worn in its presentation. Another was the *Dance of Married Intimacy*, also called the *Young Girl Dance* ; and this was probably of a nature that prevented its preservation in writing.

Popular *Sarugaku*, left behind as an undeveloped remnant by *Noh*, formed the basis of the comic interludes presented by Sanzaburo ; and in illustration of these may be mentioned *Saruwaka Daimyo* and *Hanagasa Odori*, the latter being played by lads of twelve or thirteen years of age, who, according to old pictures, wore wide-brimmed hats of straw decorated with artificial cherry-blossoms and bound under the chin with red ribbons.

In an old book of Kabuki pictures there are fragments of song which illustrate the better type of those which

followed the *nembutsu*. In one instance an actor, possibly
Sanzaburo, tells Okuni that he will sing a *Joruri-like* song,
evidently meaning a sentimental love-song as unlike the
nembutsu and the battle chants of the *Monogatari*.

> Our love is troubled,
> As the moon by clouds,
> Or flowers by winds that blow.
> To win my way of love is hard
> As passing mountain pathways for mounted horsemen.
> In some distant village,
> Beyond the mountains,
> Far from the world of prying folk,
> In secret I would love.
> As rhythm to all music,
> So is my love :
> At eve I play the entertaining flute,
> At midnight sing ;
> Upon the flageolet at dawn
> I voice my love.
> Whene'er I waking leave thy side,
> I long again for thee ;
> And when I see the blossoms droop
> Beneath the rains of spring,
> I would not have you fade like them—
> A maid unwed.

By 1603–1604 Okuni had reached the height of her
popularity, and had established stages in various parts of
the city. Her plays were addressed primarily to the
common people ; but she soon attracted the attention of
the nobility, and was invited to play at the residence of the
Shogun. There is record of at least one invitation to play
before the Imperial Court in 1603–1604.

Such success led to imitation, and the number of *Kabuki*
playhouses multiplied; but, in spite of occasional signs
of aristocratic favour, *Kabuki* remained essentially an
entertainment of the common people—in reality a protest
against social as well as dramatic conventions. Those who

devoted themselves to its interests were men without honourable employment and women from the prostitute quarters. Gross immorality and unbridled licentiousness made it a social danger; and as early as 1608 official order confined it to the outskirts of the cities. In 1629 *Onna Kabuki* was strictly prohibited, avowedly because of its immoral influence, possibly because of its being also a hotbed of dangerous thought and popular freedom.

The doom of *Onna Kabuki* seems to have been foreseen by some, for in 1617 Dansuke, who had been conducting a company of women, founded the first company composed of men-players only. Men, especially young men, had played in *Onna Kabuki*; and it probably was not difficult to build up a company from these and from men about town, as the downfall of the Ashikaga Shogunate had left many of its natural supporters without employment. As women were forbidden the stage, young men held a monopoly of the female parts; and for this reason the new companies and their plays were known as *Wakashu Kabuki*.

To compensate for the absence of women upon the stage, greater attention was given to matters of costume and scenery; and the plays appear to have retained their full measure of popular favour. The object of official prohibition, in so far as it had to do with public morality, however, was not attained, for grosser forms of prostitution became increasingly prevalent. Official disapproval of *Kabuki*, together with the generally recognized immorality of the *Kabuki* stage, was probably a contributing cause of the renewed popularity accorded *Joruri*, which was at the time enriching its presentation with the use of dolls in *Ayatsuri*. Here also may be found some explanation of the fact that Chikamatsu, who had begun to write for *Kabuki*, turned his talent exclusively to the needs of the *Ayatsuri* stage, which owes much of its abiding importance to the genius of his compositions.

In 1644, when *Wakashu Kabuki* was most popular, official prohibition was renewed to stop the employment and training of young boys, which, it was charged, was undermining the morals of the warrior class; and in 1652 this second type of *Kabuki* was banned.

Profiting not a little from the example and success of the *Ayatsuri* stage, *Kabuki* refused to be destroyed. In spite of restrictions—perhaps in part because of them—it had made for itself a place in the social life of the people which demanded satisfaction. Older men continued the *Kabuki* tradition of freedom; and there developed the *Yara* (adult male) *Kabuki*, which enriched its presentations with music and the inclusion of better dramatic material to compensate for the relative absence of debasing elements.

Maintaining its dramatic freedom, *Kabuki* developed its art eclectically from *Kagura*, *Noh*, *Kyogen*, and *Ayatsuri*, borrowing, particularly from the latter, material which it worked over into form more suited for presentation by living actors. Upon much of this material, however, the stamp of *Ayatsuri* is indelibly fixed, as may be noted in the retention of the *takemoto*, or reader, for certain passages which seem to us quite as well adapted for the dramatic actor. In the material thus brought into use upon the *Kabuki* stage four distinct classes may be discerned. There are Historical Plays (*Jidai Mono*), such as are found in *Joruri* and *Ayatsuri*, in which historic characters and a thread of fact serve to sustain a display of bravery and devotion vicariously satisfying and of inspirational value; Plays of Common Life (*Sewa Mono*), foreshadowed in *Genzai Mono Noh*; Plays of Unrestrained Action (*Aragoto*), closely associated with the great Ichikawa family and its style, which was in every particular a skilful use of exaggeration; and Pantomimic Plays (*Shosagoto*), which owed more to early dance traditions in *Kagura* and *Noh* than to any literary antecedent.

In all earlier forms of the Japanese drama the liturgic requirement, on the one hand, or the will of the author, upon the other, governed the stage. Now, for the first time, the actor is seen taking a position of control; and this in a measure accounts for the slight attention given to originality in the material of *Kabuki*. Not composition but presentation was the problem of the *Kabuki* stage. With the development of the *Yara Kabuki* actors began, more generally than before, to train themselves for specific parts. In the earlier *Kabuki* men had often played the part of women; but now, when it had become necessary that they should do so upon all occasions, a professional class of womenfolk (*onnagata*) grew into prominence. Attention to technique and pride in accomplishment secured marked results; and individual actors established family claims to certain rôles. Dramatic skill of a high order took the place of personal grace and of sex appeal upon the *Kabuki* stage. Books by the series have been written concerning the dynasties of various dramatic families which from the time of the Genroku Age contributed to the development of *Kabuki*; and Sakata-Tojuro of Kyoto and Ichikawa-Danjuro of Tokyo are still names with which to conjure.

Together with its relative freedom *Kabuki* developed its own conventions adapted from earlier forms, and applicable to manner of staging and action rather than to nature of material. The Flower-way (*Hanamichi*), along which the actor approaches the stage through the midst of the theatre audience, may be taken as an example. It is merely an adaptation of the conventional approach to the *Noh* stage; but it is significant in that it connotes a much closer contact between audience and actor. Its principal advantages are self-evident, and it marks the *Kabuki* for what it is—a play of the people for the people.

With the new emphasis upon actor rather than author there came into being a new type of criticism; and 1656 is mentioned by Ibara as the probable date of the first published article of dramatic criticism. From mere expressions of personal opinion these grew into studied declarations of judgment, and form a body of literature known as Chronicles of Fame (*Hyobanki*), which should be studied intensively for a more detailed account of the People's Theatre.

Following the Genroku Period (1688–1703), for a century and a half the Japanese drama shows no development. The time was a time of general quiescence, of rest, without inspiration from the past or hope for the future; and it was not until the middle of the nineteenth century, when a member of the famous Ichikawa family brought *Sewa Mono* again into prominence, that its vitality became evident.

The history of *Kabuki* is worthy of more careful investigation, for in its development are found elements of all preceding forms of the Japanese drama, and, in spite of serious abuses, those essentials of popular co-operation without which no truly national drama can evolve. *Kagura*, with its intimate social contacts, became stereotyped in the liturgy of Shinto; *Noh* and *Kyogen*, with their great dramatic possibilities, were refined to death; *Kabuki* alone, without patronage and amid vulgarity, wrought out a form of drama so generally satisfactory that one can but wonder what might have been its achievement had it received encouragement in freedom and guidance in art. The dramatic instinct lives in the Japanese people; and there is reason to hope for its future expression if it can conserve the riches of its past achievements and avoid the blight of modern emphasis upon things which are seen and are therefore temporal.

CHAPTER XII

SHINJU KAMIYA-JIHEI [1]

THE DEATH-LOVE OF KAMIYA-JIHEI

---

[1] A *Kabuki*, by an unknown author of the early nineteenth century, based upon a *Joruri* by Chikamatsu-Hangae, 1770.

Persons Represented :

JIHEI, *a Kamiya or Paper-merchant.*

MAGOEMON, *Jihei's Elder Brother, a Flour-merchant.*

GOZAEMON, *Jihei's Father-in-law.*

KANTARO, *Jihei's Little Boy.*

SANGORO, *Jihei's Apprentice.*

TAHEI, *a Wholesale Paper-merchant.*

SAIBEI, *Master of Kinokuniya, a House of Entertainment.*

DENKAI ⎱
ZENROKU ⎰ *Serviceable Villains.*

VILLAGER.

KOHARU, *an Inmate of Kinokuniya, with whom Jihei is infatuated.*

O-SAN, *Jihei's Wife.*

O-SUE, *Jihei's Little Girl.*

TAKEMOTO, *the Reader of Joruri Parts.*

ACT I

SCENE I. *Before the House of Jihei, the Paper-merchant.*

(*A street across the front of the stage is backed by an eighteen-foot house-front in two sections. On the left is a room with sliding doors, from which a curtained doorway leads to an inner room. A letter-holder, with letters from various provinces, and a case of account-books hang upon the grey wall. On the right is an unfloored store with a street-entrance. From the rear a doorway with yellow-brown curtains leads to the garden. This room is lined with shelves, which are surmounted by a sign of the business and loaded with various kinds of paper. A high window, over the street-entrance, shows a dark blue curtain having the sign of a paper-merchant upon it. The entire place is furnished like that of a Temma (Osaka) paper-merchant.*)

(*The scene opens to the sound of* Kagura *music.*)

(SANGORO, *dressed in a striped jacket with a dark blue apprentice apron, is playing dolls with* KANTARO *and* O-SUE. *In the box beside him are several dolls and toys.* KANTARO *is playing with a doll, and* O-SUE *has a paper crane.*)

SANGORO.

Here, you big boy, stop snarling ! I'll tell the story of the Willow-woman and the Ridge-pole of Sanju-san-gen-do,[1] which I saw at the puppet-show a little while ago, and I'll make the dolls act.

---

[1] *Sanju-san-gen-do*, a noted temple-hall in Kyoto, housing 33,000 images.

Give ear, give ear, all ye people! That which we are about to present is the scene at the home of Heitaro in the story of the Ridge-pole of Sanju-san-gen-do. It begins this way :

> (*He beats with wooden clappers and imitates with his mouth the sound of the samisen (three-stringed guitar*).)

There are famous places at Wakanoura : First, there is Gongen Temple ; second, Tamatsu Island ; third, the overhanging pine ; fourth, Shiogama's shore ; Yoi, Yoi, Yoiyasa !

> (*As he tells the story, moving the dolls about, a villager, in very ordinary dress, enters the store from the lower right.*)

VILLAGER (*in the doorway*).
Hey, I beg your pardon! Beg pardon!

> (*He calls loudly, while* SANGARO *continues to recite* Joruri *and play with the dolls.*)

VILLAGER (*loudly*).
I say, excuse me!

SANGORO (*in surprise*).
Eh! Who are you? You frightened me.

VILLAGER.
Not much were you frightened. I've been calling some time. You're a great boy, you are!

SANGORO.
Well, what do you want?

VILLAGER.

Give me fifty sheets of soft paper and two rolls of writing-paper.

SANGORO.

Oh, what a bother you are !

VILLAGER.

I never !   Do you call a customer a bother ?

SANGORO.

I had come to the most important part of the lumbermen's chant as they hauled the willow-woman willow.   Oh, bother !

> (*Still complaining, he brings from the shelves the soft paper and the rolls of writing-paper.*)

There, the paper is 48 mon ; the writing-paper, 24 mon.[1]

VILLAGER.

Well, well !   48 mon and 24 mon make 72 mon in all. Thanks, am sorry to have troubled you.

SANGORO.

From the first, of course, you're a bother.

> (*He sings, and the* VILLAGER *goes out to the right.*)

SANGORO.

There, now I'll continue the story.   Well, I declare, little girl, you're a very good little girl.   You have been making paper cranes quietly ; you're truly a nice little girl.   If you have finished the cranes, I will stretch a string and show you a crane in the air.

[1] *Mon*, twentieth of a cent.

O-SUE.

When I have finished folding this crane, please show me a play with Sannozuke [1] in it.

SANGORO.

If it's a play, I'll play any play you want.

KANTARO.

Oh, come, hurry up ! I want to see.

SANGORO.

All right ; I will, I will.

(*He takes up the dolls and gets ready to perform.*)

Here, now, the story goes on.

(*Using his mouth for a samisen, he makes the dolls perform.*)

They carry Mother Willow to the city. Yoi, Yoi, Yoi-yasa !

(*He recites the* Joruri *and manipulates the dolls. Meanwhile from the right* DENKAI, *a chanter of street-songs, enters in ragged dress with two wooden fish-gongs in his hands. Behind him comes* ZENROKU, *dressed like a samisen-player, tucking his skirt up behind and wrapping his cheeks in a towel.*)

DENKAI.

Eternally Living One, I worship Thee ! Hullo, everybody ! Just listen to mock Buddhist scripture.

ZENROKU.

Noko, noko, sai sai !

(ZENROKU *plays the samisen and* DENKAI *beats the gongs.*)

[1] *Sannozuke*: a doll character.

SANGORO.

Pass on, pass on !

DENKAI.

Say, comrade, he says " Pass on ! "

ZENROKU.

If he says " Pass," [1] let's pass in !

DENKAI.

Let's pass in !   Pass in !

(*The two pass through to the room at the left and sit down.*)

SANGORO.

Here, you dirty, ragged things, where are you going ?

DENKAI.

Look here, boy ; we came in because you invited us to come in.   Oh ! I see ; you want to have me recite the mock scriptures in the house.

ZENROKU.

That must be it !   That must be it !   If you want, we will do so here.   Say, priest, be careful and chant with a clear, high voice.

DENKAI.

Sure !   I   understand.   Ahem !   This   is   a   scripture which is current about town, but particularly in the gay quarters.   The latest one begins, the latest one begins——

(ZENROKU *takes up his samisen, and* DENKAI *beats the gongs.*)

[1] *Tori* may according to context be Pass on or in.

Dear, dear, dear!

Eternally Living One, I worship Thee; and call upon the Dora Nyorai![1] Dear, dear, dear! Now, all listen well!

With Koharu of Shinchi, in bloom like the bloom of the sea, poor Jihei, the paper-merchant, has fallen in love. His infatuation, like expensive thick Sugiwara paper,[2] became so great that at the year's end he asked postponement of accounts, and put his bills aside like paper hankies, tossing his customers here and there like cheapest toilet-paper.[3] The clothing of his family is sold; and he no longer cares for his wife, who carries the odour of pickles, but secretly, summer and winter alike, visits Koharu.

ZENROKU.

Noko, noko, sai sai; nora sai sai![4]

DENKAI.

The man is soaked through and through like wet paper, wild over a harlot; and Hokaru is like dark-blue Tosa paper,[5] while his wife is like very good but useless Chinese paper. This is the gossip in Temma.

SANGORO.

Bah! What are you saying? Are you slandering my master, Jihei, just because someone asked you to do it? What a racket! Shut up!

DENKAI.

Don't say, " Shut up," you young rascal. If you didn't want us to make a noise, why did you ask us to come in?

---

[1] *Dora Nyorai* : name of a fictitious deity.
[2] Thick paper for wrapping gifts or for formal letters.
[3] The passage is full of language drawn from the paper-market.
[4] A meaningless mockery of Buddhist chanting.
[5] Strong.

ZENROKU.

Right you are! Right you are! As for this story, no one has asked us to tell it. 'Tis the common talk of the hour.

DENKAI.

The master of this shop may not be the only Jihei in town. I don't know as the story is of this Jihei or not. It is a mock scripture, indeed.

ZENROKU.

This is our business ; we get our living by chanting and by getting paid for it.

DENKAI.

The authorities have not forbidden the chanting the words of this tale, or issued rules in prohibition.

ZENROKU.

Right you are! Right you are! And we are not going until we've had money for chanting, for holding forth as we have.

Let's smoke a bit, till we see the master or mistress and get some money out of them.

DENKAI.

That's good, that's good! Here, boy, hand us the tobacco-tray. I'm thirsty ; bring us tea.

SANGORO.

That's nothing to me. Do as you darn please!

(ZENROKU *and* DENKAI *smoke. Music.* TAHEI, *in best dress of the middle class, enters and goes directly into the shop.*)

U

TAHEI.

Jihei, are you in ? I want my money ! This worthless stuff I don't want. I want to be paid in real, true money.

SANGORO.

Sakes alive, what a day ! First there comes a peddling priest with fool scriptures, speaking ill of my master ; and here's a fellow who roars for the payment of money. Who in the world are you?

TAKEI.

Here, know-nothing youngster, if Jihei is in, go tell him that Mr. Tahei is here.

SANGORO.

I won't. If you have business, tell my highness your story in detail ; and, as I think best, I will take the trouble to inform him.

TAHEI.

What a provoking kid ! The business for which Mr. Tahei is here is as follows : The twenty dollars I received from Jihei the other day were no good. To-day, when I gave them to a wholesale dealer in settlement of an account, the counterfeit was discovered. Even I was under suspicion ! He's indeed a despicable fellow to pay me in counterfeit coin—me who took pity upon him when he was refused admission to Koharu because he had not the fee, and advanced him twenty dollars. Go and tell him to pay me the money at once.

SANGORO.

Don't be so big with your gab. There are guests since morning ; master and mistress are in conversation with them. Mr. Sangoro is in charge. Many strange, foolish

fellows have come and are saying the stupidest things. I'll see
that every one of you gets a good scolding. You just wait.

(*So saying, he goes into the house with* O-SUE *and*
KANTARO. TAHEI, *with a look of understanding,
joins* DENKAI *and* ZENROKU *in smoking. Music.*
SAIBEI *of the Kinokuniya, dressed as the keeper of
a tea-house, approaches the stage along the raised
walk from the rear of the theatre.*)

SAIBEI (*while still on the walk*).
I wish I could find Mr. Tahei.

(*He comes to the house and sees* TAHEI.)

Oh, Tahei, here you are! I've been hunting for you
everywhere.

TAHEI.
You have been hunting for me! What do you want?

SAIBEI.
What do I want! How absurd! and with such an
innocent air! Here, I return your twenty dollars. How
dared you entice Koharu to run away with you? Come,
make your apologies later, but first of all bring back the
girl whom you've hidden away.

TAHEI.
Boo! Saibei, go, wash your face! Wake up, and stop
talking nonsense. "You've hidden Koharu away; you
have made her elope." What in the world are you talking
about?

SAIBEI.
What am I talking about? You brazen-faced idiot!
Don't stop to argue, but bring back Koharu, whom you
have buried away.

TAHEI.

Look here, you ask me to bring Koharu back, as if I had hidden her away. Have you any evidence ?

SAIBEI.

Should I be talking without evidence ? Of course, I have proof.

TAHEI.

How very interesting ! Suppose you let me see it.

SAIBEI.

Certainly, you shall see it. This letter, left from her hand, is proof, good and certain.

(*Takes a paper from his breast.*)

Look at this ! Just read it.

(*He throws it at* TAHEI.)

TAHEI (*picking it up*).

What ! Koharu's ? He, he, he ! This will touch Jihei's heart. I will read it aloud. (*He opens the letter.*)
" In shame I write this farewell. You have treated me with great kindness, even until now ; but to save my lover's name I must run away."

DENKAI.

What a disgusting street drab !

ZENROKU.

After that, what did she write ?

TAHEI.

Wait, wait ! What's this ? " That I have been deeply in love with the paper-merchant Jihei until now——— "

DENKAI.

Well, well! It's just as we said——

TAHEI.

"That I have been deeply in love with the paper-merchant Jihei until now is not true." What's that, what's that?

DENKAI AND ZENROKU.

What's that, what's that?

TAHEI.

Keep quiet and listen. Really, I am in love with Mr. Tahei only.

DENKAI AND ZENROKU.

What's that, what's that?

TAHEI.

"The reason I treated him coldly was that I wanted him to strengthen his purpose and redeem me that we might become true man and wife, and live united for ever. For that reason only I treated him coldly."
Well, well! So the wind blows from that quarter!

DENKAI.

You begin to appear quite a lady-killer, Mr. Tahei.

ZENROKU.

Koharu's sincerity is apparent. Her story, indeed, seems quite plausible.

DENKAI.

I am eager to hear the rest; read on quickly.

DENKAI AND ZENROKU.

Let's hear it, let's hear it !

> (*They talk loudly. Drawing aside the curtain in the doorway to the inner room,* JIHEI *and* MAGOEMON *appear in ordinary house dress. Frowning, they overhear the conversation.* TAHEI, *with an expression of delight, continues to read.*)

TAHEI.

Oh, don't hurry me ! Somehow my heart goes pita-pat. I'm not used to this ; it seems so quite sudden ! Eh, what ? " All that I've ever said to paper-man Ji was a lie. My heart's desire is to marry Tahei. Mr. Tahei has given you twenty dollars in pledge ; but you are not at all pleased ; and I'm afraid that you won't let me marry him in the end."

Why ! Why should I not marry you ? See if I don't marry you. Marry you ! My darling !

" I am tired of myself, and have made up my mind to kill myself alone."

What, what ! Then, for love of me you plan to kill yourself ? It may be, it may be. How's this ?

" Cruel, cruel Tahei ! Will you redeem me to freedom, indeed ; or are you only deceiving me ? "

Why should I deceive you ? Why should I ? Oh, darling ! My darling !

" I cannot find rest in my heart ; and so I shall run away to a place of which Mr. Tahei knows, and there hide myself for a while."

Darling ! Darling ! What ?

" If I cannot have my desire, please keep this letter of farewell, and for me, I pray you, offer a prayer. Buddha of Mercy, I adore ! I adore ! "

Oh, darling ! My darling !

TAKEMOTO.

> " My dear one ! My dear one ! "
> In passion he cries,
> While sobs shake his being,
> And tears from his eyes
> Up-well, such as never since boyhood,
> Now twenty years passed,
> From depths have arisen.

DENKAI.

Naturally enough !

DENKAI AND ZENROKU.

No wonder, no wonder !

TAKEMOTO.

> In sympathy near him
> The friendly souls weep.
> Now drops from the sleeve
> Of his garment, all shaken
> By bodily anguish,
> A letter, which slyly
> Magoemon, seeing,
> Unnoticed picks up.

(TAHEI *drops a letter from his sleeve.* MAGOEMON *beckons to* SANGORO *and whispers in his ear.* SAN- GORO *understands and picks up the fallen letter. He hands it to* MAGOEMON *and withdraws to the inner room.*)

TAHEI.

Oh ! Saibei, since reading Koharu's words, I've grown hysterical. Oh, oh, oh, oh !

Say, Denkai, it was all for this that you took the trouble recently, wasn't it ?

DENKAI.

Why, of course, of course ! If you delay, she will die. Make haste at once to redeem her.

ZENROKU.

In her letter she mentioned " a place you know." Do you understand ?

DENKAI AND ZENROKU.

Where is it ?

TAHEI.

The place I know ? Until now I've been entirely at sea in my love for her. " The place we know ! "
I haven't the slightest idea, Saibei.

SAIBEI.

No, you can't slip out of it like that. This letter is clear proof. Come, I will take you to the Government office ; and we will inquire into the whereabouts of the hole in which you have hidden her.

TAHEI.

Oh, wait a bit ! Wait a bit ! It's quite natural for you to think thus. Let me see : " The place I know " ? Oh, Kinoi ! Come, Denkai and Zenroku ; come with me !

DENKAI. Let us make haste, for till we save Koharu——

ZENROKU.

We shall not feel at ease.

DENKAI AND ZENROKU.

Let us go !

(*As the three start out* MAGOEMON *enters from the inner room.*)

MAGOEMON.

Wait, Tahei ! I want you two fellows also.

THE THREE.

What ! Want us ?

MAGOEMON.

Yes, there's a question I want to ask you.   Stand aside and answer me.

TAHEI. Ha !

> (*The three look one at another and withdraw to the right.* MAGOEMON *crosses calmly and sits down.*)

MAGOEMON.

Here, Shaved Pate ; your name is Denkai, isn't it ?

DENKAI.

Well, what's wrong with that ?

MAGOEMON.

It was you who pretended to be a priest at the tea-house in Kiyomizu [1] the other day, wasn't it ?

DENKAI.

Eh ?

MAGOEMON.

You're a reprobate in cahoots [2] with Tahei.

DENKAI.

No, no ! I haven't even seen any Tahei or Tarobei.[3]

---

[1] *Kiyomizu* : famous temple and garden in Kyoto.
[2] Literally, in the same hole.
[3] A second possible reading of the same written word, hence further proof of his ignorance of the man intended.

MAGOEMON.

That Tahei, whom you have never seen, just said : " Say, Denkai, it was all for this that you took the trouble." And you replied, " Why, of course, of course ! If you delay, she will die. Make haste at once to redeem her."

DENKAI AND TAHEI.
What !

MAGOEMON.
Why did you say that ?

THE TWO.
Why, because——

MAGOEMON.
Because what ?
I have something else to show you.

(He takes out the letter and, opening it, reads.)

" I just want to let you know that the ten ryo [1] you gave me at the tea-house the other day has already been swallowed up in recent gambling. If your scheme of the promissory note [2] works out well at Jihei's store to-day I wish you would again lend me ten ryo. It seems better to write

---

[1] *Ryo* : about the value of 100 sen, or a Japanese dollar.

[2] In the original *Joruri*, from which this *Kabuki* was taken, Saibei, Koharu's master, would not allow her to go out with Jihei because he could not pay ; but Koharu, on the other hand, refused to go with Tahei. Therefore Denkai, in the guise of a priest acting for Tahei, asked Koharu to go with him as an entertainer. This she consented to do, feeling safe with a priest. At the tea-house, however, she met Jihei, and stayed with him, avoiding Tahei. Thus her master found her, and demanded payment from Jihei. As he had no money, he was forced to borrow from Denkai, and signed a note, which was unaddressed, since the supposed priest refused to give his name. Later Tahei wrote in his own name as payee, and presented the note to Jihei for payment. Jihei paid the twenty ryo due on the note to Tahei, who was here just come, declaring that the payment was in counterfeit coin.

than to ask you bluntly to your face.—Mr. Tahei, from Denkai."

There ! Do you still insist upon your innocence ?

THE TWO.

Well, that——

MAGOEMON.

Well, what ?

THE TWO.

Well——

THE THREE.

Well, well——

MAGOEMON.

Oh, you can't get out of it, you know !

TAHEI.

I'm in a fix ! There, now——

THE TWO.

Ready !

> (DENKAI *and* ZENROKU *spring at* MAGOEMON, *who jumps to one side and hits them over the heads with a pipe.* TAHEI *attacks with a broom, which* MAGOEMON *quickly snatches away. With it he beats the three repeatedly.*)

MAGOEMON.

And how about the note payable to an unknown name ? Your trick ! Confess all about it, just as it is. If you don't, more blows of the broom ! Do you want——

DENKAI.

Wait, wait a moment, please ! I will confess, I will confess. Yes, it was I who acted the part of the priest, at Mr. Tahei's request.

MAGOEMON.

Well, you have told the truth ! And now, Zenroku, you pretended to be the fellow who was going to redeem Koharu, didn't you ?

ZENROKU.

Since you know it all, what's the sense in denial ? Yes, it's as you supposed.

MAGOEMON.

Yes, yes, and you, too, you lady-killer, while I'm about it——

TAHEI.

As you please ! All's as you saw it to be : revenge, for love unrequited, upon Koharu, who to me, up to this hour, would not listen. What a revenge ! Ah ! there is nothing so painful as love.

MAGOEMON.

You three are regular jail-birds.

ZENROKU.

That's a bright idea !

THE THREE.

Greatly obliged !

MAGOEMON.

By rights, you three should be dragged to judgment ; but in mercy I will spare you. On condition, however, that you will have nothing further to say to Jihei.

TAHEI.

No, it is not for me to have anything to say, anything at all. On the contrary, Jihei may now rightly reproach me. Truly, Mr. Jihei, you may quite naturally be angry, having just heard of Koharu's love for me ; but be good enough to think it my fortune by Fate to have her love, and give her up without protest.

MAGOEMON.

Shut up, and get out !

(*He drives the three off towards the right.*)

Now, Mr. Master of Koharu, you have, I suppose, no further occasion for speaking. Don't be excited, but get out and go home.

SAIBEI.

Certainly, certainly ! I am sorry to have troubled you upon this my first visit here.

(*Thus speaking, he goes out to the right.*)

Look here, Tahei, if you delay in your ransom, Koharu will kill herself. In that case, you are a murderer ; and I shall not let you escape ; I shall not.

TAHEI.

Oh, I know it, I know it ! All lovers need must wear the livery of a journey dreadful. Speaking in the language of the stage, mine is the leading part in the love-scene of the second play.[1]

DENKAI.

And, as entertainment, meet for such lewd actors,

[1] The first play upon the programme was likely to be historical, the second social and much less refined.

ZENROKU.
Behold the feast of brooms !

TAHEI.
Behold my miserable self !

DENKAI.
And all for whom ?

BOTH.
Koharu !

TAHEI.
Love is pain, indeed !

TAKEMOTO.
What's this they are saying ?
What weakness of soul !
With spirits all broken,
No limbs in control,
They stagger as drunken,
Each helping and helped ;
And clatter off, limping,
Of manhood bereft.

(*The three walk off in a ridiculous manner.* MAGOEMON
watches them go.)

MAGOEMON.
Here, Sangoro ; go and call Jihei and O-San.

SANGORO.
Yes. Master ! Mistress ! The master from Dojima [1]
is asking for you.

JIHEI (*from within*).
All right ! I'll be right there.

---

[1] *Dojima:* the section of the city where Magoemon makes his home.

TAKEMOTO.

From his dressing-room Master Jihei comes out, followed shamefacedly by O-San.

(JIHEI *and* O-SAN *enter and are seated*.)

MAGOEMON.

Jihei, you have heard all that went on here, haven't you ?

JIHEI.

I heard it all from the other room.

MAGOEMON.

As you heard it there's no need of my repeating. Since Tahei went out speaking as he did, it is quite certain that he will redeem Koharu ; and you, Jihei, after having heard her letter, can have no hankering after her, I suppose.

JIHEI.

No, oh no ! I don't want to think of her again.

O-SAN.

Truly, I also heard it. Because of that letter, he certainly must have given up all thought of Koharu. There can be no deceit in my husband about that matter ; not a bit. Of that I am very sure.

MAGOEMON.

As your brother I am greatly relieved to hear that ; but your old father and mother are old-fashioned folk, and will not be content with a mere verbal promise. To remove your father's doubt, will you not sign a written agreement ? [1]

---

[1] Jihei and O-San are cousins, O-San's mother being a sister of Jihei's father. Hence Magoemon takes this interest in what the related parents think.

JIHEI.

Oh, yes ! If it's an agreement he wants, I'll sign as many as you please.

MAGOEMON.

So you should be willing. Now, O-San, bring the inkstone box.

O-SAN. Yes, yes !

TAKEMOTO.

When she had handed the inkstone and paper for writing
    the letter,
Slowly, in form of a promise of loyalty ne'er to be broken,
Pledging himself to surrender Koharu for ever and
    leave her,
Pledging himself, in a manner of words that are binding
    in promise,
Gods and the Buddhas attesting, he finally finished the
    writing.

(JIHEI *writes the pledge, and, cutting his little finger with
a knife, signs in his blood.*)

JIHEI.

Please read it.

MAGOEMON.

Ah, good, very good ! This will satisfy the hearts of your father and mother.

O-SAN.

As a result of your brotherly kindness, my heart also is quieted. Though we have children in union, now for the first time are we plighted. The children, because of this, will be happy, I am sure.

MAGOEMON.

If you continue as you now resolve, you are sure to succeed in your business. Attend to your customers carefully. All your family and relatives will rejoice. It is only because I think of your happiness and that of the family that I am impatient with you and fret as to-day I have done. Just consider the innocent charm of these children.

Ah! speaking of the children reminds me. Any grandfather is a docile slave of his grandchildren. It will be best to have his grandchild give this written agreement to Grandfather. Call O-Sue, please.

O-SAN.

Yes, oh yes! (*Turning towards the inner room.*) O-Sue, O-Sue!

O-SUE (*from within*).

Yes, I'm coming.

(*She enters, dressed as before.*)

What do you wish, Mother?

O-SAN.

I want you to go with your Uncle to your Grandfather's.

O-SUE.

Then, am I to go to Grandfather's with Uncle?

O-SAN.

Yes, run along.

MAGOEMON.

I will take O-Sue with me, and let her make peace for her Father with this letter.

(*He takes* O-SUE *by the hand, and they pass off towards the right. The husband and wife escort them.*)

x

JIHEI.

Must you go now ? I am certainly indebted to you for this day's trouble.

MAGOEMON.

Don't mention it ! We are brothers, not strangers. There may come a time when I shall need your help. No one knows what may happen on the morrow.

JIHEI.

Changeful is the heart of man !

O-SAN.

That which changes never is a mother's love.[1]

MAGOEMON.

Be faithful, each to the other, as man and wife, and take good care of the business.

JIHEI.

Good-bye, Brother !

MAGOEMON.

Good-bye, Jihei, O-San.

BOTH.

We are very glad that you came.

TAKEMOTO.

With O-Sue, hand in hand,
Magoemon,
To his home returning,
Now slowly goes.

(MAGOEMON *takes* O-SUE *by the hand and goes out to the right.* O-SAN *and* JIHEI *appear thoughtful.*)

[1] She can forgive Jihei and, though he is false, shield him for the sake of the children.

JIHEI.

Ah! I'm tired with all this confusion. I think I'll take a nap.

TAKEMOTO.

> Unquiet in mind,
> Pushing the curtains aside,
> He enters the chamber
> Just as the care-free Sangoro——

(JIHEI *enters the inner room; and* SANGORO *comes out, rubbing his eyes.*)

SANGORO.

Ma'am, what time is it now? Please, ma'am!

O-SAN.

Why, Sangoro, as if it were midnight! It will soon be evening. Close up the shop as usual, light the light, and offer lights at the shrine.

SANGORO.

Yes, ma'am! Certainly, I will, I'll do just as you say.

O-SAN.

What a chatterbox! And Kantaro?

SANGORO.

He's by the fire, in there. I was lying beside him and went to sleep without knowing it; and I dreamed that I went to see a play at Dotombori. Please, ma'am, let me go to see a play to-morrow.

O-SAN.

What are you talking about? Were you asleep without hearing a bit of the racket?

SANGARO.

What ? What racket ? I didn't hear any racket, except the cat running after the rats.

O-SAN.

Dear, dear ! That there's no cure for a dunce is a true saying.

(O-SAN *thoughtfully goes into the inner room.*)

SANGORO.

Whenever she speaks she calls me " Dunce, dunce " every other word. Makes a mountain out of a molehill ; that's what she does. I don't see why she calls such a bright fellow a dunce.

(*Looking about, he sees the fish-gongs which* DENKAI *left. Thinks a moment.*)

What's this ? Um ! Two wooden fish-gongs. These are what the singers of mock scriptures use. I see, I see ! One who does nothing but idle away his time we call a dunce. Such are the readers of mock scriptures. I'll recite the fool scripture of the—I've forgotten—double suicide, which I saw the other day at Sennichi-mae. The words of the scripture begin . . .

(SANGORO *poses humorously. Curtain.*)

ACT II

SCENE I. *Behind the House of* JIHEI, *the Paper-merchant.*

(*A street across the front of the stage is backed by the rear
of* JIHEI'S *house, the stage having been turned. To
the left is a fence of charred boards, through which
opens a door of lattice, marked " Service Entrance."
By the door stands a tub of water, a protection against
fire, surrounded by open palings of charred wood.
To the right, a space surrounded by paper-screens
represents the paper-merchant's inner room.*

*Furnishings are placed to the accompaniment of
* Joruri *music. A charcoal-heater is covered with
a quilt. Near it is a paper-covered night-lamp.
Tobacco tray, etc.*

JIHEI, *dressed as before, lies by the fire.* O-SAN
is sewing with workbox beside her.

The evening bell sounds.)

TAKEMOTO.

Having dismissed them in nonchalant haste from the
doorway in parting,

Jihei lies down as for slumber, the ruler at hand for
a pillow.

Like to the warmth of October, called little spring by
the people,

Called by the name Koharu,[1] glowed the warmth of the
brazier.

" Still are your thoughts with the harlot, and still do you
wander in Cape Town ? "[2]

> [1] The word *Koharu* means " little spring."
> [2] Where Koharu lived.

> Lifting the quilt from his shoulders and finding his face
> wet with tear-drops,
> Gazing intently upon him, she questioned, amazed and
> indignant.

O-SAN.

This is too much, Jihei. If you do miss her so, it would
have been better had you not written the promise. Why?
oh, why do you hate me?

JIHEI.

What is that you are saying? We who have children
in union——

O-SAN.

Oh, no, no! You hate me! You hate me!

TAKEMOTO.

> Is it not true that you hate me, though in October,
> Two years ago, on the second day of the boar,
> At the time of starting fall-fires,

O-SAN.

> Right here were the pillows,

TAKEMOTO.

> We couched side by side; and, since that time, deep in
> my bosom,

O-SAN.

Dwelleth a devil!

TAKEMOTO.

> Or dwelleth a serpent suspicious!

O-SAN.

Weep, if you miss her so much, weep unrestrainedly.

TAKEMOTO.

If your tears should swell the Shijimi river's flow,
Drawing, Koharu will drink. How cruel you are, Jihei!
Why, if, indeed,

O-SAN.

For her you feel deep obligation,
Have you no care for the children?

TAKEMOTO.

She sobbed from the depths of her heart,
Grief that could not be stifled.

JIHEI.

Rightly you censure. I ask forgiveness. Without a
word I could reveal my heart, if from my eyes should flow
tears of sorrow and from my ears tears of bitter shame;
but now my tears are from the eyes alone. For some three
years——

TAKEMOTO.

To you who know no jealousy I shame to speak.

JIHEI.

But listen, I implore. The other day at Cape Town I
learned Koharu's faithlessness [1]; but only now, as it were
this moment, have I awakened from my dream, my fond
illusion, and am resigned. As we were saying,[2] Tahei will
at once redeem her. Though I will not mourn for one so
faithless as to accept redemption from another within ten
days of my departure,

[1] This has reference to a part of the *Joruri* not taken over into this
Kabuki. Magoemon in disguise had visited Koharu; and she in
conversation with him, having already received a letter of entreaty from
O-San, declared her purpose to give up Jihei, rather than to commit
double suicide with him, as she had promised him that she would do,
since he did not have money wherewith to purchase her freedom. A
part of this conversation Jihei overheard in passing.

[2] This seems to imply a conversation between the acts.

TAKEMOTO.

The thought of being
Laughed at by those on Change, who do not understand, but
Say that I surrendered her for lack of money,

JIHEI.

Makes me weep.

TAKEMOTO.

O-San draws near and nearer now.

O-SAN.

Eh ? then has she said to you words of estrangement,
And in truth is she going to Tahei ?

JIHEI.

Certainly ! Why so startled ? Why that tone ?
What is the matter ?

O-SAN.

Koharu does not intend to live; she certainly does
not. She will kill herself. What shall I do ? What
shall I do ?

TAKEMOTO.

She sits down, she jumps up. Restless, the wife, the
husband unconcerned.

JIHEI.

Now, now ! Though you are a bright woman you are
merely a domestic housewife.[1] That faithless girl will not
kill herself.

---

[1] A refined woman of the home, knowing nothing of the life of the
Quarters, and hence quite unable to understand the psychology of such
women as Koharu.

O-SAN.

Oh, yes, yes, she will. She is not in the least unfaithful, not as much as a grain of mustard. You're so stolid ! As though in a dream you do not listen at all to what I am saying.

TAKEMOTO.

I was anxious lest some sad thing should happen ; and to Koharu

O-SAN.

I entreated by letter, saying, " Give up, I beseech you, Jihei, whom you adore."

TAKEMOTO.

Her answering letter declared that she understood,—that she would resign you, that her love for you meant as much as her filial duty.[1]

O-SAN.

With so sincere a heart how could she turn to Tahei ? She must have now resolved to die when once by him redeemed.[2]

TAKEMOTO.

If Koharu kills herself it will be because I have failed in my duty.[3]

O-SAN.

Indeed, I do long to save her. Think of some way, I beseech you.

[1] Koharu had become an entertainer in order to support a widowed mother—a case of self-sacrifice not uncommon.

[2] In case of her death, under such circumstances, Saibei could not charge the financial loss to her mother, but to Tahei, if to anyone.

[3] The Japanese woman of olden time was so gentle and sympathetic that she would feel it right to obliterate herself in such a case as this.

TAKEMOTO.

I am utterly at a loss what to do ! Now for the first time my wife has told the whole story.

JIHEI.

At your request, then, she made pretence of unfaithfulness ?

O-SAN.

I think——

TAKEMOTO.

Surprised at hearing,

JIHEI.

And because of love for me——

TAKEMOTO.

Because I did not realize her worth till now——

(*Music.*)

JIHEI.

Oh ! I am ashamed of myself that I was angry with her and thought her unfaithful.

O-SAN.

Stop not to grieve, but go at once and hold her back from death.

TAKEMOTO.

It is his wife who urges !

JIHEI.

But—— ; one hundred and fifty ryo will be needed to buy Koharu's life. There is no other way than to give at least half that sum in pledge and so secure her. And for one who now has reached the end in borrowing money !

TAKEMOTO.

While he stands at a loss, O-San draws near.

O-SAN.

You speak as though of that which cannot be.   The sum, indeed, is small, if it will save her.

TAKEMOTO.

She goes to the chest and opens a small drawer.   She takes out something wrapped in silk to which a twisted cord is attached.   Opening the bundle quickly, she takes out a package.   Jihei holds it up in surprise.

> (*Meanwhile* O-SAN *opens the small, sliding screen at the back of the room.   From a white-wood chest behind the screen she takes a package of fifty ryo wrapped in a small silk cloth.   This she puts before* JIHEI, *who looks greatly surprised.*)

JIHEI.

What !   Fifty ryo !   How did you——

O-SAN.

You shall know later where I got the money.   I had put this away to pay Iwakuni's bill at the end of the month ; but I think I can manage that in consultation with my elder brother.   Koharu's case is urgent.   With this fifty ryo and the rest I——

TAKEMOTO.

She goes to the chest and takes from the drawers a coloured winter dress with light-brown lining, for which she never dreamed such use—a black silk dress, unfaded, one of light purple, and children's clothes daintily fashioned.   She gathers up the dresses—even the clothes of the children. Their value, at least, will be thirty——

> (*She brings a large brown wrapping-cloth, such as is used in the shop, and from the drawers to the accompaniment of the* TAKEMOTO *reading, takes out the dresses and wraps them up.*)

O-SAN.

If we take these,

TAKEMOTO.

They will not refuse a loan.

The cloth which wraps her husband's shame and her own faithfulness is filled with love for him.

O-SAN.

Though the children and I have nothing to wear, his reputation is all-important to a man. Redeem Koharu, and yield not to that Tahei.

TAKEMOTO.

> Urging him forward, she spoke ; but with
> trembling lips he made answer,
> Clasping his hands in a gesture unconscious :

JIHEI.

> You are too kind.
> When I have given the money in pledge,
> and taken her forth,
> Where shall I leave her, or elsewhere
> or home, and what then
> Will you——

TAKEMOTO.

Abruptly he stops, and is buried in painful confusion.

O-SAN.

> Pray do not worry ! Worry not at all.
> I am content the children's nurse to be,
> Or even cook, if that be not too much—
> Too much for thee. But as a sister—
> You had a sister——

TAKEMOTO.

> Think me.
> Though thus she speaks, the tears well up ;
> They well, but are swallowed down.
> Her changeless loyalty to him
> Seems most pathetic.[1]

JIHEI.

I have nothing to say. I tell you, O-San, though the condemnation of my fathers, of heaven, of the gods and Buddhas holy, be not visited upon me, the condemnation of my wife is more than I can bear.

TAKEMOTO.

> Forgive is all that he can say ;
> And clasps his hands, adoring.[2]

O-SAN.

> I cannot, cannot, cannot bear it !
> For my husband I would bear all pain,
> To the tearing of toe-nails and fingers ; but if
> We are late there can nothing avail.
> Go, and go quickly ! Sangoro, Sangoro !

---

[1] The reader identifies himself with the audience and voices their emotions. This prompting of the audience as to how they ought to feel is not uncommon.

[2] Compare this moral blindness with the clarity of the evil king in *Hamlet*, who sees that he cannot be forgiven so long as he retains the rewards of evil.

TAKEMOTO.

    She calls him.

SANGORO (*from another room*).

             Yes.

             (*Entering.*)

             What, ma'am ?

O-SAN.

    Take this and go with master.

SANGORO.

    Go with master to North Shinchi ? [1] Good ! That's fine !

JIHEI.

    Look here ! No talking back. Take up this bundle.

SANGORO.

    What a load !

TAKEMOTO.

        To Sangoro he hands the bundle,
        And deep in his bosom hides the money,
        Preparing to depart.

    (JIHEI *puts the package of money into his bosom.* SANGORO *takes the bundle on his back. In the meantime,* GOZAEMON, *dressed as an old man, enters through the kitchen, and comes where they are through the doorway from an inner room.*)

GOZAEMON.

    Hello, Jihei, are you at home ?

    [1] Another name for the region of Koharu's place of dwelling.

TAKEMOTO.

Since he comes suddenly they are confused.

(JIHEI *and* O-SAN *look surprised*.)

JIHEI.

Why ! How do you do, Father !

O-SAN.

Why, Father ! Most unexpected !

GOZAEMON.

What's that ?

JIHEI.

We are very glad to see you.

TAKEMOTO.

Husband and wife are restless. Gozaemon looks at the bundle on Sangoro's back.

GOZAEMON.

Fool, where are you going with that bundle ? Are you off to the pawnshop again ? Hand it over to me.

TAKEMOTO.

Having it snatched from his back, Sangoro is as surprised as one might be if discovered planning a secret visit in the morning to some shrine. He goes into the next room.

(GOZAEMON *forcibly takes the bundle from* SANGORO'S *back. When the boy tries to shield the bundle he glares at him ; and, frightened, the lad runs into the next room*.)

GOZAEMON.

I was expecting this. Look here ! You pawn your clothing and waste all the money in insatiable madness after a harlot. Young fellow, a faithful harlot and a gargoyle with a smiling face are things non-existent. Come, give O-San a writ of divorcement. According to custom, the girl-child goes with the mother. O-Sue has already been taken home by Magoemon. At that time—what was it ?

(*He takes* JIHEI's *letter from his bosom.*)

This, this pledge he showed me, as if it were something important. Oh, yes ! You look wise ; but you are young and green in spots. This will not go down. Instead of a pledge, write a form of divorcement.

TAKEMOTO.

> Into small pieces he tears it, and, throwing the frag-
> ments full at the
> Face of young Jihei, sits himself down, like a mortar
> immovable,
> Where should be seated a guest whom the house
> delighted to honour.
> Able to bear it no longer, O-San from depths of
> emotion——

(GOZAEMON *tears the pledge into bits and, throwing them away, stares at the couple.* O-SAN *in emotion.*)

O-SAN.

I will not listen to you, Father ; I will not listen. You are yourself to blame for the loss of our property. You said that you had need of a silver mountain, which proved to be worthless ; and borrowed thirty ryo, and then fifty ; and in the end lost it all, principal and interest, when the venture collapsed. And when Jihei thought it not wise to make a fuss about it, since you were his father-in-law and the fault would seem in some measure his own, but in manly fashion returned to you all your notes and settled the matter in private, you thanked him with tears on your panic-stricken face, and called him in joy your household's fostering deity. This you have not forgotten, I hope. And thus you are to blame for all his wild dissipation. Though not in so many words did he say it, I well understood that he began to go to the Quarters merely to give some reasonable excuse for the loss of the property, by his family honourably given ; for, if they questioned the reason, he had no intent, making a fool of himself, of saying it had been taken by you, his father-in-law. When first he began to go to the Quarters, I very much feared that the real reason might become known ; and whenever I saw him depart I used to worship his shadow.

You have forgotten your great obligation, and now call him a fool and an idiot. What language ! Shall I patiently bear it ? Father, go home !

TAKEMOTO.

> Thus she comforts and censures.
> One between the two standing,
> Clearly her pain and her anguish
> Call for our whole-hearted sympathy.

With an equal weight of sorrow Koharu comes from Kinokuni to make clear her heart's intent ; but, seeing that something of great moment is taking place, and thinking it unwise to enter, hides behind the water-tub and listens. Of all this unconscious, Jihei places his hands on the floor in a gesture of humble entreaty.

> (KOHARU *enters the stage from the theatre passage, veiled and dressed for the street. At the kitchen door she pauses, looks in, then thoughtfully hides herself at the right.*)

JIHEI (*humbly*).

What O-San has said is but nonsense, and what I have never once dreamed of. Pray, let us remain as we are.

> (GOZAEMON *interrupts, speaking sternly.*)

Y

GOZAEMON.

No, I will not. There is nothing to be said ; nothing to be heard. Divorce O-San. ; That's all ! But I will put a mark upon all her belongings. (*He rises.*)

TAKEMOTO.

As he rises O-San is surprised.

O-SAN.

Oh, Father ! Everything is there. There's no need of looking.

TAKEMOTO.

She runs to stop him ; but he pushes her aside, and violently opens the drawers.

> (JIHEI *tries to rise, but finds it impossible to stand.* O-SAN *confronts* GOZAEMON, *who pushes her away and opens the drawers of the chest, speaking.*)

GOZAEMON.
What ! This ! Why ?

TAKEMOTO.

He opens the first, the second, all the drawers, and even the closet. Knocking the bottom of the empty drawers, Gozaemon stares with open mouth, wordless, dumbfounded.

> (GOZAEMON *opens all the drawers and looks into them, astonished, dumbfounded.* JIHEI *rises.*)

JIHEI.

I say, Father, please take this fifty ryo for O-San's clothing ; though perhaps it may be all-insufficient.

> (*He hands the package of money to* GOZAEMON.)

GOZAEMON (*taking it*).

Certainly I will take this home with me. You have, after all, some considerable property.[1] But, since I have seen your misconduct, I will take my daughter as well along with me. Come, come along at once !

TAKEMOTO.

As he bids her follow,

O-SAN.

Father, when once he has spoken, will listen to no one. I fear I must go along with him.[2] To your keeping I entrust Kantaro. Do not forget to give him Dr. Kuwayama's[3] pills each morning before breakfast. (*She weeps.*)

JIHEI.

Be not anxious, down-hearted. Matters are turning quite as we had not expected. My mind is all in a whirl. For a time we must part. You are your father's daughter, and he will not treat you unkindly. Soon, I have hope, you will be allowed to return.

O-SAN.

Jihei, be careful, I beg you ; and do not be carried away by any impulse of passion.[4]

[1] The sums of money mentioned in the play are of little significance. Three and five, with their multiples, are common combinations ; and what a woman has saved for the monthly rent is the same as the sum involved in a silver mine !

[2] In old Japan the authority of a father continued in force over a daughter even after her marriage. This served as a measure of protection against the possible tyranny of her husband's family, but left her a slave to her father's wishes, even though he might wish to re-marry her to another. Here the authority seems to be exercised by a keen-minded father who sees the real situation and wishes to save her, though against her will.

[3] A certain Kuwayama, accompanying Hodeyoshi on his expedition into Chosen, brought back a general specific for children, which was later sold in Osaka.

[4] She fears that he may kill himself since now, as she thinks, he has no money wherewith to redeem Koharu.

GOZAEMON.

What a long leave-taking ! Come, at once !

TAKEMOTO.

He drags her away, and Kantaro is awakened by the noise.

KANTARO.

Mamma ! Mamma !

TAKEMOTO.

> Hearing him calling,
> Back to him turning,
> How can she leave him,
> Child of her bosom !
> Husband and wife are
> Now like the bamboo
> Parted unnaturally
> Ever asunder.
> For the long journey
> Off are they started.

(KANTARO, *who has been sleeping by the fire, tumbles out of the blankets and staggers to his feet. O-SAN is about to take him up when* GOZAEMON *comes between them, and pushes the child violently away.* JIHEI *picks the boy up and exchanges sorrowful glances with* O-SAN. O-SAN *cannot bear to part with them and starts back ; but* GOZAEMON *glares at her.*)

GOZAEMON.

What are you so interminably weeping about ? You have been divorced, and so are nothing to them. If you meet her anywhere hereafter, Jihei, don't call her your wife. I forbid it.

TAKEMOTO.

Though he speaks thus harshly with his lips, Gozaemon leaves a heart of sympathy behind him as he goes.

(GOZAEMON *enters the inner room and goes out through the kitchen door, followed by* O-SAN, *weeping.*)

TAKEMOTO.

Watching them go, watching them go, Koharu at once runs in.

(*From her hiding-place* KOHARU *comes out ; and, watching them off, runs into the kitchen and on through the inner door.*)

KOHARU.

Oh, Jihei ! How I've wanted to see you !

JIHEI.

Why, it's Koharu ! How did you get here ?

KANTARO.

Mamma !

TAKEMOTO.

Seeing the child as he weeps for his mother,
Both with compassion deeply are moved.
Koharu takes him and woos him to slumber,
Clasped in her arms ; the while from her heart
Freshly outpoureth her passionate story.

KOHARU.

From where shall I begin ? With the sad parting from you in estrangement the other day at Cape Town ? Though I have, indeed, given you up, I have made up my mind to kill myself at once if I am redeemed by Tahei. I came here to see you once more before I say farewell to the world.

I came here ; but the time was ill-chosen and I heard all that was being said. I am the one cause of loyal O-San's heart-broken sorrow. Oh, forgive me, I beg of you !

JIHEI.

The more I know of her true heart the greater my guilt appears. Can there be another wife in all the three thousand worlds such as she ? To make amends, you and I——

KOHARU.

What ! You too ?

JIHEI.

Of course !

KOHARU.

I am so happy !

TAKEMOTO.

>Embracing each the other
>They sob ; and sobbing
>Their hearts, each to the other,
>In secret speak.

(*In the inner room* SANGORO *sings.*)

SANGORO.

Takasago ! [1] With rice cakes in a nest of boxes.

TAKEMOTO.

Babbling the song, foolish Sangoro, carrying in his hands a reading-desk with its three sacred objects, comes before them.

(*From the inner room* SANGORO *brings from the Buddhist family altar a small reading-desk with flower-vases*

---

[1] From a wedding song, the name of a place famous for its pine-trees, typical of old men and old women.

in the shape of a crane and a tortoise, and a tray of
offerings with white rice-cakes upon it.   He carries
a wine-server in one hand, and holds the desk cere-
monially a little higher than his eyes.)

SANGORO.

Say, but this is funny ! A little while ago mistress said
to me : " Sangoro, after I have gone Koharu probably will
come. If she comes, you marry her and the master. I
trust you to do it," she said. So I thought this pine, in
the crane and tortoise vases, would be appropriate. As
there's no wine in the house I've put water [1] in the server.
I'm responsible for your marriage.   In reward, just give me
some of Toraya's [2] cakes—those that I like ; and, say, quit
calling me a dunce, and drink this quickly, quickly.

TAKEMOTO.

> Though he thus presses upon them,
>   they yield not,
> Seeing in water the sign of their parting.
> Though they have made up their minds,
>   and that fully,
> Lost is their self-control ; and their eyelids
> Brim with the tears that o'erflow.

SANGORO.

Why ! You two are weeping. Don't cry, don't cry !
Oh, I see—tears of joy, are they not ?

KOHARU.

Yes, as you say, they are tears of joy. But if I marry
Jihei, what about O-San ?

---

[1] The boy does not know that water, in place of wine, is used symbolically as a cup of parting.

[2] A famous maker of *manju* cakes. His family still has its main
office in Kyoto.

SANGORO.

Why, you won't be doing her any wrong. She has made old bones [1] of herself, and for you a delicious soup. Reject not her kindness, but drink quickly and give him the cup.

JIHEI.

Indeed, if we consider this a ceremonial of marriage, as Sangoro suggests, duty——; but the cup of water in parting—

SANGORO.

Oh, then shall I pour ?

TAKEMOTO.

> Weeping, they hold up the cup ;
> Drink they the water,
> Wine of their parting for aye,
> Wine of their parting.
> Earthen the cup which they hold ;
> Earth our conclusion.
> Lonely the pine in the vase,
> Symbol of sorrow ;
> Crane and the tortoise, alike,
> Tell them of dying.
> These are the things which now break
> Hearts that are grieving.

(SANGORO *takes up the earthen cup and pours the water.* KOHARU *and* JIHEI *drink.*)

SANGORO.

Now all will be well. Is there no musician ? I wish one would come.

---

[1] The extreme sacrifice.

TAKEMOTO.

> Then, as he looks to the street,
> Wearing straw sandals,
> Dressed in a garment of black,
> Girlhood scarce seven——

(*From the right* O-SUE, *dressed in white with a black outer robe and wearing a hat of plaited bamboo, enters and goes to the kitchen door.*)

O-SUE.

Anyo temple nunnery! Constantly I pray—

SANGORO.

There it comes!

TAKEMOTO.

> Out of the door runs the fool,
> Bringing the child in again,
> Surprised at the sight of her face.

(SANGORO *brings* O-SUE *in. All are surprised to see her.*)

JIHEI.

Why, it's O-Sue! Did you come back all by yourself? And in such a strange dress!

O-SUE.

Yes, Grandpa gave me this beautiful dress; and, because it was too white, a great deal of something has been written upon it. Grandpa said, " Go and show what is written to your Papa and Auntie "; and he brought me here.

(KOHARU *and* JIHEI *go to the child, and, taking off the outer robe, look thoughtfully at the writing upon the white dress.*)

JIHEI.

What ?   What ?   " While the tears flow, I pen this brief letter.   When I returned with my father a short time ago I saw, I am sure, Koharu hiding herself ; but, as you know, under the circumstances I could not speak with her.   So I am writing."

KOHARU.

Oh, Jihei! let me read it, too ; please let me read it!   Eh ? " I asked Koharu to do an unreasonable thing, in my desire to save my husband's life ; and she consented.   My joy was as high as a mountain, as deep as the sea.   From my heart I thank her.

JIHEI.

" Indeed, to repay her kindness there is no way but to make you two husband and wife for ever.

KOHARU.

" And, understanding now my father's true intent, I will give you up, and think our union destined to be broken. I will, with the very milk of my bosom, bring O-Sue up ; and I do beg Koharu to be good to Kantaro."

Eh ?   What can she mean ?   What can she mean ?   You are all wrong, O-San !   I have done nothing to deserve your thanks.   Do you mean to break my heart ?   I have given him up, in truth.   Come back, come back, at once !   Oh, Jihei !   Call her home.

TAKEMOTO.

> Rising in haste, she stands up ;
> Sitting again—
> Wildly bewildered she sinks—
> Tearful confusion.
> While with the reading again
> Jihei continues.

Jihei.

What's this ?   What ?   " Your father, Gozaemon, wishes
to add his word."

Eh ! How's that ?   That ungrateful man cannot write
anything decent, I'm sure. Eh ?   What ?

" Your father, Gozaemon, wishes to add his word.   Six
years ago, when through the silver mine I caused you loss,
you returned the bonds because of the relation between us
of son and father-in-law.   For that I am greatly obliged."
You ought to be obliged, I am sure.   What ?

" To afford an excuse to your family for the loss of the
money you began to frequent the Quarters.   That which
at first was a sham became a reality.   'Twas a common
experience. Well, I remember my youth."   Hum !   " When
I had heard the explanation, all the whole story, from my
daughter, I put one hundred and fifty ryo—little enough to
be sure—in the big drawer of the chest when I looked for
the dresses."

Oh ! Open the drawer of the chest.   No, the lower one.

(Jihei *tells* Koharu, *who with hesitation thoughtfully
opens the drawer.*)

Koharu.

Oh, here it is !

Jihei.

It's there, is it ?   " With that money redeem Koharu,
and be happy hereafter."

Koharu.

Why, then his unkindness of manner was all intended
as kindness."

Jihei.

What !   What's this ?   " My daughter and O-Sue have

this day become nuns." Oh, listen to this, Koharu!
O-San has become a nun. (*He weeps.*)

KOHARU.

Oh! If O-San has become a nun, what shall I do?

(*Sinks into tears.*)

JIHEI.

Oh dear! O-San has become a nun, become a nun!
Eh? "My daughter and O-Sue have this day become
nuns; and their new names are Teigyoku—chaste jewel—
and Chigetsu—moon wisdom. I took them to Anyoji at
Tengachaya, and paid the money you gave me to the temple
for their support.

TAKEMOTO.

> Reading not to the end,
> There they together
> Lift up their voices and weep,
> Bursting with tears.

JIHEI.

That is selfish! Truly, O-San, you put me in the
wrong, you put me in the wrong. Now that I must die,
who will take care of the children? I will not have it so,
O-San.

TAKEMOTO.

Kindness proves unkindness, he complains. Even the
fool weeps, and Koharu chokes with tears.

KOHARU.

Selfish!

TAKEMOTO.

O-San!

KOHARU.

In gratitude for your kindness in allowing me to see him unhampered by jealousy up to this time, I granted the request in your letter ; but that now proveth a fetter.

TAKEMOTO.

If you intended this, why at the time did you not tell me so ?

KOHARU.

Oh, Jihei dear !

TAKEMOTO.

Call O-San back, and with her remain loyal for ever.

KOHARU.

Not merely such a woman, but also such a—

TAKEMOTO.

Child as that before you,
Do you not love ?
Sweeter still he seemeth,
The more I look !
To take him from his mother's breast,
Where else in mother-love he'd be o'erwhelmed !
That he is orphaned is my doing !

KOHARU.

Forgive !

TAKEMOTO.

With that she bursts into tears, distrait. In sympathy Sangoro cries aloud. He cries so hard it seems his throat will break. Their tears fall like rain upon the broken leaves of the banana-tree and fall incessantly.

(ZENROKU *and* TAHEI *enter.*)

TAHEI.

Look here, Jihei ! I'm going to redeem Koharu and make her my wife. Why did you tempt her in ?

ZENROKU.

Now, Tahei, you need no longer complain of small matters. As for this Jihei, against whom you have so great a grudge, just knock him down ; kill him, and so give vent to your anger.

TAHEI.

Right, I will !

TAKEMOTO.

From two sides they start to spring upon him ; but with all his strength he grasps their arms.

JIHEI.

Sangoro, take O-Sue and Kantaro to father's in Dojima.

SANGORO.

You'd be helpless without me.

JIHEI.

Well, don't stop to chatter ; go at once.

SANGORO.

I will.

(*In prompt obedience* SANGORO *goes out to the street, taking the two children with him.*)

KOHARU.

Oh !

JIHEI.

Do not be frightened, Koharu. Keep quiet. (*He shields her.*)

TAKEMOTO.

Zenroku and Tahei from opposite sides thrust at Jihei ; but, turning aside, he avoids them, and they strike each the other.

TAHEI.

Jihei has wounded me !

> (*Frightened at the cry*, JIHEI *loses his presence of mind, and strikes wildly, at last sitting upon them and giving the death strokes.*)

KOHARU.

Awful ! What, both ? (*Frightened.*)

JIHEI.

Behold !

> (*Appropriate music.*)

Behold, be not frightened ! Nothing can save us now. As we had planned, the temple of Daicho at Amijima is the place for our last moments. Come at once !

KOHARU.

Before anyone comes !

JIHEI.

Yes, hasten!

TAKEMOTO.

He takes her by the hand, and they hasten to their fate. The end of ill-starred love is tears, tears, and the seed of a story.

AUTHORITIES

MUCH of the material utilized in this study was gathered in conference, at various shrines and temples, with various Shinto and Buddhist priests whose uniform kindness is worthy of comment.

ENGLISH.

ASIATIC SOCIETY OF JAPAN, THE. Transactions.
ASTON, W. G. The Way of the Gods.
 A History of Japanese Literature.
BRINKLEY, CAPTAIN F. Japan: Its History, Art, and Literature,
CHAMBERLAIN, BASIL HALL. A Translation of *Ko-ji-ki*.
 Japanese Poetry.
KINCAID, ZOE. Kabuki, The Popular Stage of Japan.
KURE, B. The Historic Development of the Marionette Theatre in Japan.
LOMBARD, F. A. Pre-Meiji Education in Japan.
MURDOCK, JAMES. History of Japan.
STOPES, MARIE C. Plays of Old Japan. The Nō.
WALEY, ARTHUR. The Nō Plays of Japan.

JAPANESE.

Suggested by TAKANO TATSUYUKI, Tokyo, Japan.

KOMA-NO-CHIKAZANÉ. Kyōkunsho (Instructions), 1233.
KANZÉ MOTOKIYO (Seami). Seami Jūrokubu Shu (Seami's Sixteen Booklets), 1400–1436.
TOYOHARA MUNEAKÉ. Taigensho (Records of Music and Musical Instruments), 1504–1520.
OGAWA MORINAKA. Kabu Himmoku (Varieties of Song and Dance), 1898.
IHARA SEISEIEN. Nihon Engeki Shi (History of Japanese Drama), 1904.
NOMURA HACHIRŌ. Nō-Kyōgen no Kenkyū (Studies in Nō and Kyogen), 1916.
SAITO YOSHINOSUKÉ. Nō Men Taikan (Illustrations of Nō Masks), 1920.

IWAHASHI KOYATA. Nihon Butō Shi (History of Japanese Dance), 1922.
OTSUKI JODEN. Bugaku Zusetsu (Illustrations of Musical Dances), 1927.
TAKANO TATSUYUKI. Kabu Ongyoku Kōsetsu (Considerations of Music and Dancing), 1915.
Nihon Kayō Shi (History of Japanese Songs), 1926.
Nihon Engeki no Kenkyū (Studies in Japanese Drama). Vol. I, 1926; Vol. II, 1928.

Suggested (in supplement) by TOMITA KOJIRO, Museum of Fine Arts, Boston, U.S.A.

ICHIJŌ KANEYOSHI. Ryōjin Guan Shō (Notes on Kagura and Saibara).
IKEUCHI NOBUYOSHI. Nōgaku Seisui (Rise and Fall of Nō), 1925.
KONAKAMURA KIYONORI. Kabu Ongyoku Ryakushi (Brief History of Dances and Music), 1896.
KUMAGAI NAOSHI. Ryōjin Kōshō (Further Notes on Kagura and Saibara).
YOKOI HARUNO. Nōgaku Zenshi (Complete History of Nō), 1917.
NŌGAKU DAIJITEN. (Encyclopædia of Nō).

Suggested (on Kabuki) by YARAMOTO SHUJI, Kyoto, Japan.

GOTO KEIJI. Nihon Gekijō Shi (A History of the Japanese Theatre), 1925.
IHARA SEISEIEN. Kinsei Nihon Engeki Shi (History of Modern Japanese Drama), 1913.
IITSUKA TOMOICHIRO. Kabuki Saiken (Synopsis of Kabuki Plays), 1926.
MITAMURA ENGYO. Shijitsu Kara Mita Kabuki Shibai (The Kabuki and its Sources), 1910.
TSUBOUCHI SHŌYŌ. Tōzai no Senjō-teki Higeki (A Study of the Eastern and Western Melodrama), 1923.

INDEX

Achime, 36, 38
Acrobatic skill, 27, 61, 63
Actors, 20, 61
  of Kabuki, 288, 290 ff.
  of Noh, 90, 181
Ama-terasu, 19 ff., 51
Ame-no-usume, 20, 38, 91
Ayatsuri, 185 ff.
Azuma asobi, 31 ff.
Azumae, 30 ff., 61

Bamboo, 41, 42, 66
Biwa, 79 ff., 184
Biwa bozu, 184
Buddhism—
  Influence of, 33, 73, 161 ff.
  Sects of, 171 ff.
  Spread of, 73, 88
Busu (a kyogen), 164 ff.

Chamberlain, Basil Hall (translation by), 19 ff.
Chants, 22, 23
Chikamatsu, 188, 292
  Play by, 192 ff.
Children, 65
  Boys, 75
China—
  Influence of, 31, 33, 73 ff., 82, 183, 287
Chorus, 23, 76, 90 ff., 163
Chosen, 33, 59, 65, 161
Chrysanthemum (a Dengaku), 83 ff.
Costume, 29, 60 ff., 71, 76, 174, 186, 292
Criticism, 295

Dance, 17, 20 ff., 60 ff., 74
  Chinese, 161
  Eastern Provinces, 31
  Field, 27, 57
  Korean, 161
  Labour, 26
  Worship, 34 ff.

Denbu, 27, 57 ff.
Dengaku, 27 ff., 61, 63, 70 ff., 161
  Dai, 70
  Kachi, 71
  Maiko, 70
  Mura, 71
  Play (Kikusui), 83 ff.
  Schools of, 71
  Shiba, 70
  Sho, 70
  Titles of, 81
Dojoji (a Mibu Kyogen), 176 ff.
Dolls, 63, 65, 67, 68, 185, 188
Drum (hand), 29, 35, 52, 69

Eguchi (a Yurei Noh by Ujinobu), 115 ff.
Engaku, 172, 176
Ennen Mae, 72 ff., 93

Flageolet (hichiriki), 31, 36, 38, 52
Floats, 63, 67 ff.
Flute (wabue), 31, 35, 36, 38, 69
Folk-songs, 23 ff., 31
Fuji (a Seirei Noh by Yasukiyo), 126 ff.
Fujiwara, 28, 51, 76
Furyu, 75 ff.
  A Furyu (Music for the Biwa), 79 ff.

Geisha, 20
Gempei Seisuiki, 183
Genji Monogatari, 68, 183
Ghosts, 89
Gion, 62 ff., 71
Gods—
  Ancestral, 20
  Cosmic, 20
  Plays of, 21 ff.
Gohei, 20, 41
Gorobei, 187
Goryo, 62

Hagoromo, 32